The Pleasures of Memory in Shakespeare's *Sonnets*

SHAKE-SPEARES

SONNETS.

Neuer before Imprinted.

AT LONDON
By *G. Eld* for *T. T.* and are
to be folde by *William Aſpley.*
1609.

Frontispiece. Title page, *Shakespeare's Sonnets Never before Imprinted* (1609).
STC 22353, A1r, used by permission of the Folger Shakespeare Library.

The Pleasures of Memory in Shakespeare's *Sonnets*

JOHN S. GARRISON

OXFORD
UNIVERSITY PRESS

OXFORD
UNIVERSITY PRESS

Great Clarendon Street, Oxford, OX2 6DP,
United Kingdom

Oxford University Press is a department of the University of Oxford.
It furthers the University's objective of excellence in research, scholarship,
and education by publishing worldwide. Oxford is a registered trade mark of
Oxford University Press in the UK and in certain other countries

Published in the United States of America by Oxford University Press
198 Madison Avenue, New York, NY 10016, United States of America

British Library Cataloguing in Publication Data
Data available

Library of Congress Control Number: 2023937965

ISBN 9780198857716

DOI: 10.1093/oso/9780198857716.001.0001

Printed and bound in the UK by
Clays Ltd, Elcograf S.p.A.

Contents

List of Figures

Acknowledgments

I feel so lucky to be part of a scholarly community that allows for such productive dialogue about ideas. Many people have helped this project grow as I have shared draft portions of it during conference panels and seminars, as well as in exchanges with colleagues. And, of course, there are the more informal conversations in scholarly and non-scholarly settings. A list of such helpful interlocutors (which is, with my apologies, surely partial) would include Leah Allen, Gina Caison, David Campbell, Stef Craps, Emma Depledge, Dustin Dixon, Paul Edmondson, William Engel, Lynn Enterline, Margie Ferguson, Susan Ferrari, Andrew Fleck, Huw Griffiths, Stephen Guy-Bray, Rebeca Helfer, Marianne Hirsch, Kristine Johanson, Rory Loughnane, Randall Martin, Jeffrey Masten, Carla Mazzio, Johanna Meehan, Joe Neisser, Sarah Purcell, Vanessa Rapatz, Karolyn Reddy, Melissa Sanchez, Ralph Savarese, Helen Saxenian, Robert Stagg, Goran Stanivukovic, Robert Stretter, Andrea Kaston Tange, Will Tosh, Jan Frans van Dijkhuizen, Stanley Wells, and Grant Williams. In class conversations, too, many talented and thoughtful students helped advance my understanding of the *Sonnets* and their relationship to the themes of this volume.

This project was supported by generous grant funding from the Grinnell College Center for the Humanities, Guggenheim Foundation, National Endowment for the Humanities, Newberry Library, and Renaissance Society of America.

At Oxford University Press, Eleanor Collins and Alexander Hardie-Forsyth have been enormously helpful in taking the current volume from idea to book, and the press's anonymous readers provided invaluable feedback along the way. Raja Dharmaraj was a wonderful guide in the production processs.

My former students (and now excellent scholars) Caryn McKechnie, Nicole Polglaze, and Saiham Sharif provided crucial support in early research and formatting of the manuscript.

Quotations from Maureen Owen, "Sonnet 147" are reproduced with permission from the poet and from S. Cohen and P. Legault (eds.) (2012). *The Sonnets: Translating and Rewriting Shakespeare*. Brooklyn, US: Nightboat/Telephone Books.

I must give special thanks to two people. First, I cannot express enough my gratitude to my frequent collaborator Kyle Pivetti, who always models for me the thinking and writing of an outstanding scholar. Second, I also am at a loss for words to describe how essential Marissa Nicosia has been to this project: brainstorming early on over tacos one afternoon in Los Angeles and then encouraging me at every step of the way.

Finally, I extend the deepest of thanks to my family. My mother and father instilled in me a deep love of reading. It is especially meaningful for me that I have been able to choose J. M. W. Turner's painting *Queen Mab's Cave* as the cover image for my book. It is apt for the theme as Shakespeare mentions the faerie figure in *Romeo and Juliet* and Turner referred to *A Midsummer Night's Dream* in this depiction of the fantasies that come to us in our sleep. Moreover, my father chose Turner's *Rain, Steam, and Speed - The Great Western Railway* as the cover image for his book, also published by Oxford University Press. My father did not live to see me choose the same artist or publish with the same press, but it's meaningful to me that this link between us extends into the afterlife. I also thank my husband Chris, who closely read every page of this book and heard me read sections of it countless times. And Roland sat by, patiently listening as the work continued.

Introduction

Remembering the *Sonnets*

The word "pleasure" appears only twelve times across the 154 poems in Shakespeare's *Shakespeare's Sonnets Never before Imprinted* (1609), and the word "memory" appears only eight times. Yet the interplay between these two elements flows throughout the volume. Recollection constantly shapes romantic and sexual experience, all the while that erotics fuel what is remembered and how those memories are formed. The *Sonnets* ultimately elucidate how pleasure and memory not only drive each other but also co-constitute each other.

To paint in quick brushstrokes how such interplay works, I would like to begin not with a poem by Shakespeare but with a poem I have always loved by Constantine Cavafy. His "One Night" (1916) reads:

> The room was shabby and sordid,
> concealed above the seedy tavern.
> From the window you could see the alley,
> squalid and narrow. From below
> came the voices of some workmen
> playing cards and reveling.
> And there, upon the lowly, humble bed
> I had the body of love, I had the lips,
> the sensuous, rosy, intoxicating lips—
> the rosy lips of such sensual ecstasy that even now,
> as I am writing, after so many years,
> in my lonely home, I feel drunk again. (1–12)[1]

The scene opens in what might not appear to be an erotic setting. The dirty room and the suspect nature of the tavern below suggest something shameful about the subsequent encounter. The voices of the card-playing workmen outside the window, like the shabbiness of the room, might seem distractions to concentrating on intimate connection. But the encounter itself has such an intense, transformational quality. The details about the partner are at once specific—those intoxicating lips

---

[1] C. P. Cavafy, "One Night," in *The Collected Poems: With Parallel Greek Text* (Oxford: Oxford University Press, 2009), 71–3.

The Pleasures of Memory in Shakespeare's Sonnets. John S. Garrison, Oxford University Press. © John S. Garrison (2023). DOI: 10.1093/oso/9780198857716.003.0001

to which the speaker returns again and again—and abstract—this person is the very embodiment of "love." In the glow of the encounter, the surroundings take on an erotic charge: the "concealed" room containing the secret of the lover's tryst, the laughing men outside unknowingly contributing to a sense of communal joy, and the seediness of the tavern implying the scene is its own little world where every element is saturated with sensuality.

And then we discover that the "now" of the poem is, in fact, many years later. The speaker revivifies the encounter in his mind and, in turn, that memory pulses sensation through his body. The feeling is so intense that he is "drunk again," and by implication reaching a physical climax again, overcome with an ecstasy that dismisses the loneliness of his empty house. The rejuvenation of the aging speaker dramatizes how, as Thomas Wilson puts it in his 1560 treatise *The Art of Rhetoric*, "the same is memory to the mind, that life is to the body."[2] And we can recognize that the comfort and distance of retrospect allows the speaker to choose which details to recall and how to "remember with advantage," to borrow that phrase that Henry V uses with his men at Agincourt. The sordid nature of the room can be mined for meaning without experiencing its less savory sensory elements. The men below, if they were even there at all in the original experience, can add to the rich homoeroticism of the queer poet's depiction. And those lips, those intoxicating lips of love's body. The encounter may have occurred just once, but the speaker can visit those lips and that body as many times as he likes in memory and, as he notes in his penultimate line, in writing.

The "one night" of the poem's title is not just the time of the encounter but also the time of its recollection, which can be summoned on any night (or day) when the speaker desires a renewed encounter with love. This one night certainly merits the descriptor "flashbulb memory," a term that cognitive psychologist Martin Conway coined to describe how heightened emotion at the time of experience can increase the likelihood that the experience will be remembered.[3] And Cavafy reminds us that this memory may indeed shine even brighter every time he returns to it, rearranges it, and adds more meaning to it.

Consider, then, how different Sonnet 129 reads in light of Cavafy's depiction of pleasurable recollection:

> Th' expense of spirit in a waste of shame
> Is lust in action, and, till action, lust
> Is perjured, murd'rous, bloody, full of blame,
> Savage, extreme, rude, cruel, not to trust,
> Enjoyed no sooner but despisèd straight,
> Past reason hunted, and, no sooner had,

[2] Thomas Wilson, *The Arte of Rhetoric*, ed. G. H. Mair (Oxford: Clarendon Press, 1909), 209.
[3] Conway's original formulation has influenced much work in the cognitive sciences regarding how memories are formed and encoded in the brain, a process which I discuss throughout the book. Martin A. Conway, *Flashbulb Memories* (Brighton: LEA, 1995).

> Past reason hated as a swallowed bait
> On purpose laid to make the taker mad,
> Mad in pursuit, and in possession so,
> Had, having, and in quest to have, extreme,
> A bliss in proof and proved a very woe,
> Before, a joy proposed; behind, a dream.
> All this the world well knows, yet none knows well
> To shun the heaven that leads men to this hell. (1–14)[4]

The speaker here finds his memories to be traumatic and all the more so because of their erotic charge. His "expense of spirit," or semen, is certainly a flashbulb memory for him, but the brief moment when he "enjoyed" the physical climax has been transformed into a source of equally powerful negative emotions. That "bliss" so quickly turned to "woe" as soon as it was viewed in hindsight. The poem's use of anadiplosis, where "mad" ends one line and repeats to start the next, emphasizes that his continual return in memory only makes him more irrational and more unhappy. Indeed, the endgame of this madness is the last word of the sonnet: "hell." One way to read that word is to see it as early modern slang for "vagina." So we may see here Shakespeare's misogyny, where he blames female sexuality for his suffering. At the same time, the term also suggests recollection as an afterlife of perpetual torture.

The speaker's madness derives, to some extent, from his inability to generate a traceable narrative that can make sense of the pleasure he received. Raphael Lyne locates such tension in the poem's "combining resonantly contrasting keywords ('bliss ... woe,' 'joy ... dream') with the language of logical organization ('proof, and prov'd ... propos'd')."[5] In turn, "the outcome is an arresting mixture of the inexpressible maelstrom of desire with some clear moral processing."[6] Shakespeare's speaker is far from achieving the mastery over erotic memory that Cavafy's speaker demonstrates, a mastery akin to one described in Levinus Lemnius's *The Touchstone of Complexions* (1576): "Those things therefore which a man would gladly remember, it shall be good for him to think upon, and many times with himself in mind to meditate and revolve."[7] Instead, Sonnet 129 dramatizes the opposite as its speaker dwells on those things "such as he would feign shake off and forget, as hurtful and pernicious to his mind," unable to "with reason and judgment stoutly resist and strive against [them]."[8]

---

[4] All references to the *Sonnets* are drawn from William Shakespeare, *The Oxford Shakespeare: The Complete Sonnets and Poems*, ed. Colin Burrow (Oxford: Oxford University Press, 2008). All subsequent references to the poems are cited by line number in the body of the chapter.

[5] Raphael Lyne, *Shakespeare, Rhetoric, Cognition* (Cambridge: Cambridge University Press, 2011), 212.

[6] Lyne, *Shakespeare, Rhetoric, Cognition*, 212.

[7] Levinus Lemnius, *The Touchstone of Complexions*, 2nd edition, trans. Thomas Marsh (London: Thomas Marsh, 1576), 122.

[8] Lemnius, *The Touchstone of Complexions*, 122.

We might say that what Cavafy's speaker achieves is a kind of integration, bringing his past forward in such a way that it can address present loneliness and rewrite possibly negative aspects of previous experience. Shakespeare's speaker, on the contrary, seems unable to accurately remember what pleased him and finds himself profoundly alone.[9] Adam Phillips may be right when he states that "a good memory makes us more efficient, productive, and better problem-solvers, which means more successful pleasure-seekers."[10] Sonnet 129 reminds us, though, that part of deriving pleasure from memory entails avoiding *too much* recollection, managing how one reacts to their recollections, and knowing when to forget.

The *Sonnets*

The Pleasures of Memory in Shakespeare's Sonnets pursues new lines of inquiry into Shakespeare's poems, in part, by setting aside long-held assumptions about them. As Heather Dubrow has observed, "Indeterminate in their chronology, destabilized by their textual cruxes, and opaque in their language, Shakespeare's sonnets nonetheless have attracted curiously positivistic claims."[11] That is, scholars have argued (often vigorously) for the poems' intended order, definitive meanings, or ties to the author's own biography.[12] My study embraces the evocative ambiguities of the poems. Rather than binding the discussion within the terms of an overall narrative structure to the poems, I trace shared operations and tropes that give us insight into Shakespeare's thinking on pleasure's peculiar relationship to memory. I thus follow scholars such as Paul Edmondson and Stanley Wells to favor a view where "the poems are more properly regarded as a collection than as a sequence."[13]

---

[9] The poem showcases failures in memory in the quest to achieve intimacy. Richard Levin interprets the series of strophes as signaling a "fading out in the speaker's memory," and Goran Stanivukovic sees this sonnet as part of a pattern where "masturbation is only one of several examples that illustrates a 'lack of reciprocity' in the *Sonnets*." Goran Stanivukovic, "Sex in the *Sonnets*: The Boy and Dishonourable Passions of the Past," in *Shakespeare / Sex: Contemporary Readings in Gender and Sexuality*, ed. Jennifer Droin (New York: Bloomsbury Arden Shakespeare, 2020), 183; and Richard Levin, "Sonnet 129 as a 'Dramatic' Poem," *Shakespeare Quarterly* 16 (1965): 179.

[10] Adam Phillips, *Side Effects* (New York: Harper Perennial, 2006), 101.

[11] Heather Dubrow, "'Incertainties now Crown Themselves assur'd': The Politics of Plotting in Shakespeare's Sonnets," *Shakespeare Quarterly* 47, no. 3 (1996): 291.

[12] Such efforts are clearly not ones of the past. Take, for example, Neil L. Rudenstine's *Ideas of Order: A Close Reading of Shakespeare's Sonnets* (New York: Farrar, Straus, and Giroux, 2014), which argues strongly for an an overarching narrative to the *Sonnets*, or Elaine Scarry's *Naming Thy Name: Cross-Talk in Shakespeare's Sonnets* (New York: Farrar, Straus, and Giroux, 2016), which identifies the male addressee of Sonnets 1–126 as Catholic exile Henry Constable. An older study that pursues the poems as an overall narrative but is nonetheless groundbreaking is Joseph Pequigney's *Such Is My Love: A Study of Shakespeare's Sonnets* (Chicago: University of Chicago Press, 1986), which takes the poems as autobiographical record of a homoerotic relationship. An intriguing, alternative take on a similar theme is Paul Innes's *Shakespeare and the English Renaissance Sonnet: Verses of Feigning Love* (New York: Macmillan, 1997), which looks at the instability of the poetic persona, as well as of femininity and masculinity, across sonnets of Shakespeare and his contemporaries.

[13] Paul Edmondson and Stanley Wells, *Shakespeare's Sonnets* (Oxford: Oxford University Press, 2004), 28.

However, as Wells has put it, they may not be a "unified sequence" but "nor are they a totally random assemblage of diverse poems."[14] Dilating on the intertwined themes of my study, I find connections across even seemingly disparate sonnets.[15] A strain of previous scholarship has been deeply invested in questions of "homosexual" or "heterosexual" desire in the poems, and this is also a place where my analysis seizes on the possibilities inherent in ambiguity.[16] I draw upon the ways that our understandings of desire have been productively complicated by scholars of sexuality in the early modern period. In doing so, I share Michael Schoenfeldt's belief that "the sonnets analyze love in its most heterodox incarnations."[17] And I hope this book can help meet Valerie Traub's challenge to scholars to rethink our "presumptive knowledge" about sex, to reconsider "*how* we know as much as *what* we know."[18] I draw from Traub's work the challenge to accept as unstable or inexact the depictions of sexual experiences in early modern literature and to embrace those ambiguities that put pressure on the notion of any kind of categorizable eroticism.[19] Indeed, I am fascinated by the way that Shakespeare seems to meditate on the at-times queer implications of being in love.

The very genre of Shakespeare's poems has ties not only to expressions of desire but also to the operations of memory. Hester Lees-Jeffries observes that by the

---

[14] Stanley Wells, *Looking for Sex in Shakespeare* (Cambridge: Cambridge University Press, 2004), 50.

[15] As Matthew Harrison remarks, "Caught between the infinite interpretability of a poem and our awareness that the patterns we find refract our own desires back to us, Shakespeare's sonnets have long invited us to confront our own methodologies and to reflect on which connections we are justified in making." Which sonnets speak to me, or which theories most resonate with me, ultimately are informed by my own experience and curiosities. Matthew Harrison, "Desire Is Pattern," in *Shakespeare's Sonnets: The State of Play*, ed. Hannah Crawforth, Elizabeth Scott-Baumann, and Clare Whitehead (New York: Bloomsbury Arden Shakespeare, 2017), 186.

[16] In a recent edition that reorganizes the poems in their likely chronological order, Paul Edmondson and Stanley Wells emphasize that there is little reason to perpetuate the idea that one set of the *Sonnets* is addressed to a "Young Man" and the other to a "Dark Lady." The editors make clear that some poems might be addressed only to a man or to a woman (though not always the same person across poems) while others could be addressed to either a female, gender-fluid, or male addressee, and that some lack any indication of a gendered addressee. Paul Edmondson and Stanley Wells, "Introduction," in William Shakespeare, *All the Sonnets of Shakespeare*, ed. Paul Edmondson and Stanley Wells (Cambridge: Cambridge University Press, 2020), 1–37.

[17] Michael Schoenfeldt, "Introduction," in *A Companion to Shakespeare's Sonnets*, ed. Michael Schoenfeldt (New York: John Wiley & Sons, 2006), 5.

[18] Valerie Traub, *Thinking Sex with the Early Moderns* (Philadelphia: University of Pennsylvania Press, 2016), 34. For another excellent volume on how our modern language and concepts around sex might estrange us from fully comprehending early modern sexualities, see Jeffrey Masten's *Queer Philologies: Sex, Language, and Affect in Shakespeare's Time* (Philadelphia: University of Pennsylvania Press, 2017).

[19] Throughout the book, I strive to consider as broadly as possible what might constitute the sexual in the poems. I do also comment on the role of romantic love in the poems. However, to favor the latter and ignore the former—in other words to follow Carl D. Atkins's urging for readers to "take from *The Sonnets* what is universal to all loving relationships heterosexual, homosexual, or passionate friendship, namely, true love"—risks overlooking the full expression of pleasures depicted in the poems. Carl D. Atkins, "The Context of the Sonnets," in William Shakespeare, *Shakespeare's Sonnets: With Three Hundred Years of Commentary*, ed. Carl D. Atkins (Madison and Teaneck: Farleigh Dickinson University Press, 2007), 15.

time Shakespeare's book was published in 1609, "the sonnet sequence was an old-fashioned, perhaps even nostalgic, genre."[20] Emily Vasiliauskas has argued that the "outmodedness" of the sonnet as Shakespeare's chosen form is part of his strategy to interleave memory and desire. "In giving up its ambitions either for timeliness or timelessness," she writes, "an outmoded poem suffers from neglect, and with neglect comes privacy."[21] That is, an intentionally outmoded style shields the writer from critiques in the moment while also investing the poem with a nostalgic mood. And this, too, motivates my approach to avoid seeking evidence of lived experience or biography in the *Sonnets*. As David Lowenthal puts it pointedly, "nostalgia tells it like it wasn't."[22] But, even if the *Sonnets* are works of the imagination, their backward-looking perspectives encourage me to see them as narratives of and about memory. The poems may or may not detail actual events of Shakespeare's life, but they do instantiate a speaker telling stories about the past as he makes sense of how it fits together to explain his present and to imagine his future.

My book does not argue that the *Sonnets* are somehow biographical, especially with regards to the poet's sexuality. "William Shakespeare was almost certainly homosexual, bisexual, or heterosexual," Stephen Booth remarks in his introduction to the 1977 edition; "the sonnets provide no evidence on the matter."[23] But we should also recall that, in Edmondson and Wells's estimation, "121 of the sonnets do involve people, real, or (and remember these poems are from the quill of an expert dramatist) imaginary."[24] One cannot do more than speculate about Shakespeare's own sexual interest. However, Shakespeare's *Sonnets* do importantly give readers access to a poetic voice that feels longing for male, female, and gender-fluid beloveds, and that voice may be very welcome to readers who feel it is lacking in the canon.

When we talk about Shakespeare's sonnets, we most often think of those 154 poems that were published in 1609 with the title *Shakespeare's Sonnets Never before Imprinted* (see the frontispiece). It is important to note, though, that there is no evidence that Shakespeare had a hand in publishing them or in how they are ordered. While Shakespeare was better known as a poet than as a playwright in his lifetime, the *Sonnets* did not seem to experience the great popularity and significance that they do today.[25]

[20] Hester Lees-Jeffries, *Shakespeare and Memory* (Oxford: Oxford University Press, 2013), 137.

[21] Emily Vasiliauskas, "The Outmodedness of Shakespeare's Sonnets," *ELH* 82, no. 3 (Fall 2015): 760.

[22] David Lowenthal, "Nostalgia Tells It Like It Wasn't," in *The Imagined Past: History and Nostalgia*, ed. Christopher Shaw and Malcolm Chase (Manchester: Manchester University Press, 1989), 18–32.

[23] Stephen Booth, *Shakespeare's Sonnets* (New Haven: Yale University Press, 1977), 548.

[24] Edmondson and Wells, "Introduction," 26.

[25] Despite Shakespeare's status as a widely read poet in his lifetime, the *Sonnets* did not experience as much popularity as his other works. *The Rape of Lucrece* was published in six editions while he was alive, and *Venus and Adonis* appeared in ten editions before he died. While certainly many people would have seen Shakespeare's plays, they did not circulate as widely as the poems did among readers. The

Though I am primarily a scholar of gender and sexuality studies, the "pleasure" that I explore in this book is not exclusively erotic and romantic. However, the *Sonnets* themselves do place such desires at the center of many of their depictions of recollection and thus this book reflects that.[26] Yet I also explore how the possible objects of desire and love, as Lauren Berlant's work captured so vividly, can be capacious:

> When we talk about an object of desire, we are really talking about a cluster of promises we want someone or something to make to us and make possible for us. This cluster of promises could be embedded in a person, a thing, an institution, a text, a norm, a bunch of cells, smells, a good idea—whatever.[27]

Thus, when I am discussing desire in the book, I address not just sexual or romantic objects of desire but also other sought-after objects such as canonicity, forgiveness, health, time, and even memory itself.

My book visits familiar sonnets as well as what will be less familiar ones for some readers. In doing so, I seek to put forth new readings, which pursue what Barbara Hardy finds to be "animated and strange" in Shakespeare's depictions of memory.[28] As I discuss below, my focus on memory in the poems is as much about retrospect as it is about anticipation. Thus I am drawn to them for their status as, in the words of Colin Burrow, "objects not fully knowable, stubbornly full of futurity."[29]

---

most popular were *Richard III* and *Richard II* (five editions each), *Romeo and Juliet* (four editions) and *Hamlet* (three editions). The *Sonnets* did not appear in the First Folio. The growth of the posthumous popularity can be attributed in part to John Benson's 1640 edition, which I discuss in Chapter Two. See Faith Acker, "John Benson's *Poems* and Its Literary Precedents," in *Canonising Shakespeare: Stationers and the Book Trade, 1640–1740*, ed. Emma Depledge and Peter Kirwan (Cambridge: Cambridge University Press, 2017), esp. 105–6.

[26] I do not mean to valorize erotic pleasures over others nor do I want to imply that such desires are universal. I am not sure that we can go as far as to say, as psychoanalyst Stephen Mitchell does, that "no realm of human experience is more fraught with conflict, conundrum, and confusion than sexuality." Certainly, those individuals who self-identify as asexual or aromantic, or characters who we might interpret to be so, can experience a fully enriched and complex life. However, I would agree with Mitchell that "the interpenetration of bodies required by the sexual act makes its endless variations ideally suited to represent desires, dreads, conflicts, and negotiations in the relations between self and others." For a useful overview of scholarship on Shakespearean asexuality, see Melissa E. Sanchez, "Protestantism, Marriage, and Asexuality in Shakespeare," in *Shakespeare / Sex: Contemporary Readings in Gender and Sexuality*, ed. Jennifer Drouin (London and New York: Bloomsbury Arden Shakespeare, 2022), 98–122. An excellent resource for scholarship related to premodern asexuality has been developed by Liza Blake, Simone Chess, Catherine Clifford, and Ashley "Aley" O'Mara. It can be accessed at https://tinyurl.com/earlymodacebib. Stephen Mitchell, *Can Love Last? The Fate of Romance over Time* (New York: W. W. Norton & Co., 2002), 58 and 59.

[27] Lauren Berlant, *Cruel Optimism* (Durham: Duke University Press, 2011), 1.

[28] Barbara Hardy, "Shakespeare's Narrative: Acts of Memory," *Essays in Criticism* 39, no. 2 (1989): 114.

[29] He goes on to say, "Any attempt to relate a poem to a single occasion necessarily ignores what we might term the uncooperative principle of lyric, which is central to the trans-historical vitality of poetry." Colin Burrow, "Shakespeare's Sonnets as Event," in *The Sonnets: The State of Play*, ed. Hannah Crawforth, Elizabeth Scott-Baumann, and Clare Whitehead (New York: Bloomsbury Arden Shakespeare, 2017), 112.

Part of my motivation in writing this book is to share what I have learned—and what I am still learning—about the *Sonnets* in the classroom and as the focus of student research.[30] I admit that many of the interests here are personal to me, too, or involve sonnets about which I love to puzzle and ponder with others.[31]

While the *Sonnets* are appealing for literary study broadly, I find them particularly compelling for the exploration of the nature of memory. Consider psychologist Mark Freeman's contention that there is a "parallel between hindsight and poetry." He writes, "just as hindsight might expose meanings that might have been unavailable in the immediacy of the moment, poetry might disclose meanings or truths that might otherwise have gone unarticulated."[32] I would add that both poetry and recollection entail an ordering process. And because this process is explicitly narrativized on the written page, the *Sonnets* offer a complement to modern theories that focus on unconscious processes. Indeed, The *Sonnets'* status as primarily love poetry makes them useful for my line of inquiry into the interoperations of desire and memory. Toni Morrison remarks that writing entails "not simply recollecting or reminiscing" but also "It is doing: creating a narrative."[33] I find such active work in Shakespeare's poems especially as he uses the formal elements of the sonnet to make sense of how he remembers and how he desires.[34]

Part of what interests me is how this collection of poems can help us understand what cognitive psychologists term *the autobiographical self*. While recent scholarship has largely dismissed the idea that the *Sonnets* are a sequence or that they tell a coherent story, they are utterances of a speaker addressing a beloved, a reader, or himself. That is, these poems tell us about the speaker (not necessarily Shakespeare) and how he desires and remembers, among other things. The poet constructs his speaker through a process that mirrors how neuroscientist Antonio Damasio describes the generation of the autobiographical self through "reiterated display of some of our own personal memories, the *objects of our personal past*, those that can easily substantiate our identity, moment by moment, and our

---

[30] As Edmondson and Wells observe, "coupled with the compression and density of the poems themselves, the Sonnets can soon become the most difficult and complicated part of the Shakespearean canon to read and discuss." Edmondson and Wells, *Shakespeare's Sonnets*, 50.

[31] Brian Boyd argues that the lasting power of the *Sonnets* lies in their complex use of expectation and surprise, which uniquely stimulate pleasure centers in the brain because "the proliferation of patterns upon patterns that Shakespeare incorporates into his sonnets [...] makes the detection of pattern an ongoing pleasurable, a hide-and-seek game." Brian Boyd, *Why Lyrics Last: Evolution, Cognition, and Shakespeare's Sonnets* (Cambridge, MA: Harvard University Press, 2012), 162.

[32] Mark Freeman, *Hindsight: The Promise and Peril of Looking Backwards* (Oxford: Oxford University Press, 2010), 43.

[33] Toni Morrison, "Rememory," in *The Source of Self-Regard: Selected Essays, Speeches, and Meditations* (New York: Alfred A. Knopf, 2019), 323.

[34] As Jyotsna Singh observes, the speaker "frequently reveals an impulse to *aestheticize* his passions, typically associated with the frustrations of desire, in the solace of memory of previously shared love." Jyotsna G. Singh, "'Th' expense of spirit in a waste of shame': Mapping the 'Emotional Regime' of Shakespeare's Sonnets," in *A Companion to Shakespeare's Sonnets*, ed. Michael Schoenfeldt (New York: John Wiley & Sons, 2006), 285.

personhood."[35] Yet these objects are by no means concrete or fixed. Memories are, as Martin Conway puts it, "peculiar experience-near symbols of the self that both reveal and conceal goals, purposes, desires, and images of the self in the past."[36] I find particularly useful the way that Conway pairs the terms "experience-near" and "symbols," underscoring that recollection shares with literature its inherent fictionality and elements of analogue, metaphor, and simile.

Memory and Pleasure

The book argues that we should develop a richer understanding of how memories are formed by considering literary depictions—especially early modern depictions—of the recollective process. I contend that modern scientific and psychoanalytic accounts of the memory-formation process largely leave out the possibility of *agential* techniques for memory making, techniques that were explored by a number of early modern thinkers, including Shakespeare. Current brain science understands memory as an adaptive faculty that suits contextual purpose. Neuroscientists, for example, see memory as a repository but one clearly affected by emotional context, which feeds biochemical stressors.[37] Psychoanalytic frameworks interpret our impulse to repress some memories as movement between the conscious and subconscious components of the mind.[38] Early modern writers predicted the insights of both these fields in many ways, but they also approached memory as an art and a technique.[39]

[35] Antonio Damasio, *The Feeling of What Happens: Body, Emotion, and the Making of Consciousness* (Orlando: Harcourt, 1999), 196.

[36] Martin Conway, "Memory and Desire: Reading Freud," *The Psychologist* 19, no. 9 (2006): 549.

[37] Shakespeare's work has recently been the object of analysis by scholars interested in cognitive science. However, such work has focused primarily on the plays and on audiences' experience of them. See, for example, Donald Beecher, "Recollection, Cognition, and Culture: An Overview on Renaissance Memory," in *Ars Reminiscendi: Mind and Memory in Renaissance Culture*, ed. Donald Beecher and Grant Williams (Toronto: Centre for Renaissance and Reformation Studies, 2009), 367–426; Mary Thomas Crane, *Shakespeare's Brain: Reading with Cognitive Theory* (Princeton: Princeton University Press, 2000); Evelyn Tribble, *Cognition in the Globe: Attention and Memory in Shakespeare's Theatre* (Basingstoke: Palgrave Macmillan, 2011); Evelyn Tribble and John Sutton, "Minds in and out of Time: Memory, Embodied Skill, Anachronism, and Performance," *Textual Practice* 26 (2012): 587–607; and Evelyn Tribble and John Sutton, "Cognitive Ecology as a Framework for Shakespearean Studies," *Shakespeare Studies* 39 (2011): 94–103.

[38] As Valeria Finucci and Regina Schwartz remark, in their introduction to the essay collection *Desire in the Renaissance: Psychoanalysis and Literature*, "For all their differences—Shakespeare did not read Freud (if Freud did read Shakespeare)—Renaissance literature and psychoanalysis are both obsessed with the 'inner life' and the ways in which it interacts with the more external spheres." Valeria Finucci and Regina Schwartz, "Introduction: Worlds within and without," in *Desire in the Renaissance: Psychoanalysis and Literature*, ed. Valeria Finucci and Regina Schwartz (Princeton: Princeton University Press, 1994), 3.

[39] In addition to those works already cited in this introduction, I would note this long (and certainly incomplete) list of recent work: William E. Engel's *Death and Drama in Renaissance England: Shades of Memory* (Oxford: Oxford University Press, 2002), *Forgetting in Early Modern English Literature and Culture*, ed. Christopher Ivic and Grant Williams (London: Routledge, 2004), Garrett A. Sullivan's

Those early moderns writing on memory conceived of it as a faculty to be developed and managed, especially through the use of rhetoric. In this way, their approaches presage modern psychology, which increasingly understands the self to be constructed as we tell ourselves stories to explain patterns or to link experiences in our lives. This book places Shakespeare's *Sonnets* at the center of a discussion about how Renaissance writers consciously shaped their own self-narratives. In doing so, I trace more broadly how early modern thought suggests ways that contemporary neuroscientific and psychoanalytic understandings of recollection might be expanded and deepened.[40]

Early moderns saw that memories are not necessarily representations of actual experiences but instead are tools for shaping affective experience (sometimes toward pleasurable ends but other times for harmful ends). We perhaps know this phenomenon best in the form of what modern memory studies scholars call *postmemory*, a term that Marianne Hirsch has introduced to describe the ways in which historical events are reshaped as they are later recalled by members of a culture.[41] I extend the use of this term to describe the way that an individual's memory is reshaped after the fact, as exemplified in the *Sonnets*. Further, even expectation in the *Sonnets* functions as a form of what I would term *pre-memory*, where memories are pre-formed prior to the actual experience. These pre-memories are influenced by recollections of previous experience but, more importantly, involve an individual imagining a future event in the way that one hopes to remember that event after the fact. For the speaker of Shakespeare's *Sonnets*, the *now* of the poems is often preoccupied with thoughts of reunion with his beloved. In Sonnet 29, for example, "thy sweet love remembered" allows the speaker to withstand compounding emotional loss by imagining the presence of the poem's addressee (29.13). However, irreconcilable details about the seasons in Sonnets 97–9 reveal that recalled encounters with the male beloved are partially fictions generated to combat loneliness in the present even as they suggest the speaker's doubt about his own desirability. Further, the hoped-for reunion between the poems' speaker and addressee is desired for its capacity as material for future memories.

Memory and Forgetting in English Renaissance Drama: Shakespeare, Marlowe, Webster (Cambridge: Cambridge University Press, 2005), Grant Williams's *Ars Reminiscendi: Mind and Memory in Renaissance Culture* (Toronto: Center for Reformation and Renaissance Studies, 2009), Andrew Hiscock's *Reading Memory in Early Modern Literature* (Cambridge: Cambridge University Press, 2011), Rebeca Helfer's *Spenser's Ruins and the Art of Recollection* (Toronto: University of Toronto Press, 2012), Kyle Pivetti's *Of Memory and Literary Form: Making the Early Modern English Nation* (Newark: University of Delaware Press, 2015), and John S. Garrison and Kyle Pivetti, eds., *Sexuality and Memory in Early Modern England: Literature and the Erotics of Recollection* (New York: Routledge, 2015).

[40] Let me be clear that my study is not trying to convince us that Shakespeare somehow envisioned neuroscience, something like Jonah Lehrer, *Proust Was a Neuroscientist* (New York: Houghton Mifflin Harcourt, 2007). Nor is it some sort of primer on brain science such as Paul M. Matthews, Jeffrey McQuain, and Diana Ackerman, *The Bard on the Brain: Understanding the Mind through the Art of Shakespeare and the Science of Brain Imaging* (New York: Dana Press, 2003).

[41] Marianne Hirsch, "Family Pictures: Maus, Mourning, and Post-Memory," *Discourse* 15, no. 2 (Winter 1992–3): 3–29.

Part of my argument, then, is that memories are generated agentially to accomplish certain affective goals and that those memories are sometimes generated ahead of time. Because subjects look forward to new experiences based on what has come before—whether they seek to avoid negative experiences or repeat positive ones—anticipation can be framed as a form of memory. In fact, recent research has found that the same areas of the brain are involved in recollection and in prediction.[42] Yet I argue that Shakespeare's *Sonnets* help us see how an individual might begin to prefigure pleasurable experiences in the mind based not just on past recollection but also on hope for how the future self will look back upon these experiences.

I hope that *The Pleasures of Memory in Shakespeare's Sonnets* expands our conceptual vocabulary for discussing the role of *remembering* in the *Sonnets*. Critical discussions of these poems typically consider recollection only in terms of what scholars of memory studies call *cultural memory* or *collective memory*—how past events or figures are kept alive in the public recollection shared within a group or groups. That is, the *Sonnets* are analyzed and taught in terms of how they seem designed to immortalize both Shakespeare and his "fair" and "dark" beloveds through everlasting fame (or infamy) in the minds of future readers. While my study acknowledges this effort to secure a literary afterlife for the figures in the poems, I am mainly interested in *individual memory*, an operation of primary interest to fields in the cognitive sciences and psychoanalysis. I trace the speaker's efforts to understand how his own memory functions and how he might influence the memories of his addressees in the collection of poems. While the author seeks to control how future generations will regard his writing, the poetic speaker seeks to control his own future memories and thus points to a conscious dimension to memory formation.[43]

My analysis locates the *Sonnets* within the context of treatises on the early modern memory arts, while also setting the stage for how the book excavates historical ideas that have purchases on modern notions of memory. In a similar vein, I look at early modern discourses on love and sexuality and counterpose them to contemporary ideas about desire.

---

[42] I describe this research in Chapter Seven.

[43] Rather than simply seeking instances of commonplaces from the early modern memory arts in Shakespeare's poems, I seek also to trace how he personalizes or reacts against those models. I take inspiration from the way Tony Judt, near the end of his life and unable to write due to loss of the use of his limbs from ALS, would compose essays in his head at night and then memorize them by using his own personalized version of the memory arts. In his posthumously published memoir, he notes how he "had long been fascinated by the mnemonic devices employed by early-modern thinkers and travelers [yet] could no more have imagined in my still and silent nights such a memory palace than I could have sewn myself a star-spangled suit of pantaloon and vest." Instead, he drew upon "nostalgic recollections of happier days spent in cozy central European villages," coming to settle on a model that was meaningful for him: "if not a memory palace, why not a memory chalet?" Tony Judt, *The Memory Chalet* (New York: Penguin, 2011), 6.

Just as I focus on the profound complexity of the romantic impulses described in the *Sonnets*, I also show how the poems productively complicate our understanding of recollection. I examine memory as an active, dialectical process—one that can only function in tandem with forgetting; one that requires fantasy to make convincing narrative of past experience; and one that is a communal experience as well as a private one. The book thus expands our conceptual vocabulary for discussing the role of *remembering* in the *Sonnets* beyond what Hester Lees-Jeffries refers to by that helpful phrase "the eternizing conceit."[44] It thereby builds on extensive and insightful scholarship in recent years on memory in the early modern period, work which often includes some mention of Shakespeare.[45]

I take as my focus how recollection is co-constitutive of pleasure in the poems. Indeed, because the speaker so often laments the absence of the beloved, memory becomes the primary means by which he can achieve the pleasure of erotic union. And these memories are often shaped by what he hopes will happen in the future. As my analysis shows, both the speaker's moments of anticipation and his moments of recollection represent efforts to bring pleasure in the present. Yet, both expectation and retrospect involve the imagination. On the one hand, the *Sonnets'* hopeful instances seem to embody Casanova's notion that "the best moment of love is when one is climbing the stairs."[46] On the other hand, the richest erotic moments sometimes instantiate Foucault's notion that "the best moment of love is likely to be when the lover leaves in the taxi."[47] Yet we should also recognize the pessimism in each of these viewpoints, both of which the regretful speaker of Sonnet 129 captures with the phrase "Before, a joy proposed; behind, a dream."[48]

Rather than Casanova and Foucault articulating opposite positions, we can consider their shared implication: the most erotic moments lie not in the encounter but in the recreation of the encounter in the mind, when the power of fantasy begins to assert its narrative over the material provided by memory. And it is important to note that this material is never truly *raw material*. Recollection, even

[44] Lees-Jeffries, *Shakespeare and Memory*, 9.

[45] Books which take Shakespeare and memory as their primary focus include Peter Holland, ed., *Shakespeare, Memory and Performance* (Cambridge: Cambridge University Press, 2006), Lina Perkins Wilder's *Shakespeare's Memory Theatre: Recollection, Properties, and Character* (Cambridge: Cambridge University Press, 2010), Jonathan Baldo's *Memory in Shakespeare's Histories: Stages of Forgetting in Early Modern England* (New York: Routledge, 2012), Isabel Karremann's *The Drama of Memory in Shakespeare's History Plays* (Cambridge: Cambridge University Press, 2015), and Andrew Hiscock and Lina Perkins Wilder, eds., *The Routledge Handbook of Shakespeare and Memory* (New York: Routledge, 2018).

[46] Michel Foucault, "Sexual Choice, Sexual Act," in *Foucault Live: Collected Interviews, 1961–1984*, ed. Sylvère Lotringer (New York: Semiotext(e), 1996), 330.

[47] Foucault, "Sexual Choice, Sexual Act," 330.

[48] Wilfred Bion, a mid-century psychoanalyst whose thinking drew from Sigmund Freud and Melanie Klein, writes, "Memory and Desire [...] deal respectively with sense impressions of what is supposed to have happened and sense impressions of what has not yet happened." Here, memory is only about the past, and desire focuses on the future. What we will see in the *Sonnets* problematizes such binary distinctions. Wilfred R. Bion, "Notes on Memory and Desire," *The Psychoanalytic Forum* 2 (1967): 272.

moments after the fact, is shaped by one's point of view and one's own personal experience as well as by the genre—confession, self-reassurance, sonnet—in which one resuscitates the memory.[49] And these operations are by no means solitary. Indeed, the memory-inflected pleasures in the *now* of the poems often figure themselves as efforts to draw the beloved (and even the reader) into the situation of the speaker.

The other productive complication I would like to note here is that memory is not always backward-looking and desire is not always forward-looking. As I argue throughout this book, the *Sonnets* provide a compelling case study for the future-inflected nature of memory. The notion that memory relates to and shapes the future has been explored by scholars of memory studies, and I build on their work here.

Overview of the Chapters

The book is divided into seven chapters, which combine historicist and presentist close readings. More often than not, I reproduce the entire sonnet being examined. I do this both for the ease of the reader to not need to consult a second volume and to acknowledge that the pleasures of reading poems is part of the reason that many of us study them. I place Shakespeare's *Sonnets* in dialogue with other texts that may have informed them or would inform a reader's experiences of them because, as Raphael Lyne puts it, "Theories of memory can tell us things about literary intertextuality; but literary intertextuality can tell us things about theories of memory."[50] I also consider some poems that are explicit adaptations of Shakespeare's as I believe they can both tell us about how the *Sonnets* have been received over time and also cast the original poem in a new interpretive light.[51] Other contemporary texts are included to throw into relief patterns of thought in the *Sonnets* in order to encourage new readings of them. I concur with Valerie Traub that "What requires new theorizing is how to stage a dialogue between *one*

---

[49] This is an insight shared by cognitive science and by psychoanalysis, though the causes might be in dispute. As Conway and Freeman have noted above, individuals remember in ways that fulfill their sense of self and their desires for the future. Bion notes that "Memory is always misleading as a record of fact as it is distorted by the influence of unconscious forces." Bion, "Notes on Memory and Desire," 272.

[50] Raphael Lyne, *Memory and Intertextuality in Renaissance Literature* (Cambridge: Cambridge University Press, 2006), 2.

[51] Useful starting points for drawing such genealogies are Faith D. Acker, *First Readers of Shakespeare's Sonnets 1590–1790* (London: Routledge, 2020); Jane Kingsley-Smith, *The Afterlife of Shakespeare's Sonnets* (Cambridge: Cambridge University Press, 2019); Bruce R. Smith, "Shakespeare's Sonnets and the History of Sexuality: A Reception History," in *A Companion to Shakespeare's Works*, Vol. 4: *The Poems, Problem Comedies, Late Plays*, ed. Richard Dutton and Jean E. Howard (Oxford: Blackwell, 2003), 4–26.

past and *another*."[52] In using this approach, I acknowledge historical difference while exploring how such transhistorical conversation might prove fruitful.

Chapter One, "Time, Hope, and Desire," considers how desirous memory might alter the speaker's experience of temporality. It integrates a conventional reading of time in the *Sonnets* as a swift-footed force that threatens to devour all that the speaker holds dear—his beauty and reputation, as well as those of his beloveds. However, the analysis also explores how the poet attempts to deploy the power of retrospective and anticipatory memory to summon the past—and even the future—into the present. I trace how the speaker attempts to gain control over time when he seizes upon the narrative component to identity and to recollect. The second chapter, "The Pleasure of the *Sonnets*," pursues two interrelated questions: what constitutes pleasure in Shakespeare's poems and what pleasure does the reader derive from reading them? The discussion utilizes Roland Barthes's *The Pleasure of the Text* as a heuristic framework for pursuing these questions, and the chapter takes Sonnet 18 as its central case study, as this poem captures an elevated state of love that is at heart indescribable. The discussion underscores how memory—both the speaker's and the reader's—cannot be disaggregated from the pleasures described in the poem

Chapter Three, "Embracing Absence," begins by considering the evocative apostrophe to absence itself in Sonnet 39. When we recognize the absence of the beloved as a persistent theme, Shakespeare's *Sonnets* suggest that the absence associated with mourning and unfulfilled romantic longing should not be taken as entirely negative. The speaker of the *Sonnets* at times seems to prefer the beloved in his absence as he can explore strategies for new forms of erotic experience that find longing—not union—as the marker for the most heightened form of pleasure. The fourth chapter, "Body, Remember," takes its title from Cavafy's poem of the same name. I explore how Shakespeare, like Cavafy, viewed the body as a repository for memories and an access point for an archive of erotic experience. I examine the vexed operations of bodily memory, which both enable and threaten the private intimacy that the speaker seeks.

Chapter Five, "Scenographies of Waiting," continues the discussion from the previous chapter and centers on the ways in which the speaker promises he can function as a double for the beloved. The poet draws upon a variety of dyadic models—idealized friends and married partners, as well as the master and the enslaved person—but finds that each undermines the promise of the double to store and carry forward memories of their other half. The sixth chapter, "Remembering, Repeating, and Writing Through," adapts its title from Freud's early essay on the repetition compulsion entitled "Remembering, Repeating, and Writing Through." The chapter attempts to answer a question that has vexed many readers: why does repetition abound in the *Sonnets*, both within certain key poems and

---

[52] Valerie Traub, "Friendship's Loss: Alan Bray's Making of History," *GLQ* 10, no. 3 (2004): 357.

across the poems? This chapter argues for repetition as a form of erotic memory, revealing that persistent phrases and tropes emphasize that recollected pleasure intensifies with each instance. The chapter concludes with a discussion of efforts to forget in the *Sonnets*, focusing on an erotics of oblivion that adds a new dimension to the selective operations of postmemory.

My final chapter, "Contagious Memory," represents the study at its most presentist. I engage in a close reading of Sonnet 147 in tandem with a meditation on a recent adaptation of the poem by Maureen Owen. I set this discussion in the context of recent research about the nature of memory replication as well as the function of prediction in relation to recollection in the brain. This forms the foundation for final thoughts on the unique purchase of early modern literature on our understanding of the pandemics of our time.

1

Time, Hope, and Desire

In William Faulkner's *The Sound and the Fury*, Quentin is given his grandfather's watch and is told to think of it as "the mausoleum of all hope and desire."[1] I cannot remember when I first heard or read this phrase, but it has been deeply embedded in my memory for a long time now. It pinpoints vividly for me that Renaissance aphorism *tempus edax rerum*. Time will devour all things. When Quentin looks at this watch, he will see foreclosed and foreclosing possibilities. He will recall the things he wanted to do but has not done, the things he wishes he had done differently, and the things he cannot do within the time he has left. And the watch will serve as a mausoleum not just commemorating Quentin's unfulfilled hopes and desires but also those of his father and grandfather who wore it before him. These sentiments dovetail with a conventional reading of the *Sonnets*, one where the speaker again and again laments his and his beloveds' dissipating youth and beauty as well as the uncertainty of future fame.[2] While such a reading certainly characterizes the urgency that motivates many of the poems, it does not fully capture the ways in which the interplay between desire and memory offers the speaker reprieve from such a doomed sense of temporality.

It was only recently, when I revisited Faulkner's novel while writing the present book, that I realized that there is more to the description of the watch. When Quentin's father passes on the heirloom, he adds, "I give it to you not that you remember time, but that you may forget it now and then for a moment and not spend all your breath trying to conquer it."[3] I find in Shakespeare's *Sonnets* this same dialectic, this same collision of opposing senses of the operations of time. On the one hand, the poems' speaker admits that time's passage intensifies the weight of inevitability and generates remorse about lost opportunities. On the other hand, his growing understanding of the story he tells himself about time produces the possibility of liberating himself from time's grasp. Indeed, Shakespeare's choice of genre for this meditation has close kinship with Quentin's watch. "The sonnet form is always a timekeeping device," Wendy Beth Hyman remarks, "a lyric whose

---

[1] William Faulkner, *The Sound and the Fury: The Corrected Text* (New York: Vintage, 1991), 76.
[2] Dympna Callaghan observes the financial urgency that may motivate Shakespeare's focus on time's swift progress: "While Petrarch spends a lifetime of excruciating introspection on the *Canzoniere*, it is precisely time that the poet in the sonnets, hustling for patronage in the burgeoning metropolis, simply does not possess." Dympna Callaghan, "Confounded by Winter: Speeding Time in Shakespeare's Sonnets," in *A Companion to Shakespeare's Sonnets*, ed. Michael Schoenfeldt (New York: John Wiley & Sons, 2006), 104.
[3] Faulkner, *The Sound and the Fury*, 76.

The Pleasures of Memory in Shakespeare's Sonnets. John S. Garrison, Oxford University Press. © John S. Garrison (2023).
DOI: 10.1093/oso/9780198857716.003.0002

rhythmic structure foregrounds its imminent end."[4] The fourteen lines of iambic pentameter tick away an allotment of heartbeats for the reader with little variation. Yet the *Sonnets'* frequent subjects—loss, love, the bearing of the past on the present and on the future—involve feelings and experiences with time-defying effects.[5]

Desire can do strange things to the perception of time. Consider the statement (attributed to Albert Einstein but probably apocryphally so) "When a pretty girl sits on your lap for an hour, it seems like a minute. When you sit on a hot stove for a minute, it seems like an hour. That's relativity."[6] Here, in this simple object lesson that counterposes pure somatic sensation to a more complex interweaving of bodily pleasure and mentalization, the speed of time's passage correlates to the degree to which the experience is desired. And this relativity is best realized after the fact. The situations in the quotation engage the memory of an experience: it is only when the speaker looks at their watch during that hour spent with someone attractive or looks at the clock after pulling the hand away from the burner does he realize how much or how little time has passed. The statement usefully crystallizes the queerness inherent in the relativity conjoining desire, memory, and time, a queerness which extends into the Shakespearean imaginary. As Elizabeth Freeman notes, "when Prince Hamlet says that 'the time is out of joint,' he describes time as if its heterogeneity feels like a skeletal, or at least deeply somatic, dislocation."[7] We find such differential bodily experience of temporality in Einstein's comment and, as we will see, in the *Sonnets* as well. Not only is time felt by the body but the experience of pleasure or pain dislocates the body's connection to an objective, universal experience of time's passage.

---

[4] Wendy Beth Hyman, "Patterns, the Shakespearean Sonnet, and Epistemologies of Scale," *Spenser Studies: A Renaissance Poetry Annual* 36 (2022): 331.

[5] There may also have been a more ambiguous relationship to time's passage in the Renaissance than we conceive today. Paul Glennie and Nigel Smith call our attention to "the sheer diversity of ways in which clock time has been counted, a topic with a complex history which has been almost entirely lost in contemporary daily life." They remind us that, until the late seventeenth century, "clock time revolved around public devices and public spaces, rather than being something that was kept privately." The parish church or town hall would be the place to generate a sense of time markers through the public tolling of bells. Queen Elizabeth wore a wristwatch that did not function. People were aware of time's passage but did not track its specificity in ways we do today. Paul Glennie and Nigel Smith, *Shaping the Day: A History of Timekeeping in England and Wales 1300–1800* (Oxford: Oxford University Press, 2011), 24.

[6] There are numerous permutations of the quotation appearing in newspapers, quotation compendiums, and trade books since 1929. This version appeared in "Here You Have It," *The Circleville Herald* (September 27, 1929), page 2, column 4. Qtd in Albert Einstein, *The Ultimate Quotable Albert Einstein*, ed. Alice Calaprice (Princeton: Princeton University Press, 2010), 409.

[7] Amanda Bailey nicely articulates how the temporal flow of *Hamlet* seems to be anything but straight: "For Hamlet, his father's death and ghostly return is untimely, his uncle's assumption of the throne preemptive, and his mother's remarriage premature. For us, Hamlet's move from contemplation to action occurs too late, even as the play itself is seen as ahead of its time." Amanda Bailey, "Hamlet without Sex: The Politics of Regenerate Loss," in *Sexuality and Memory in Shakespeare's England: Literature and the Erotics of Recollection*, ed. John S. Garrison and Kyle Pivetti (London and New York: Routledge, 2016), 221; and Elizabeth Freeman, *Time Binds: Queer Temporalities, Queer Histories* (Durham: Duke University Press, 2010), 11.

The presence of the beloved is so thrilling in the lap of the supposed Einstein that afterwards he declares, "That's relativity," as if the sometimes counter-intuitive experiences of the mechanics of the universe find their best analogue in the experience of erotic desire. And his ability to recall this moment has the capacity to expand his sense of time's elasticity. That is, his perceived minute with a beloved may only last an hour, but the mental return to that encounter in memory can occur over and over again, extending the duration of the time one might spend there. I am reminded here of the central idea in Hirokazu Kore-eda's *After Life*.[8] In the film, the newly deceased choose their happiest memory which, in turn, they will re-experience for eternity as they forget all other events from their lives. Kore-eda's film uses a speculative premise to imagine an experience of time that is made elastic through recursivity, and it is enabled by an active choice in how one dwells in memory.[9] The film thus dramatizes what Carolyn Dinshaw describes as "the possibility of a fuller, denser, more crowded *now* that all sorts of theorists tell us is extant but that often eludes our temporal grasp."[10] Each of these imagined objects—an inherited watch that allows Quentin to forget time, a pretty girl who speeds time, a snowglobe-like afterlife which transforms a moment into eternity—grants access to such an expanded now. I would add the sonnet—that "scanty plot of land" where nonetheless William Wordsworth found "brief solace"—to such a list of time-warping devices.[11]

"Scanty" and "brief" might seem apt descriptors for the fleeting moments in which Shakespeare perceives his moments of happiness with a beloved. The final lines of Sonnet 64 express this so compellingly:

> Ruin hath taught me thus to ruminate,
> That Time will come and take my love away.
> This thought is as a death, which cannot choose
> But weep to have that which it fears to lose. (11–14)

The story the speaker tells himself characterizes time as a relentless march toward decay, and that story is so compelling that it casts a depressive shadow across even the present experience of love. Even in the moment when the object of his affection is alive and possessed by him, the lover thinks only of impending loss. And that

---

[8] *After Life* (known in Japan as *Wonderful Life*), directed by Hirokazu Kore-eda (Engine Film and TV Man Union, 1998).

[9] Kore-eda describes his thinking behind the film this way: "Although the memories in *After Life* are presented as real experiences that are later reconstructed as film, you can't really distinguish the stories characters tell as 'truth' and the recreations as 'fiction'. They intertwine with great complexity." Qtd from the original film press pack in Calum Russell, "*After Life*: Hirokazu Koreeda's Meditative Analysis," *Far Out Magazine* (August 10, 2021).

[10] Carolyn Dinshaw, *How Soon Is Now? Medieval Texts, Amateur Readers, and the Queerness of Time* (Durham: Duke University Press, 2012), 4.

[11] William Wordsworth, "Nuns Fret not in Their Narrow Rooms," in *William Wordsworth—The Major Works: Including The Prelude*, ed. Stephen Gill (Oxford: Oxford University Press, 2008), 286.

vision of the future is informed by "ruin," a macabre figure of a teacher who takes the form of the decaying external world or of aging bodies.[12] The lines express how, as studies by contemporary cognitive psychologists have found, "rumination involves a kind of obsessive recycling of thoughts and memories regarding one's current mood or situation which produces an even worse outcome."[13] Yet the speaker's dire tone serves as a reminder that this is just one variation of possible self-talk as he seems to fail to realize "the difference between generating useful narratives and endlessly ruminating."[14] He might instead embrace an alternative story about his life that could alleviate the negativistic pain of recursivity. This sonnet, like others I will examine in this chapter, help us see how storytelling is not just the purview of literature but also of the mode by which individuals make sense of their lives. Studies in the field of cognitive psychology have found that "the act of turning turbulent emotions into narrative form influences important physiological symptoms," including "positive mood."[15] The foreclosed possibilities for the future stated so definitively at the end of Sonnet 64 throw into relief how an alternative narrative might assuage the speaker. In turn, a re-contextualizing and retroactive sense-making regarding past experience might generate positivity. What the speaker seems to lack in this poem is clarity around the narrative component to memory and how that might shape his relationship to time.

Telling Time

Sonnet 12 and Sonnet 60 are perhaps the most overt examples of Shakespeare telling himself a story about his and the beloved's relationship to time. Both of these poems might seem simply to reinforce the conventional *tempus edax rerum* message. Sonnet 12, whose numbering calls our attention to the passing hours on the clock, portrays Time as a violent adversary with the ability to terminate possibility in a definitive stroke. It opens with the speaker watching the clock and thinking about decay, "When I do count the clock that tells the time, / And see the brave day sunk in hideous night" (1–2). The poem ends by suggesting, as the other so-called "procreation sonnets" do, that the addressee should have a child because "nothing 'gainst Time's scythe can make defence / Save breed to brave him when he takes thee hence" (13–14). This couplet posits a resistance tactic, one that is all the more potent in light of the Renaissance notion that the child is a

---

[12] The poet describes "lofty towers" (3), "brass" (4), and waves eroding the "shore" (6), but he also describes "outworn buried age" (2) and "state itself confounded to decay" (10). The notion of the decaying, once-desirable body is amplified when we realize that "state" carried a now-obsolete meaning of "Stature, bodily form, or shape," in the early modern period. "state, n.5b" OED online.

[13] Daniel L. Schacter, *The Seven Sins of Memory: How the Mind Forgets and Remembers* (Boston and New York: Houghton Mifflin Harcourt, 2001), 171.

[14] Schacter, *The Seven Sins of Memory*, 171.

[15] Schacter, *The Seven Sins of Memory*, 171.

copy of the father. However, to resist time's threat of foreclosure by having a child serves to undergird a worldview of time inevitably marching forward at a set pace. The figure of the child, which Lee Edelman has located at the center of ideology that privileges continuation of the family line within a positivistic "reproductive futurism," places the beloved's genealogy in lockstep with time's march forward.[16]

The notion that forward progress of father to child is inevitable has the suspect straightforwardness of Claudius's counsel to his nephew Hamlet, "But you must know your father lost a father; / That father lost, lost his" (1.2.89–90).[17] But in Elsinore, as in the *Sonnets*, the progress of time is not so teleological or straight. And the past does not remain so inaccessible. Prince Hamlet encounters his friend Horatio, who has seen the ghost the night before, and tells him:

HAMLET: My father—methinks I see my father.
HORATIO: O where, my lord?
HAMLET: In my mind's eye, Horatio.
[...]
HORATIO: My lord, I think I saw him yesternight.
HAMLET: Saw? Who?
HORATIO: My lord, the King your father. (1.2.183–90)

In terms of the plot of the play, the major revelation here is that the prince's deceased father still roams the castle grounds. We also learn, though, that Hamlet thinks often of his father and feels as if he too has seen him even after his death. The parallel structure of Horatio's and Hamlet's claims in the dialogue above points to a likeness in the experiences. The father can break the barrier between the living world and the afterlife to haunt the present in the form of a ghost and in the form of personal memory. The emotional pull of recollection resists Claudius's advice that one should curtail mourning in order to simply move forward along with the family line. Memory demands a rumination on the past, a necessity punctuated by the ghost's final edict to his son in their subsequent encounter: "Remember me" (1.5.91).

The bluntness of Sonnet 12's numbering and final couplet suggests a world apart from Elsinore, where "the time is out of joint" (1.5.189). However, the body of the poem reveals a more nuanced understanding of time's relativity. The first line emphasizes the speaker's volition in marking the passage of his life with the measured passage of time: "When I do count the clock that tells the time" (1). Susan J. Wolfson reads this phrase as an instance where "Time's active agency activates

---

[16] Lee Edelman, *No Future: Queer Theory and the Death Drive* (Durham and London: Duke University Press, 2004), 2.

[17] All references to Shakespeare's plays are drawn from William Shakespeare, *The New Oxford Shakespeare*, ed. Gary Taylor, John Jowett, Terri Bourus, and Gabriel Egan (Oxford: Oxford University Press, 2016).

this speaker's attention" such that "he remorselessly tells the time, to himself and to us, line to line."[18] She keenly observes that the speaker renders himself passive in the face of time's activity and that he translates the passage of time into a passage of text. Yet, if we think about the structure of a sonnet and the location of this phrase at the very opening, we can consider it as an articulation of a problem to be addressed or a point of view for which to seek an alternative. At the onset, the speaker implies that there are times when he does not note time's passing ("When I") and that this attention is an active choice on his part ("do count"). The fact that the opening line reads "When I do count," rather than "when I count," introduces possibilities for how the speaker may be learning to compensate for time's passage. What he tells himself about time actively contributes to his mood and to his construction of self. Like Wolfson, John Kerrigan characterizes the speaker as shackled to the passage of time. He finds the speaker "counting the chimes of a clock" in this sonnet to instantiate how "Shakespeare was fascinated by the idea that, appearing to possess time, man was possessed by it."[19] However, attention to how Shakespeare contemplates how his narrative about time contributes to the story he tells about himself suggests a liberation for the speaker from that possession. As Mark Freeman puts it, "Living and telling, at least to the extent that telling has to do with deliberate reflection on one's past, are indeed two quite different phenomena."[20]

The peculiar wording of the poem's first line links the active counting of the hours with generating a narrative. Since the turn of the thirteenth century, "tell" carried the meaning of factual ordering or revealing: "To mention, narrate, relate, make known" and "to describe in order."[21] The term also carried connotations of generating fiction: "With the narrative, etc., as object."[22] As the object of "tell," the "time" upon which the speaker reflects can be understood as a narrative. Indeed, the verb "tell" began to carry even strong connotations of narration at the beginning of the seventeenth century when it took on the meaning "to admit of being told in a particular way."[23] The speaker may indeed be watching the clock in this sonnet, but he may also be admitting the story he tells himself about time's passage. The latter interpretation is bolstered by the fact that "count" carried in Shakespeare's time a now obsolete meaning of "To tell, relate," functioning as a synonym for "recount."[24] Seen in light of these etymologies, Sonnet 12's first line

---

[18] Susan J. Wolfson, "Reading Intensity: Sonnet 12," in *Shakespeare up Close: Reading Early Modern Texts*, ed. Russ McDonald, Nicholas D. Nace, and Travis D. Williams (London: Bloomsbury, 2012), 147.

[19] William Shakespeare, *The Sonnets and a Lover's Complaint*, ed. John Kerrigan (New York: Penguin, 2000), 38.

[20] Mark Freeman, *Rewriting the Self: History, Memory, Narrative* (New York: Routledge, 1993), 105.

[21] "tell v.1 and v.2a" OED online.

[22] "tell v.2b" OED online.

[23] "tell v.2c" OED online.

[24] "count v.6" OED online.

frames clock watching as an activity not just fertile for rumination but also as generative of more useful and positive narratives.

The when/then logics of the sonnet further underscore how the speaker reflects on a narrative he has imposed upon himself. Consider:

> When I behold the violet past prime,
> And sable curls all silvered o'er with white;
> When lofty trees I see barren of leaves,
> Which erst from heat did canopy the herd,
> And summer's green all girded up in sheaves,
> Borne on the bier with white and bristly beard:
> Then of thy beauty do I question make[.] (3–9)

By only seeing the violet "when" the flower is "past prime" (3) and the trees "when" they are "barren of leaves" (5), the speaker "Then of thy beauty do I question make" (9). The aging of the elements listed here allows the speaker to rehearse the onset of age for him and his beloved before it transpires. The personification of these elements in nature progresses in the sonnet for effect, culminating in their ossification when gathered "on the bier with white and bristly beard." These memories of previous decay in the natural world set the pattern for what he is certain will come for his beloved's beauty. And the recollections also crowd out the present. Dwelling in thoughts about previous and forthcoming winters as well as about the inevitable decay of the addressee, the speaker ignores the positive elements of the beloved in his prime in the present. The poem thus echoes Sonnet 64, where "ruin" drove the speaker to "ruminate." This negativistic story has him prematurely enduring the hardship of mourning, convincing himself that he and the beloved cannot be happy until a new object—whether a child or a portrait of the young man immortalized in verse—is guaranteed to replace the lost one. As Freud understood it, this cycle drives states of longing.[25] The mourner will masochistically endure loss and waiting (and at times experience them as forms of pleasure) because, as Marilia Aisenstein and Donald Scott put it, "Desire commemorates what has been lost and pursues the possibility of re-finding its semblance."[26] Considered in light of this definition of desire, the speaker looks only into the past in order to remind himself that he might be happy in the future. In the Janus-headed chronology of

---

[25] "We believe that we possess a certain capacity to love, called the libido," Freud writes, "which at the earliest stages of development applied to our own ego. Later, though still very early on, it turns away from the ego and towards the objects which are thus to an extent absorbed into our ego. If those objects are destroyed or if we lose them, our capacity for love (the libido) becomes free once more." Sigmund Freud, "Transience," in *On Murder, Mourning, and Melancholia*, trans. Shaun Whiteside (New York: Penguin, 2005), 198–9.

[26] Marilia Aisenstein and Donald Moss, "Desire and Its Discontents," in *Sexualities: Contemporary Psychoanalytic Perspectives*, ed. Alessandra Lemma and Paul Lynch (London: Routledge, 1989), 72.

Fig. 1.1. Janus, facing opposite directions, in Sebastian Münster, "Cosmographia." Basle: Heinrich Petri (1552), © The Trustees of the British Museum.

Sonnet 12, the semblance of the lost object of desire lies in the future but it is based in memory, specifically Shakespeare's memory, of the fading beloved (Fig. 1.1).

In Sonnet 60, with its numbering that invokes the measurement of an hour, we find the speaker similarly assessing how self-narrative shapes his relationship to the past and to the future. It opens:

> Like as the waves make towards the pebbled shore,
> So do our minutes hasten to their end,
> Each changing place with that which goes before,
> In sequent toil all forwards do contend. (1–4)

The waves' progress might at first seem to emblematize the sense of unidirectional progress toward an endpoint inherent in teleology, echoing the logic of Claudius's claim about fathers and sons throughout time. Such a reading finds support when we note the internal rhyme that ties "towards" to "forwards." On the other hand, the waves' similarity to each other problematizes such a sense of progress. Present action replaces previous action with little variation, a point which could also be supported by this rhyme between these words whose only difference is a single letter. These two readings of the poem remind us that repetition is a narrative technique that calls our attention as much to the forthcoming element as to the past elements that render a pattern visible. The speaker's rumination on the never-ending waves recycles previous thoughts and imbricates them into present ones. The wave approaches the shore yet can be recognized to be not simply a duplicate. The intensity of each subsequent wave's meaning is increased because it is encoun-tered with knowledge of the previous one, and its meaning is further affected by the fact that the observer has changed. Sonnet 60's wave—like Sonnet 12's violet flowers and tree leaves—are as much new chronological events as they are specters of old ones.

The poem ends with the turn to verse, rather than children, as that which can defend against time. As Jonathan Bate observes, "Sonnet 60 frees itself from eternal repetition by claiming that the verse itself will endure."[27] And this endurance relies on the power of recollection in the sense that the poet avers that his work, as well as the figure praised within it, will be continually revivified:

> And nothing stands but for his scythe to mow.
> And yet to times in hope my verse shall stand,
> Praising thy worth, despite his cruel hand. (12–14)

Just as a child would have encouraged new generations to recall the father, the poem will compel readers to recall the beloved. Recognizing the backward-looking impulse in the poem does not exclude the canonical reading of the sonnets where if the young man refuses to have a child, Shakespeare's poetry can immortalize them both. But it surfaces another way to think about the poem's message: In light of the way that narrative contributes to self-identity, verse itself is a space in which time and memory can be manipulated.

While the focus of the poem oscillates between the past and the future, we can still locate within it an expanded present or *fuller now* for the speaker. Con-sider how Sonnet 60, like many others, addresses a beloved who is absent in two senses: he is not there in the present when the poet writes the poem, and he will not be there in the future when a reader encounters the commemoration of the

---

[27] Jonathan Bate, "Ovid and the Sonnets; or, Did Shakespeare Feel the Anxiety of Influence?," *Shakespeare Survey* 42 (1990): 73.

beloved. For Jonathan Culler, such expressions of apostrophe should be "immediately associated with what might be called a timeless present but is better seen as the temporality of writing."[28] The "temporality of writing" gives us a way to think about the expansive nature of narrative and memorial time. Memories in the *Sonnets* call the past into the present, and the memory arts allow the management of this admixture. One who has mastered their memory might forget the watch and the time it tells. They might return to a favorite memory as access to a heavenly paradise. Or they might re-experience the stimulation of a desirable body that was once perched in their lap. Yet the *now* of the recollection, like the memory itself, is not static. Because "we cannot separate our memories of the ongoing events of our lives from what has happened to us previously,"[29] memories are dynamic based on the ordering of them in alignment with other past experiences. These processes— ordering, excluding, including, editing, revising—are not only those by which the sonneteer crafts the fourteen-line poem but also the steps often involved in the manner by which the past is recounted or told as a narrative.

Telling Time and Telling Stories in Sonnet 30

Sonnet 30 exemplifies the artistry—both the poetic artistry and the memory artistry—involved in the ordering work necessary for self-narrative. It admits both the negative and positive aspects of recycling thoughts, and it posits the past as prologue in such a way as to both valorize the beloved and to justify the speaker's previous suffering. By constellating himself and his love objects in relation to each other, the speaker is able to construct a positive story that makes loss endurable and one that affirms his choice of beloved. The poem begins with the conjuring of the past into the present:

> When to the sessions of sweet silent thought
> I summon up remembrance of things past,
> I sigh the lack of many a thing I sought,
> And with old woes new wail my dear time's waste[.] (1–4)

These famous lines, of course, have their own place in cultural memory. C. K. Scott Moncrieff chose *Remembrance of Things Past* as the title for his monumental English translation of Proust's *À la recherche du temps perdu* in the early part of the twentieth century. Though the French title would be better translated (and has been subsequently translated) as *In Search of Lost Time*, Moncrieff's choice points

---

[28] Jonathan Culler, *Theory of the Lyric* (Cambridge, MA and London: Harvard University Press, 2015), 152.
[29] Daniel L. Schacter, *Searching for Memory: The Brain, The Mind, and the Past* (New York: Basic Books, 1996), 5.

to a profound kinship between Shakespeare's and Proust's shared interest in the pleasures of memory.

The opening of Sonnet 30 nicely captures the complexity of present desire poised in the wake of previous failure. The work of recollection has a maudlin quality in the first quatrain as the speaker seems to rehearse an archive of those things he desired but did not attain and to ruminate on time poorly spent. Yet we are told at the onset that these thoughts are "sweet," implying their desirability. George Puttenham's *Arte of English Poetrie* (1589) identifies love and death as appropriate motivations for "poetical lamentations," and he links the two by stressing the limitations of mourning as it cannot overcome "death the irrecoverable loss, death, the doleful departure of friends that can never be recontinued by any other meeting or new acquaintance."[30] Even in the presence of the new lover, memory alerts us to not only the threat of loss but also to our own state of being alone. Roland Barthes writes that "isn't desire always the same, whether the object is present or absent? Isn't the object always absent?"; this sentiment rings true for Shakespeare's Sonnet 30.[31] The beloved is not actually present in the poem, but the speaker does conjure him in his mind's eye. So, first we have the memory of lost friends, then the invocation of the present friend in the mind. As visceral as his reactions may be to this invocation of desirable friends, they are all, in fact, recollections.

Elegiac Erotics

As much as they overtly celebrate the beloved, the *Sonnets* often frame the beloved as absent. Sonnet 30's elegiac mode dwells on absent bodies while at the same time showcasing the speaker's bodily expression. Francis Meres, in his assessment of the state of English poetry in *Paladis Tamia* (1598), equates classical poets "famous for elegie" with a list of English poets that includes Shakespeare.[32] He describes these writers as "the most passionate among us to bewail and bemoan the perplexities of love," suggesting that the most powerful of love poets were those composing elegies.[33] We can detect the crossing of the funeral elegy and the love elegy in "bewail and bemoan." The single genre term denotes two apparently different classes of poetic expression, but Meres's choice of phrase here underscores how outpourings

---

[30] George Puttenham, *The Art of English Poesy*, ed. Frank Whigham and Wayne A. Rebhorn (Ithaca, NY and London: Cambridge University Press, 2007), 135, 136.

[31] Roland Barthes, *A Lover's Discourse: Fragments*, trans. Richard Howard (New York: Hill and Wang, 2010), 15.

[32] For an excellent discussion of the popularity of the love elegy in Shakespeare's time, see Victoria Moul, "English Elegies of the Sixteenth and Seventeenth Century," in *The Cambridge Companion to Latin Love Elegy*, ed. Thea S. Thorsen (Cambridge: Cambridge University Press, 2013), 306–19.

[33] The list includes Daniel, Drayton, Gascoigne, Shakespeare, Spenser, Surrey, and Wyatt. Frances Meres, *Paladis Tamia, Wit's Treasury* (London, 1598).

of grief can appear similar to articulations of pleasure. The cries in Sonnet 30 that mourn lost friends resemble an outpouring of sexual release. Georges Bataille insists that "inevitably linked with the moment of climax, there is a minor rupture suggestive of death; and conversely the idea of death may play a part in setting sensuality in motion."[34] The narrative progression of Sonnet 30 dramatizes this link, where the speaker meditates on loss in order to achieve loving joy.[35]

Not only does Meres name Shakespeare as one of these poets who conflate death and erotism in their poems, but Shakespeare himself names the intersection in the elegy genre in *As You Like It*, when Orlando "hangs odes upon hawthorns and elegies on brambles; all, forsooth, deifying the name of Rosalind" (3.2.350–1). The character laments the loss of his beloved while he also exclaims his abiding love for her in a single utterance. Indeed, Meres might have had in mind the shared element of absence that connects mourning and unrequited love. John Harington's *A Brief Apology of Poetry* (1591) defends the erotic elegy by stating that while it might contain "lewdnesse," its meditation is "still mourning."[36] The close proximity between death and eroticism—a proximity which leads Shakespeare to declare "desire is death" in Sonnet 147—lies at the heart of the love elegy and resonates in the genre's influence on Shakespeare's *Sonnets*.

The absence of the beloved's body associated with mourning and unfulfilled romantic longing should not be taken as entirely negative in Sonnet 30 and in others like it. Meres nods to such a possibility for relations elsewhere in his volume, noting that "The memory of dead friends doth bite the mind, but not without pleasure."[37] Meres's point about the pleasure of memorializing deceased friends finds powerful expression in Sonnet 30, where the speaker draws upon the capacities of memory to re-imagine an isolated state as an opportunity for connection. George Puttenham's *The Art of English Poesy* (1588) identifies love and death as appropriate motivations for "poetical lamentations," and he links the two by stressing the limitations of mourning as it cannot overcome "death the irrecoverable loss, death, the doleful departure of friends that can never be recontinued by any other meeting or new acquaintance."[38] Shakespeare suggests that memory can obviate the problem posed by Puttenham by resuscitating lost friends in the mind. Barbara Hardy observes, "the poem is not entirely given up to retrospect; sorrow is

---

[34] Georges Bataille, *Erotism: Death and Sensuality*, trans. Mary Dalwood (San Francisco: City Lights Publishers, 1986), 107.

[35] This type of cry might express what neuroscientist Antonio Damasio describes as "*primordial feelings*," which emerge in "the feeling state that I regard as simultaneous foundation of mind and self." If so, Sonnet 30 progresses from wordless, bodily emotive expression to what will become the narrative self. Antonio Damasio, *Self Comes to Mind: Constructing the Conscious Brain* (London: Heinemann, 2010), 256.

[36] John Harington, *A Preface, or rather a Briefe Apologie of Poetrie*, prefixed to the translation of *Orlando Furioso* (London, 1591).

[37] Meres, *Palladis Tamia*, R3r–v.

[38] Puttenham, *The Art of English Poesy*, 48.

played again to release a sense of happy present."[39] Yet this "happy" present is surely still robustly populated by retrospect. It is not simply that the present friend can assuage negative feelings about previous lack. Instead, he can embody all missing friends and enable a memory function that brings the lost friends into the present.

This "eye" that is drowned in Sonnet 30 might imply tears either of sadness or joy, and it might also more broadly speak to an "I" who is overflowing with emotion and sensation. Thus, we can read this as an instance once more intermingling mourning and erotic pleasure in a single expression. Elizabeth Freeman has coined the term "erotohistoriography" to describe a practice that "does not write the lost object into the present so much as encounter it already in the present, by treating the present itself as a hybrid."[40] While we need not necessarily read Sonnet 30 as an expression of orgasm, the shared tropic language of emotional and liquid release invokes for us that bodily experience which ties to previous ones. In the moment of erotic memory, the bodily explosion of pleasure recalls a past one, mirroring the present experience with the past one. Orgasm occurs in the present but is so often a replaying of what did happen or a rewriting of what might have happened or might yet happen. In Sonnet 30, all absent friends (including the present beloved) collapse into this single, fantasized entity. While the absent figures may not be bodily presences, the effect of the speaker's memories is visceral. Freeman adds that erotohistoriography "uses the body as a tool to effect, figure, or perform that encounter," and that certainly holds true as the speaker "drown[s] an eye (unused to flow)."[41]

The opening lines express a personal reflection on the past for the speaker and a literary reflection on the past for the author. Sonnet 30 begins by invoking the first-person "I" three times within the first three lines, while the phrasing might recall for some early modern readers the Earl of Surrey's phrase "remembrance / of thoughts and pleasures past."[42] Shakespeare's poem recalls Surrey's but innovates its memorial impulse. The poem does not simply recall past pleasure; it recalls friends to life. As Shakespeare revisits his memories of loss at the opening of Sonnet 30, he finds a sense of corporeal pleasure emerging from sites of lack and nostalgia. It seems as if the speaker has forgotten his claim in Sonnet 29, where he tells the beloved that "thy sweet love remembered" (29.13) makes him not want to be like anyone else. Hester Lees-Jeffries nicely observes, "The experience of reading of Sonnet 30 is sometimes (but, of course, not always) shaped by the recollection of Sonnet 29."[43] We see here the operations of what Raphael Lyne describes as "the poem's memory," which "is not the same as the author's memory" because

---

[39] Hardy, "Shakespeare's Narrative," 99.

[40] Freeman, *Time Binds*, 95.

[41] Freeman, *Time Binds*, 95.

[42] Henry Howard, Earl of Surrey, "Complaint of the Absence of Her Lover, Being on the Sea," in *The Broadview Anthology of Sixteenth-Century Poetry and Prose*, ed. Marie Loughlin, Sandra Bell, and Patricia Brace (Peterborough, ON: Broadview Press, 2011), 192, lines 8–9.

[43] Lees-Jeffries, *Shakespeare and Memory*, 171.

"the moment of remembering, what elicits what, is governed at least partly by the reader's encounter with the text."[44] The reader may or may not relate this poem to previous sonnets in the sequence, other poems with similar themes, or personal experiences. However, as Edmondson and Wells note, the "When/Then" structure of the poem generates a situation where "the reader is made to experience the intensity of the poet's meditation on memory and sadness."[45] Thus, the *now* of Sonnet 30 is the reader's *now*, the time of reading, because readers may reflect on what they have previously read or experienced. In this poem that not only begins by invoking the word "lack" but also suggests the entire lyric may be that "sigh" of lack, we hear a variety of absences: a night without date, a sight that has vanished, and unpaid debts. Vendler notes how lack is crucial to constructing the self as the speaker "willingly—for the sake of an enlivened emotional selfhood—calls up the griefs of the past."[46] The poem's use of the habitual present tense underlines how memories of the past inform the experience of the speaker's present.

The speaker's use of the active verb "summon" further tells us that he actively calls the past into the present, and the use of the plural "sessions" lets us know that the present-tense verbs in the poem should be read as conjugated in the habitual present. He is doing this in the *now* of the poem as he has done it in the past and will continue to do it in the future. What he summons up are not only past grievances but also recollections of "precious friends hid in death's dateless night," which drive him to

> [...] weep afresh love's long-since-cancelled woe,
> And moan th' expense of many a vanished sight;
> Then can I grieve at grievances fore-gone,
> And heavily from woe to woe tell o'er
> The sad account of fore-bemoanèd moan[.] (7–11)

The recycled nature of the thoughts is underscored by repetition of words as well as by the use of polyptoton, where words echo others as they are derived from the same root. The poet's propensity to resuscitate even those things that are "fore-gone" emphasizes that even those things foreclosed or gone from this world are still available in recollection. The "sad account" in Sonnet 30 echoes the use of the word "count" in Sonnet 12 as both words evoke numerical measurement and also the intentional generating of a narrative.[47] This rumination may have its pleasurable aspects, especially given the resonances of masturbatory pleasure found in the

---

[44] Lyne, *Memory and Intertextuality in Renaissance Literature*, 13.

[45] Edmondson and Wells, *Shakespeare's Sonnets*, 54.

[46] Indeed, the poet's "multilayered self, receding through panels of time" makes it possible for the sonnet "to construct a richly historical present-and-preterite-and-pluperfect-self" that marks this poem as "a tour de force." Helen Vendler, *The Art of Shakespeare's Sonnets* (Cambridge, MA: Harvard University Press, 1997), 165.

[47] Beginning in 1561, "account" took on the meaning of "A statement or narrative of an event or experience; a relation, report, or description." "account n.11a" OED online.

speaker's repeated moans, which derive from the *sweetness* of this memory.[48] The release from the rumination (and, possibly, from sexual tension) occurs late in the volta: "But if all the while I think on thee (dear friend) / All losses are restored, and sorrows end" (13–14).

The level of active thinking shows the speaker occupied with what Freud termed "the work of mourning."[49] Jacques Derrida describes this phrase as Freud's "confused and terrible expression," and I find Freud's phrase to be a particularly apt description for the activity depicted in Sonnet 30.[50] The dead do not stay buried in the speaker's psyche but instead demand to possess him, to be expressed through his moaning and wailing, to be remembered. As David Eng and David Kazanjian have recently remarked, "as soon as the question 'What is lost?' is posed, it invariably slips into the question 'What remains?'"[51] Shakespeare has the body perform the revenant voices of the deceased here. They re-enter the world of the living through the speaker's active summoning, and they persist in his utterances in reaction to their presence. Complicating Freud's understanding of desire and mourning as processes where the subject detaches from the lost object in favor of its newfound replacement, he transfers his affection to a new person but retains echoes of his old loves. The notion that the woe has already been "canceled" yet the speaker is drawn back into it expresses an emotional state much more akin to Freud's diagnosis of melancholia, which Eng and Kazanjian describe in these terms: "unlike mourning, in which the past is declared resolved, finished, and dead, in melancholia the past remains steadfastly alive in the present."[52] Like the lights from distant stars now extinguished, the deceased friends conjured in the speaker's mind still shine upon the present at the end of the poem, only reaching the speaker now in the time of writing.

Confused and Terrible Expression

Eric Zboya's twenty-first-century adaptation of Sonnet 30 stunningly renders how the work of mourning both confounds language and also demands reordering

---

[48] As discussed in Chapter Three, the term "sweet" carried erotic, particularly homoerotic, connotations in the early modern period.

[49] Freud, *On Murder, Mourning, and Melancholia*, 215.

[50] Jacques Derrida, *The Work of Mourning*, ed. Pascale Anne-Brault and Michael Naas (Chicago: University of Illinois Press, 2001), 200.

[51] The authors take Freud's conception of melancholia as their point of departure. David L. Eng and David Kazanjian, "Introduction: Mourning Remains," in *Loss*, ed. David L. Eng and David Kazanjian (Berkeley: University of California Press, 2003), 2–4.

[52] Judith Butler argues that while Freud "suggested that successful mourning meant being able to exchange one object for another [...] Perhaps, rather, one mourns when one accepts that by the loss one undergoes one will be changed, possibly forever." Sonnet 30 suggests a third way. We do not know if the speaker has changed, but we can say that the story he tells himself about loss has changed. Judith Butler, *Precarious Life: The Powers of Mourning and Violence* (London: Verso, 2006), 20–1. Eng and Kazanjian, "Introduction: Mourning Remains," 2–4.

through language (Fig. 1.2).[53] By offering the viewer a visual display of scrambled letters from the poem, this "translation" becomes unrecognizable because it has no immediate relationship to the original poem and because it refuses to offer a

Fig. 1.2. "Sonnet 30." Eric Zboya, used by permission of the artist.

[53] Eric Zboya, "Sonnet 30," in *The Sonnets: Translating and Rewriting Shakespeare*, ed. Paul Legault (Brooklyn: Nightboat Books, 2012), 48.

readable text. The viewer is confronted with what seems to be a starry night sky, a black background with white letters of various sizes. Nonetheless, this visual representation rejects readable language to offer a much more visceral reworking of the poem's themes.

The scrambled text effectively translates the affective experience of mourning depicted in the seventeenth-century poem. While Shakespeare uses the English language to describe the loss of self experienced upon the death of friends, Zboya uses the loss of language to describe the emotional effects of mourning. Jonathan Dollimore's claim that "Aesthetic order compensates for loss" in the *Sonnets* holds true both for the original Sonnet 30 and its adaptation.[54] Zboya's translation of the sonnet gives us a representation of the shattered self that must be reconstituted through language and memory but also removes the facade of such reconstitution. The contemporary adaptation helps us see that Sonnet 30 fits well with Dollimore's notion that when Shakespeare meditates on mutability, "the poet empowers himself through a coherent expression of desire's incoherence."[55] Shakespeare nods to the incoherence caused by mourning when, for the first two thirds of the poem, the speaker expresses himself through wailing, moaning, and sighing. June Jordan's evocative definition for poetry, "Poems are voiceprints of language," seems particularly apt here. Shakespeare paradoxically gives voice to that feeling and expression that is beyond language but does so through written language.[56] For all his claims to have found a solution, the speaker still shows himself at his least intelligible, which somehow logically leads to the happy ending of the poem. The ordering of his lost friends as a chain of catastrophes that have brought him to present joy—as cohesive and compelling a compensation it may be for the loss the poet describes—must also be acknowledged to be a fiction. The original Sonnet 30 exposes how mourning is stubbornly difficult to describe in written language, and Zboya's translation's indecipherability accurately translates Shakespeare's thinking into compelling visual representation.

The adaptation simply gives us a constellation of characters, a night sky with language approaching us from an interstellar distance and from a time long ago. The whole endeavor might seem nonsensical until we realize these are the letters of the poem. Just as the speaker recalls the new beloved to make sense of the inventory of lost friends, the reader recollects the ordered, original poem to make sense of Zboya's storehouse of letters. The visual representation of the raw material which we place in order to generate meaning illustrates how, as Martin Conway puts it:

---

[54] Jonathan Dollimore, *Death, Desire, and Loss in Western Culture* (London and New York: Routledge, 1998), 102.

[55] Dollimore, *Death, Desire, and Loss in Western Culture*, 102–3.

[56] June Jordan, "Introduction," in *Soulscript: A Collection of Classic African American Poetry* (New York: Crown, 2004), xx.

Memories are an intrinsic part of us—they are the database or the content of the self. They ground it in remembered reality that constrains what the self can be now and in the future, and what it could possibly have been in the past.[57]

The past friends or random letters are the raw data from which the speaker or reader brings meaning to light in language and in feeling. Barthes writes of losing a beloved, "Isn't the most sensitive point of this mourning the fact that I must lose a language—the amorous language? No more 'I love yous.'"[58] The disappearance of a friend or lover means not only the emotional loss of shared love but also the ontological loss of the ability to say "I" directed toward someone's "you." The implications of this are particularly acute in the context of early modern ideals of friendship, where friends are mirrored images of each other. To recover himself, the speaker must move from wailing to speaking, from a focus on loss to a focus on the present absence of the living beloved.

In Shakespeare's original poem, the final couplet finds the self reconstituted with a renewed focus on the present beloved. The poem thus captures how the past can be embedded in the present but also how the present itself is just an expectation of the future:

> But if the while I think on thee (dear friend)
> All losses are restored, and sorrows end. (13–14)

Here, we have what cognitive psychology describes as the ordering of thoughts to generate a positive mood. Nonetheless, the final couplet retains an elegiac quality. The operations of recollection help us see that this reconstitution involves an active, intentional alignment of elements from memory and from language, a point made beautifully by Zboya's reimagining of the poem. The renewed promise of future pleasure seems to be only fulfillable by the arrival or reciprocal expression of love from the new friend. And this does not occur in the poem. Seen in light of that contingency, the praise of the friend in this poem might constitute an act of self-abnegation. Hugh McIntosh has argued that Shakespeare deploys the language of sexualized masochism in the *Sonnets* in order to express class difference and to position himself to ascend in the class system: "The sexualized, abject persona that appears [...] in the Sonnets, then, might record Shakespeare's attempts to charm an audience that outclassed him."[59] Sonnet 30 positions the poet as having endured such pain while waiting for someone like the beloved, and ends by

[57] Conway, "Memory and Desire," 548.
[58] Barthes, *A Lover's Discourse*, 107.
[59] Hugh McIntosh, "The Social Masochism of Shakespeare's Sonnets," *Studies in English Literature, 1500–1900* 50, no. 1 (Winter 2010): 115.

positioning the poet as waiting for a response from the friend, fitting with the power relations that McIntosh supposes. As Barthes opines, "*To make someone wait*: the constant prerogative of all power, age-old pastime of humanity."[60] However, we might also say that the balance of power is not so clear-cut in the poem. In some sense, the speaker waits for the beloved. Yet the speaker also makes a claim to possess him already. Just as he can and does conjure his absent friends into his thoughts to wail about them, he can now do the same with the present beloved.

Bottling Pleasurable Memories

"I have only to break into the tightness of a strawberry," Toni Morrison writes in *The Bluest Eye*, "and I see summer—its dust and lowering skies."[61] I find this to be a remarkable sentence, both for its lyricality and for how it showcases the way that sensory detail swings open the door to memory. The sentence echoes the moment when Proust's narrator Marcel tastes the madeleine and finds himself steeped in the involuntary memory of Combray. Unlike Marcel, however, Morrison's Claudia voluntarily calls upon her memories. Rereading her sentence now, I find Morrison's use of "tightness" to be the most striking word choice in the sentence. It seems so effortless for Claudia to "only" break into a single strawberry, yet it is *tight* with the fullness of all the emotions and the sensoria of summers past.

The narrator's tapping into the specific seasonal remembrance is volitional, though she nonetheless notes an ego-dissolving power to her own session of silent thought:

> But my memory is uncertain; I recall a summer storm in the town where we lived and imagine a summer my mother knew in 1929. There was a tornado that year, she said, that blew away half of south Lorain. I mix her summer with my own. Biting the strawberry, thinking of storms, I see her.[62]

Claudia's access point found inside the strawberry takes her to a summer of storms and to her mother as well as to her mother's memory of summer storms. It is simultaneously an invocation of past experience and an instance of ego dissolution with an absent loved one. She can "see" her mother in her mind's eye, just as Hamlet tells Horatio that he regularly sees his deceased father. The strawberry offers a way to experience the beauty of summers past and the presence of her mother, but it is also subtended by threatening elements: a summer of dust and of tornadoes, a

---

[60] Barthes, *A Lover's Discourse*, 40.

[61] Toni Morrison, *The Bluest Eye* (New York: Vintage, 2007), 187.

[62] The passage from *The Bluest Eye* has resonances of Borges's "Shakespeare's Memory," discussed in the next chapter. In that short story, it is unclear whether the narrator inherits the poet's recollections or simply knows so much about Shakespeare that he cannot help but see his memories through the lens of the earlier man. Morrison, *The Bluest Eye*, 187.

post-memory of a trauma experienced by her mother, and an ambivalent loss of ego boundaries.

In Shakespeare's Sonnet 5, the speaker's access point to summers past and the absent beloved is a glass perfume bottle. The vessel itself, variously interpretable as a female womb to contain the beloved's heir or a male womb to contain the poet's imagination, offers a time capsule which can ignite recollection and deliver an edited version of previous experience. Raphael Lyne notes how the work of distillation evokes the volitionality of the memory arts, given how it "suggests that the creation of something memorable, and the burden of remembering, require some strain."[63] Summer—replete with its erotically charged "sap" and "lusty leaves"—is captured in perfume, a "liquid prisoner pent in walls of glass":

> Those hours, that with gentle work did frame
> The lovely gaze where every eye doth dwell,
> Will play the tyrants to the very same,
> And that un-fair which fairly doth excel:
> For never-resting time leads summer on
> To hideous winter, and confounds him there,
> Sap checked with frost, and lusty leaves quite gone,
> Beauty o'er-snowed and bareness everywhere.
> Then, were not summer's distillation left
> A liquid prisoner pent in walls of glass[.] (1–10)

This multivalent vessel—a poem, a womb, the poet's mind—rewards the one who waits.[64] Holly Dugan notes a pattern across this and other sonnets, as well as *Venus and Adonis*, where the art of distillation describes "smell [as] a key part of sexual attraction," and moreover "poetry is like a perfume, a distillate of material beauty, captured for others' pleasure and saved from the ravages of time."[65] Tinged with the sensory implications of sexual pleasure inherent in its sweetness, the olfactory fuel is ready to deliver memories of a past season to those waiting to smell it.[66]

---

[63] Lyne, *Memory and Intertextuality in the Renaissance*, 92.

[64] In the use of the term "prisoner," Sonnet 5 instantiates what Jane Kingsley-Smith describes as "the Sonnets' claustrophilia," where "Shakespeare's speaker seeks to enclose the beloved, but also to feel limits around himself, to reinforce a subjectivity that is constantly threatened by desire." Jane Kingsley-Smith, "Shakespeare's Sonnets and the Claustrophobic Reader: Making Space in Modern Shakespeare Fiction," *Shakespeare* 9, no. 2 (2013): 189.

[65] Holly Dugan, *The Ephemeral History of Perfume: Scent and Sense in Early Modern England* (Baltimore: The Johns Hopkins Press, 2011), 58.

[66] Research on the human brain has found smell to be a particularly charged sense for evoking memories of the past. See, for example, Sandrine Lombion, Blandine Bechetoille, Sylvie Nezelof, and Jean-Louis Millot, "Odor Perception in Alexithymic Patients," *Psychiatry Research* 177, nos. 1–2 (2010): 135–8, Marieke Bianca Jolien Toffolo, Monique Smeets, and Marcel van den Hout, "Proust Revisited: Odours as Triggers of Aversive Memories," *Cognition and Emotion*, 26, no. 1 (2012): 83–92, and Roxanne Khamsi, "Unpicking the Link between Smell and Memories," *Nature* 606, S2–S4 (June 2022).

Yet the poem emphasizes that the nature of the sweet liquid is much more than a replication of summer flowers or the unadulterated memory of summer. It both *is* and *is not* the scent of summer. At the close of the poem, we are told

> Beauty's effect with beauty were bereft,
> Nor it nor no remembrance what it was.
> But flowers distilled, though they with winter meet,
> Lose but their show; their substance still lives sweet. (11–14)

If we read this to describe the perfume and the person waiting to smell the perfume, the lines imply that beauty has departed with winter and with aging, and the subject needs the scent to remind them of the summer's day they have forgotten.[67] But we can also read these two lines to address the complexity of distillation as well as of recollection. "Beauty's effect," the scent of the flower or the pleasure in smelling the flower, is separated from the flower itself. The scent invokes the flower's essence but it is not the scent of the flower in its original context or state. The flower itself is resuscitated in the speaker's mind through the use of memory.

Reminiscent of Sonnet 116's "love is not love" (2), these final lines of Sonnet 5 emphasize that a memory of a thing is not the thing itself in the same way that a memory of an experience is not wholly accurate to the experience itself. Richard Halpern, in tracing the resonances of the discourses of alchemy within Sonnet 5, observes the active work done in the poem's central metaphor as the perfume returns the smell of the flower but not the dirt and other elements that might accompany such a scent in nature: "the poem depicts only the perfume as distillate, while the waste matter or remainder of distillation has disappeared."[68] Just as Morrison admits to the storm, Shakespeare too leaves room for such negative elements, although he edits it from the experience. In Sonnet 5, the operations of distillation deliver something sweeter and more potent than any flower. It exceeds quotidian sensory experience and reels into a state akin to the state of bliss discussed in the following chapter.[69]

---

[67] Sonnet 65 counterposes memorial monuments—of "brass," "stone," or "earth"—to "summer's honey breath" (1, 5). This calls back to Sonnets 5, 6, and 18. The sonnet may overtly reinforce the immortality of poetry ("in black ink my love may still shine bright," 14), yet this must also be personal memory. There are always multiple readerships: Shakespeare, the beloved, and his audience.

[68] Richard Halpern, *Sodomy and Sublimity in the Sonnets, Wilde, Freud, and Lacan* (Philadelphia: University of Pennsylvania Press, 2016), 16.

[69] Such experiences of olfaction-induced memory need not be positive but even negative ones are concentrated, powerful experiences. Robert Burton records how "*Cornelius Agrippa* relates out of *Gulielmus Parisiensis* a story of one, that, after a distasteful purge which a Physician had prescribed unto him, was so much moved, *that at the very sight of physic he would be distempered*; though he never so much as smelled to it, the box of physic long after would give him a purge; nay, the very remembrance of it did effect it." Robert Burton, *The Anatomy of Melancholy*, ed. A. R. Shilleto (London: G. Bell and Sons, 1912), Vol. 1, 390–1, italics in original.

The work of distilling something or someone has its negative connotations, especially in Sonnet 5. Halpern goes on to note that the removed elements are not entirely gone: "The sublimating rhetoric of the sonnets separates out an impeccably refined and aestheticized form of desire from a sodomitical discourse that is then abjected as fecal remainder."[70] Even if we do not accept the whiff of sodomy about the poem, we can acknowledge that the beloved is being objectified (in the truest of senses: turned into an object) and that the notion that he can be edited down into a more perfect version of himself implies negativity about his current self. The eroticism generated here is at once identity-obliterating—the beloved is no longer a person but rather distilled into an object—but also optimizing—the beloved is an alternate version of himself, edited to excise less savory elements he has in his embodied life. The operation is analogous to the operations of memory that we have seen. Retrospection allows the subject to order elements to fit a desired logic or achieve an aesthetic goal. One might choose to think only of the best of times, often because the emotions present at the point of experience enhance the memory. If heightened emotion at the time of experience in turn improves recollection of that experience in flashbulb memories, then we find an agential version of that process as the speaker deploys the obverse. In other words, the rememberer chooses to invoke a desired memory, resuscitating it as a distilled version much more pure and powerful than the original experience. This act then imbues the original experience with much more emotion and reinforces its flashbulb-like resonance for the rememberer after the fact.

I am reminded here of the moment when Ennis smells the shirt of his deceased lover Jack in *Brokeback Mountain* (Fig. 1.3). It is true that the shirt's smell powerfully reinvokes memory of Jack but it is also crucial that the object that generates the smell, an old plaid workman's shirt, embodies the traditionally masculine essence that attracted Ennis to Jack in the first place.

The scene is movingly depicted in both the film and the short story upon which the film is based, where Annie Proulx describes how Ennis

> pressed his face into the fabric and breathed in slowly through his mouth and nose, hoping for the faintest smoke and mountain sage and salty sweet stink of Jack but there was no real scent, only the memory of it, the imagined power of Brokeback Mountain of which nothing was left but what he held in his hands.[71]

---

[70] He goes on to observe that the very act of distillation nevertheless carries with it the memory of that which has been removed: "This remainder is not, however, expelled to a space outside the poems, but is rather relegated to a nonspace within the poems. That is to say, it abides in the half-light of wordplay, implication, and insinuation. Sodomy subsists as the speaking of the unspeakable, as the topos of the inexpressible or unnameable. Perhaps it is more correct, then, to identify Shakespearean homosexuality with both sublime and remainder, or indeed with the very separation that produces this double product. The Shakespearean sonnet gives off a perfume that contains just the slightest hint of feces." Halpern, *Sodomy and Sublimity in the Sonnets*, 21.

[71] Annie Proulx, "Brokeback Mountain," in *Close Range: Wyoming Stories* (New York: Scriber, 1999), 281.

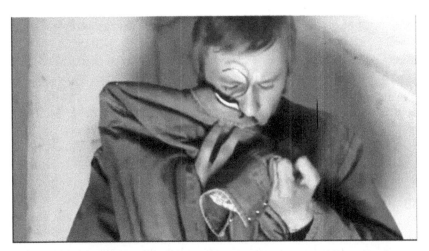

Fig. 1.3. *Brokeback Mountain* (Dir. Ang Lee, Focus Pictures and River Road Entertainment, 2005), screenshot from the film.

In the film, the audibly deep and repeated inhalation that audience members witness implies that the scent of Jack is still captured (or "pent," in Shakespeare's terms) within his shirt. The short story tells us otherwise. Nonetheless, the result is the same. What the object delivers is a distillation of the beloved, an incitement to memory and an access point to all the emotions associated with that memory. It invokes the object by symbolizing the lost status of the desired object. Aisenstein and Moss remark that a subject in mourning, "though lacking the object, must nonetheless preserve its representation."[72] Hugging the empty shirt simultaneously emphasizes the absence of the beloved's body while it also permits Ennis to hold him closer—Jack can fold Ennis into him—than the bodily form would have allowed in life.

Sonnet 5 posits memory as a counterforce to the dulling of sensation over time. Such dulling is portrayed in Sonnet 12, which urges the beloved to have a child "Since sweets and beauties do themselves forsake, / And die as fast as they see others grow" (11–12) and in Sonnet 19 where "Devouring Time" extends across "the wide world and all her fading sweets" (1, 7). However, the space of Sonnet 5 is able to preserve the pleasures of sweetness. It emphasizes the work of memory in the composition of loving verse as the perfume bottle achieves what is promised in the ending couplet of Sonnet 19: "Yet do thy worst, old Time: despite thy wrong, / My love shall in my verse ever live young" (13–14). The perfume is future-looking but also backward-looking. Yet we might begin to wonder if "verse" is not an immortalizing device but also one that allows the flow backward in time.

---

[72] Aisenstein and Moss, "Desire and its Discontents," 71.

Sonnet 5, like Sonnet 30, embraces the pleasure of delay. In Sonnet 30, there are at least two kinds of waiting: for contact with the addressee (either through reading or through a future meeting) or for death (itself a working metaphor for sexual release). Yet here, in Sonnet 5, waiting to taste something distilled yields an even stronger taste—in the short-form verse or in the bottle of perfume—and it is a taste experienced during the absence of the desired object. Just as Jack's shirt can invoke not just the man but also the time and place of romantic connection at Brokeback Mountain, the distilled perfume invokes the memory that conflates a person, place, and time. The poem shows us that, while a child or verse might offer a means to escape the ravages of time, the act of recollection holds such power as well.

Forgetting Time Now and Then

Watching the clock. Sessions of silent thought. Releasing a liquid prisoner. Perhaps these are all ways that the speaker of the *Sonnets* finds ways, as Quentin's father encouraged his son, to forget time now and then for a moment. While that urging asked that his son disregard time in order to "not spend all your breath trying to conquer it," we might say that Shakespeare does the opposite. He expends breath—in his counting; his sighing, wailing, and moaning; his inhaling; and, of course, in his writing—in order to work diligently to combat time. The speaker thus attempts to gain mastery over loss through manipulation of memory.

Such efforts extend beyond personal memory to encapsulate figures in collective memory as well. In Sonnet 106, the speaker gazes into "the chronicle of wasted time" to study those objects of affection of earlier writers in "descriptions of the fairest wights" (1–2). Yet he finds that

> In praise of ladies dead, and lovely knights;
> [...]
> I see their antique pen would have expressed
> Even such a beauty as you master now.
> So all their praises are but prophecies
> Of this our time, all you prefiguring[.] (4–10)

Previous beauties, like the previous friends of Sonnet 30, collapse in the recent memory of the present beloved. As a realization predicted by all of these past beauties, the beloved is a culmination of them, both in the speaker's personal memory in terms of his fantasy formation and in the collective memory into which his *Sonnets* now enter. And so it is like a *becoming*, both in the sense that the beloved is the evolution of all those beauties before him and also that the speaker is becoming a desiring subject.

In the imaginative space of the text, the speaker is able to compensate for loss by resuscitating past moments and to reorganize his romantic history. Memory is, in Adam Phillips's words, "both the object and the instrument of our desire [because] a good memory makes us more efficient, productive, and better problem-solvers, which means better pleasure seekers."[73] Sonnet 106 places the beloved in the story of a long history of beloveds and places the poet within the canon of still-remembered writers. As we have already seen, while such feats may seem like simply the work of creative memoir or of fiction, the approach mirrors those in the memory arts and the functioning of memory in the brain. As we will see in subsequent chapters, the speaker claims a type of agency over how he experiences time in terms of when he seizes upon the power of memory to call the past—and even the future—into the present. The poet's ability to alter his perception of time's passage and the story he tells himself about it, while not always successful, promises at times to lead to pleasurable ends.

---

[73] Phillips, *Side Effects*, 101.

2

The Pleasure of the *Sonnets*

In order to further explore how memory and erotic desire intertwine in Shakespeare's *Sonnets*, this chapter considers the various ways that the poems depict and consider pleasure. Given the complex operations by which the texts function both as a seemingly private communication to specific addressees and as public communication to a wide body of readers, this exploration involves thinking about the act of reading itself. Consequently, the following analysis pursues two interrelated questions: what constitutes pleasure in Shakespeare's *Sonnets* and what role does recollection play in engendering that pleasure? The title of this chapter nods toward *The Pleasure of the Text* (1973), that evocative and enigmatic volume where Roland Barthes attempts to sort out the unique pleasures of an encounter with literature. To open the discussion in this chapter, I draw upon Barthes's thinking as a useful heuristic lens for my extended line of inquiry throughout this chapter. As we will see, Shakespeare's notions of pleasure do not always track directly to those of Barthes, especially as the earlier writer is more willing to admit the displeasure involved in seeking pleasure. Nonetheless, placing the two authors in dialogue helps render visible how attempts to achieve pleasurable recollection in the *Sonnets* engage with early modern ideas about not only the art of memory but also the practice of reading.

Central to Barthes's theorization of reading is the distinction between *pleasure* and *bliss*. Although Shakespeare does not use these particular words in the same ways that Barthes does, the dynamics between these two elements as envisioned by the later writer can help us understand the thinking of the earlier one. For Barthes, "pleasure" (*plaisir*) indicates the thrill of desirous pursuit and initial excitement of an encounter with another's writing. When a reader finds an overwhelmingly satisfying textual moment in an author's work, then it is possible to achieve a totalizing state of "bliss" (*jouissance*). Barthes's French term for "bliss," as many readers will recognize, has become a vital keyword for thinkers attempting to describe a form of joy which has the characteristics of sexual excitement and can be accompanied by a sense of self-shattering. For Shakespeare, intense forms of pleasure and bliss offer starting points for delineating the unique characteristics of memory-inflected eros.

The Pleasures of Memory in Shakespeare's Sonnets. John S. Garrison, Oxford University Press. © John S. Garrison (2023). DOI: 10.1093/oso/9780198857716.003.0003

Seeking Pleasure in the *Sonnets*

The word "pleasure" appears twelve times across the *Sonnets* and, though Shakespeare's use is not synonymous with "*plaisir*," the early modern word did have some of the same connotations that characterize Barthes's use of the term.[1] Beginning in the fourteenth century, the English word "pleasure" denoted "the condition or sensation induced by the experience or anticipation of what is felt to be good or desirable."[2] Even in its earliest definitions, "pleasure" evinces operations common with memory. Both pleasure and memory proceed from distinct experiences, as the mind translates a sensation or event into thought and attempts to make sense of it.[3] The *Oxford English Dictionary* makes clear that pleasure can also precede an experience because anticipation of future joy is shaped by recollection of similar experiences, and here too memories of the past help us envision how future experiences will transpire and how we will in turn remember them.[4] As William Fulwood puts it in *The Castle of Memory* (1562), "memory doth always go before remembrance, for a man cannot remember except those things whereof he hath the memory."[5] Private thoughts and reflection come between lived experience and the sense we make of that experience. And perhaps erotic pleasure relies on fantasy and factual recollection, especially in the *anamnesis* that Barthes associates with the memory of love, where "the amorous scene, like the first ravishment, consists only of *after-the*-fact manipulations."[6] Pleasure and memory thus both rely on experience regardless of whether that experience is conjured in recollection or whether it is speculated in terms of previous pleasure. As we will see,

---

[1] Instances of "pleasure" are found in Sonnets 8, 20, 48, 52, 58 (twice), 75, 91, 97 (twice), 121, and 126. "Bliss" appears only once, in Sonnet 129.

[2] The term "pleasure" carries strong sexual connotations, as indicated by the second definition cited by the *OED*, "the indulgence of physical, esp. sexual, desires or appetites; sensual or sexual gratification." "pleasure, n.1a and n1b (respectively)". OED online.

[3] We might also think about memory as a tool with which a subject might attempt to rewrite the negative aspects of pleasure or to determine how to live with the memory of having indulged oneself. As Corey McEleney notes, "Perhaps the biggest obstacle to theorizing (let alone valorizing) pleasure is that it slides far too easily into the negative registers of irresponsibility, disengagement, hedonism, self-indulgence, self-abuse, quietism, passivity, narcissism, errancy, foolishness, superficiality, excess, waste, vulgarity, inconsequence, distractedness, irrelevance, irreverence, abandon, insufficiency, and incoherence. This list of epithets could, of course, go on." Corey McEleney, *Futile Pleasures: Early Modern Literature and the Limits of Utility* (New York: Fordham University Press, 2017), 39.

[4] As we saw in the previous chapter, pleasure and memory also share a particular relationship to temporality. Carolyn Dinshaw observes that "experiences of memory and expectation contribute to a sense of the present that is complex and multifold," and the same claim can be made of pleasures which can seem to suspend or collapse time. Dinshaw traces an intriguing line of thought from Augustine through canonical works by medieval authors to the work of Paul Ricoeur in *Time and Narrative* to examine "the 'noncoincidence' of memory, attention, and expectation." The phrase emphasizes that memory cannot be disaggregated from the experience of the present or the anticipation of the future. Dinshaw, *How Soon Is Now?*, 15, 13.

[5] The text is a translation of Guglielmo Gratarolo's *De memoria reparanda, augenda confirmandaque ac de reminiscentia* (Basel, 1533). William Fulwood, *The Castel of Memorie* (London, 1562).

[6] Barthes, *A Lover's Discourse*, 216.

Shakespeare goes beyond formulations such as Fulwood's and Barthes's as his poems manipulate recalled experiences to enhance pleasure and speculate about future experiences from which new memories can be made.

It should be noted, too, that pleasure was not a universally sought-after experience in the early modern period. For example, Katherine Philips's "Ode against Pleasure" warns readers that "We covet pleasure easily, / But ne'er true bliss possess" (1–2).[7] Unlike Barthes, who sees accumulated levels of pleasure leading to bliss, Philips suggests that such easily attained minor joys should be avoided if one desires the higher state of bliss because

> For by our pleasures we are cloy'd
> And so desire is done;
> Or else, like rivers, they make wide
> The channels where they run;
> And either way true bliss destroys,
> Making us narrow, or our joys. (13–18)[8]

The acceptance of quickly delivered joys comes with the danger of never truly experiencing bliss because one might feel satisfied and thereby narrow the understanding of what other pleasures await. While the use of these terms, "pleasure" and "bliss," is not necessarily consistent across writers even within a given time period, Philips's conception of bliss seems to elevate it so high that it might never be obtained. The poem might dismiss too easily how a chain of remembered experiences of pleasure might contribute to preparing someone to recognize truly sublime experiences. Drawing on recent neuroscientific studies of the brain's relationship to feeling, Antonio Damasio makes the distinction between "joy and sorrow" as "the two emblems of our affective life."[9] These feelings intertwine memories of past encounters with drivers of our emotions because an encounter with a stimulus (present or imagined) "leads to the selection and execution of a pre-existing program of emotion [and] in turn, the emotion leads to the construction of a particular set of neural maps of the organism to which signals from the body-proper contribute prominently."[10] This encourages interpretation of experiences of bliss in the *Sonnets* not just as successive and mounting encounters with pleasure but as cumulative remembrances of past pleasures distilled into a particularly charged moment of recollection, as we saw in the previous chapter with the discussions of Sonnets 5 and 30. Damasio acknowledges that fantasy has a role in the

---

[7] Katherine Philips, "Ode against Pleasure," in *Poems* (London, 1664), sig. K4.
[8] Philips, "Ode against Pleasure," sig. K4r–K4v.
[9] Damasio, *Looking for Spinoza*, 137.
[10] Antonio Damasio, *Looking for Spinoza: Joy, Sorry, and the Feeling Brain* (New York: Houghton Mifflin Harcourt, 2003), 137.

selecting and executing of the remembered emotions because joy and sorrow can occur in the present whether "those states may be actually happening or as if they were happening."[11]

The central argument of Barthes's *The Pleasure of the Text* is that erotic pleasure can be derived from reading, and we see such a formulation in Shakespeare's Sonnet 48. When the speaker describes, "Within the gentle closure of my breast, / From whence at pleasure thou mayst come and part" (11–12), we hear something akin to Barthes's encounter with a book. What the latter writer describes as the experience of any text—"I read on, I skip, I look up, I dip in again"—aptly describes the speaker's description of the beloved's only occasional attention to his pining heart. A crucial difference, though, is that Barthes wonders at how he might pleasure in how he imagines another writer's text speaking to him. In some ways, Shakespeare takes a safer route by depicting the text where he finds pleasure as his own. The earlier writer's tactic ensures that he can trust his own reading of the text but risks emphasizing his own isolation or betraying his own narcissism.

We see the clear connection between a heart and a book in *Twelfth Night* during the first conversation between Olivia and Viola:

VIOLA: Most sweet lady—
OLIVIA: A comfortable doctrine, and much may be said of it. Where lies your text?
VIOLA: In Orsino's bosom.
OLIVIA: In his bosom? In what chapter of his bosom?
VIOLA: To answer by the method, in the first of his heart. (1.5.212–17)

In *Twelfth Night*, as in the *Sonnets*, the heart functions as not simply a book to be read but a text to be memorized. Here, Orsino has authored testimony of his love for Olivia, which in turn has been copied into two texts: first, the book inside his own heart and second, the memory of the messenger he has sent to deliver the testimony. He surely hopes that reading and rereading this text—in the case of Olivia's hearing it and his repeating it in his thoughts—will engender desire in his beloved. Those of us who have read the play—or who have read any Shakespeare play, or who have seen any romantic comedy recently—know that the person who reads this book of love and falls head over heels for its author will in fact be the messenger Viola, its unintended addressee.[12] So once more Shakespeare is thinking in the same logical terms as Barthes, where reading has the capacity to generate romantic pleasure—but he does not go as far as to imagine a pure encounter between a reader and a text to do so. He still requires a body to be present, as it is Viola's

---

[11] Damasio, *Looking for Spinoza*, 137.

[12] Elsewhere, Shakespeare suggests that receiving the text of a sonnet becomes a source of pleasure for the recipient. Consider, for example, the sonnet constructed during the exchange between the young lovers in Act 1 of *Romeo and Juliet* and the introduction of halting sonnets written by Beatrice and Benedick to each other in the final act of *Much Ado about Nothing*.

gender-ambiguous body which reads the text and incites desire within Olivia not for the writer or the text but for the communal reader.

The incessant return to recollections of the beloved which drives both the sonnet speaker's and Orsino's (and eventually Viola's) desires speaks to the active work of conjuring pleasurable memories. Reflecting on the capriciousness of recollection, Montaigne posits in his *Essayes* (1603) that "memory represents unto us, not what we choose, but what pleases her."[13] We need to endeavor to subdue such recall in order to make room for the remembrance of pleasing things from the past. He adds, "nothing so deeply imprints anything in our remembrance, as the desire to forget the same."[14] That is, the more we try to forget something, the more it stays with us. Raphael Lyne suggests that Montaigne's formulation is "particularly suggestive for Hamlet," whose inability to keep in his mind his father's example exemplifies "memory's tendency to operate associatively in an uncontrolled way."[15] Viola's memorization of Orsino's love testimony, like the regularized structure of the sonnet form within which Shakespeare attempts to make sense of erotic desire, might be seen as an attempt to control the unruly nature of both memory and pleasure.

Barthes's description of skipping through and dipping into a text aptly describes the experience of reading the *Sonnets*. While it is of course possible to read the collection in its entirety, few readers would find that pleasurable. C. L. Barber posits, "To read through the sonnets at a sitting, though it is useful for surveying the topography they present, [...] can produce a sensation of hothouse oppression."[16] One's encounter with the constellation of 154 poems is typified by choosing one or a handful to read at a time. Pleasure, both within *The Pleasure of the Text* and in one's encounter with the *Sonnets*, involves a brief interaction with a satisfying object. Such a sense of transitory pleasure finds much expression in the *Sonnets*, as the speaker draws the reader into the present moment of the feeling or event he describes, all the while demanding that the reader recall a past experience analogous to the depicted situation. Patrick Fuery suggests, "The act of reading is creative because the reader is constantly having to fill in gaps and absences in the text," and these lacunae surely engage a reader's memory.[17] In turn, such engagement makes possible the experience of pleasure, as Fuery notes: "This model of the act of reading [...] figur[es] desire as something without satisfaction, continuous, motivating and, ultimately, pleasurable."[18] This formulation of desire nicely describes the "pleasure" named in the title of *The Pleasure of the Text*, which points

[13] Michel de Montaigne, *The Essayes or Morall, Politike and Militarie Discourses of Lord Michaell de Montaigne*, trans. John Florio (London: Val. Sims for Edward Blount, 1603), 286.

[14] Montaigne, *Essayes*, 286.

[15] Lyne, *Memory and Intertextuality in Renaissance Literature*, 39.

[16] C. L. Barber, "Shakespeare in His Sonnets," *The Massachusetts Review* 1, no. 4 (1960): 652.

[17] Patrick Fuery, *Theories of Desire* (Melbourne: Melbourne University Press, 1995), 72.

[18] Fuery, *Theories of Desire*, 72.

to a form of joy that motivates reading and constitutes the initial experience of finding joy from the activity. Such pursuit seems to drive the *Sonnets'* speaker, as well, who at times reaches a profound state of bliss. And this state, although rarely achieved, involves recollection.

The Sonnet as Bliss

Sonnet 18 offers a compelling case study for what Barthes describes as "the moment when by its very excess verbal pleasure chokes and reels into bliss."[19] The poem showcases how erotic satiation has obliviating effects that shatter the ability to articulate how one feels. In a 2017 talk at the Shakespeare Association of America conference, Laurie Shannon incisively linked the poem to the sentiments expressed in the song "Nothing Compares 2 U."[20] The speaker of that song (written by Prince in the 1980s but made famous by Sinead O'Connor in 1990) attempts to describe similar joys to that of spending time with its addressee.[21] Birdsong, flowers, and fancy dinners approach the heightened pleasures achievable when in the presence of the beloved, but ultimately these things cannot accurately describe the beloved. The complaint ends with a refrain that repeats the couplet "Nothing compares / Nothing compares to you." Like the song, Sonnet 18 is all that much more memorable for its insistence that it cannot name a point of comparison for what it seeks to celebrate. However, it does name those things that cannot compare to the beloved, and these offer points at which the reader and the speaker can meet. These constitute an "abrasion" on the surface of the text, in Barthes's terms, that makes legible an experience characterized by indescribability.[22] Despite its insistence on the inarticulability of its particulars, Sonnet 18 is one of the most familiar of Shakespeare's poems, just as perhaps "Nothing Compares 2 U" is one of the most memorable songs of the 1990s, or at least of O'Connor's career.

Sonnet 18's opening line, "Shall I compare thee to a summer's day?" functions as an invitation for readers to enroll themselves in the text. It is not necessarily that we imagine ourselves as the intended respondent for the question. However, the line's use of the second-person interrogative does for a moment ask us to imagine that someone might pose this question to us or that we ourselves might ask

[19] Roland Barthes, *The Pleasure of the Text*, trans. Richard Miller (New York: Hill and Wang, 1975), 8.

[20] Laurie Shannon, "'Nature's Changing Course': Asking Questions with Sonnet 18," Plenary Panel: "Queer Natures: Bodies, Sexualities, Environments," 45th Annual Meeting of the Shakespeare Association of America, Atlanta, Georgia (April 7, 2017).

[21] The song was written by Prince and, while his original 1984 recording was released in 2018, most people will recognize the version that appeared on Sinead O'Connor, *I Do Not Want What I Haven't Got* (Chrysalis Records, 1990).

[22] Barthes, *The Pleasure of the Text*, 11.

such a question. And, of course, readers also might find themselves speculating at Shakespeare's historical object of affection, even while aware that the specifics of this are unknowable.[23] Colin Burrow notes that this dynamic, "as we feel ourselves being manoeuvered now within and now outside the social situation partially implicit in the poems, looking now from an imagined inside and now from an imagined outside," makes the poem "generate a readerly restlessness."[24] And this "restlessness" helps us see the reader's contribution to the dynamic that Barthes describes where a writer

> must seek out this reader (must "cruise" him) *without knowing where he is.* A site of bliss is then created. It is not the reader's "person" that is necessary to me, it is this site: the possibility of a dialectics of desire, of an unpredictability of bliss.[25]

We see the Barthesian dialectic at the point when Shakespeare describes pleasure by describing its indescribability. The "unpredictability" that Barthes describes can be located in what the reader might imagine to be the exceptional qualities of Sonnet 18's beloved.

The poem's dialectical energies highlight the imagined qualities as simultaneously the site of estrangement between writer and reader as well as the site of connection between them. The result of the "readerly restlessness," for Burrow, is that "it encourages readers to feel themselves now part of the poem" because they "are invited to experience not the poem's historicity as much as their own futurity in relation to the poem, and perhaps also the future potential of the poem—that another world, another tongue, might read the poem again, differently."[26] To engage one's own personal memories in order to imagine the qualities of so superlative a beloved as that in Sonnet 18 involves engaging the collective memory of contemporaneous and future readers who will do the same. Such engagement offers the promise of the ecstatic pleasure of being taken outside oneself while also tapping into distinctly individual feelings. Nonetheless, the experience remains pleasurable and deeply personal. Helen Vendler's recollection of her own teenage years pinpoints how we internalize poems and make them our own: "It wasn't until I was fifteen, when I read and memorized a whole batch of Shakespeare's sonnets, that I saw a poem could tell the truth about one's

---

[23] The question of the identity of Shakespeare's intended addressees is one of relentless pursuit. William Boyd returns to the question of the addressees in a 2005 article in *The Guardian*, driven by the belief that "it is impossible to read Shakespeare's Sonnets without concluding that in this case the particular human predicament that he is so remorselessly curious about and so sympathetic to is, in fact, his own." More recently, Elaine Scarry has dedicated a book-length study to trace cryptograms in the poems that would suggest the Catholic exile Henry Constable. See William Boyd, "Two Loves Have I," *The Guardian* (November 18, 2005) and Scarry, *Naming Thy Name.*
[24] Burrow, "Shakespeare's Sonnets as Event," 112.
[25] Barthes, *Pleasure of the Text,* 4.
[26] Burrow, "Shakespeare's Sonnets as Event," 112–13.

inner being."[27] Memory and memorizing are the operations by which we internalize a poem and, in doing so, find ourselves co-constituted by the literary texts that attract us. Barthes suggests that a "text of pleasure" is one that "contents, fills, grants euphoria; the text that comes from culture and does not break with it," while a "text of bliss" is one that "unsettles the reader's historical, cultural, psychological assumptions, the consistency of his tastes, values, memories, brings to a crisis his relation with language."[28] Reading Burrow's claim and Vendler's recollection in tandem helps us see why the *Sonnets* offer a compelling case study for locating both pleasure and bliss. To find "bliss" in a sonnet is to connect with the timely pronouncement of pleasure and to tap into the timelessness of the pleasure that the poem describes.

Shakespeare's *Sonnets* further encourage readers to place themselves within the poems' described dynamics by embracing the indeterminability of the textual "I" and "thee."[29] As Jonathan Culler has put it, "lyric is spoken by a persona, whose situation and motivation one needs to reconstruct."[30] That is, interpreting the speaker's expression necessarily involves making connections to a reader's own recollected experiences. The various moments when the speaker of the *Sonnets* addresses a beloved instantiate lyric's frequent expression of what Culler terms "triangulated address," when we find the poet "addressing the audience of readers by addressing or pretending to address someone or something else."[31] As a love poem, Sonnet 18 has at its heart the idea of romantic or erotic connection between two or more people, though we should acknowledge that not every reader might experience or desire such feelings.[32] When we acknowledge this, we perceive how the "thee" of Sonnet 18's first line includes the reader but not necessarily every reader.[33] The pronoun thus reflects the same problematic dynamics of the "we" that appears in the first line of Sonnet 1 and elsewhere in the *Sonnets*. Shakespeare assumes a universal experience—and indeed his promise to secure the beloved's

---

[27] Helen Vendler, *The Ocean, the Bird, and the Scholar: Essays on Poets and Poetry* (Cambridge, MA and London: Harvard University Press, 2015), 6.

[28] Barthes, *Pleasure of the Text*, 14.

[29] For an excellent discussion about how the preponderance of pronouns in the *Sonnets* suggests many possible erotic arrangements and invites diverse readers to imagine themselves as a speaker or addressee, see Bruce R. Smith, "I, You, He, She, and We: On the Sexual Politics of Shakespeare's Sonnets," in *Shakespeare's Sonnets: Critical Essays*, ed. James Schiffer (Routledge, 2000), 411–29.

[30] Culler, *Theory of the Lyric*, 2.

[31] Culler, *Theory of the Lyric*, 8.

[32] Indeed, Culler goes on to say that "love poems, addressed to a beloved, named or unnamed, real or imagined, accessible or inaccessible, are the primary example of poems ostensibly addressed to another individual that indirectly address an audience." Culler, *Theory of the Lyric*, 206.

[33] Hannah Crawforth and Elizabeth Scott-Baumann suggest that "when Shakespeare imagines his own poems as 'the living record of *your* memory,' he speaks of each reader's ability to bring life to his verse, as well as his verse's ability to memorialize the beloved." The authors refer to Sonnet 55, where lines 7–8 reassure the beloved that "Nor Mars his sword, nor war's quick fire shall burn / The living record of your memory." Hannah Crawforth and Elizabeth Scott-Baumann, "Preface," in *On Shakespeare's Sonnets: A Poet's Celebration*, ed. Hannah Crawforth and Elizabeth Scott-Baumann (New York and London: Bloomsbury, 2016), xiv–xv.

immortality may rely on it—yet when that "we" is used without consent or without qualification, it runs the risk of sounding naive or reinforcing who might be excluded from the experience his poem describes. This also represents a departure from Barthes's desire for a text to "cruise" him. Rather than coyly expressing an interest in the reader's attention, Shakespeare's poems start or end with the conclusion that the reader will enroll in the memories and pleasures reflected within.

The *Sonnets* nonetheless engage in this strategy to encourage the reader to imbricate the poems within one's own personal memories. Amanda Watson argues that the *Sonnets* "look ahead to a time in the future when others, or at times the young man himself, will look back and try to remember."[34] Indeed, Adena Rosmarin connects this notion to the *Sonnets* because a love poem:

> sounds as if it is spoken by a lover to the beloved, yet it repeatedly testifies that it is written by a poet to a reader. It displays the infidelity of its words to what they claim to represent, yet it simultaneously protests against itself, convincing us that those words are indeed faithful, as is the lover who wrote them.[35]

This helps explain the appeal of the *Sonnets*, as Rosmarin goes on to note that "such radical contrariness defines a genre at once compelling to experience and difficult to explain."[36] The *Sonnets*' status as lyric poetry and as love poetry informs the dynamics by which their engagement with memory ties to pleasurable experience.

Sonnet 18 has strong ties to Barthes's notion of the "*will to bliss:* just where it exceeds demand, transcends prattle, and whereby it attempts to overflow" all the while that it may complicate the theorist's notion.[37] In the second line of Sonnet 18, "Thou art more lovely and more temperate," we hear language's failure to articulate the qualities of the beloved. If the speaker desires to memorialize the addressee— for future readers or even for himself—then it is a surprising strategy to argue that no image offers an accurate comparison. Indeed, the strategy strikingly diverges from early modern thinking about the function of memory. Renaissance strategies for improving memory drew upon ancient theories that relied on visuality. For example, the *Rhetorica ad Herennium* (c.86–82 BC) advises that memory functions best when associated with powerful images. The author posits that one should "set up images of a kind that can adhere longest in the memory [to] establish

---

[34] Amanda Watson, "'Full character'd': Competing Forms of Memory in Shakespeare's *Sonnets*," in *A Companion to Shakespeare's Sonnets*, ed. Michael Schoenfeldt (Oxford: Blackwell Publishing, 2010), 356.

[35] Adena Rosmarin, "Hermeneutics versus Erotics: Shakespeare's Sonnets and Interpretive History," *Publications of the Modern Language Association of America* 100, no. 1 (January 1985): 20.

[36] Rosmarin, "Hermeneutics versus Erotics," 20.

[37] Barthes, *The Pleasure of the Text*, 13.

similitudes as striking as possible."[38] This tactic was reiterated across Renaissance handbooks and treatises on the memory arts. For example, Peter of Ravenna's *The Art of Memory* (1548) advises that one imagine a series of rooms and populate them with "images [that] be the similitudes of the things that we will retain in the mind."[39] Sonnet 18 seems to do the very opposite: introducing a striking image only to dismiss it as inadequate for achieving similitude. Further, to be "more temperate" than an idealized summer's day introduces a seeming paradox. The adjective "temperate" denotes "keeping due measure, self-restrained, moderate," and thus the beloved is extreme in his lack of extremity. It remains an open question whether Shakespeare means that no image can compare to the beloved or that he simply will not share the image that does. John Wayland's *The Pastime of Pleasure* (1509/54) offers an extended meditation on the art of memory, reiterating the strategy of associating memorized elements with visual images but underscoring that these images should be "inward directed."[40] Perhaps by praising the beloved but not sharing the details of his pleasurable characteristics, Shakespeare emphasizes the private quality of their intimacy. Fulwood's *The Castle of Memory* (1562) posits that "memory is a retaining of the images or similitudes first perceived of the soul."[41] Perhaps Shakespeare avoids overtly describing his beloved to stress the private nature of his own memories, though that in turn risks obstructing the reader's ability to connect to the pleasure he leaves so abstract.[42]

Sonnet 18 partially fulfills Barthes's promise of readerly bliss where a text "exceeds demand" in another way: by linking eternity to limitless pleasure. The promise of eternity obviates the temporal inevitability that "Rough winds do shake the darling buds of May." These "winds" threaten to curtail pleasure before it can transition into bliss, just as in *Cymbeline*, Imogen laments that she could not give her lover a parting kiss before "comes in my father / And, like the tyrannous breathing of the north, / Shakes all our buds from growing" (1.4.36–8). The lines

[38] The text was widely influential and attributed to Cicero during the Renaissance. Anonymous [Cicero], *Rhetorica ad Herennium*, trans. Harry Kaplan (Cambridge, MA: Harvard University Press, 1954), 3.22.37.

[39] Peter of Ravenna, *The Art of Memory, That Otherwyse Is Called the Phenix*, trans. Robert Copland (London, 1548), 13.

[40] Stephen Hawes, *The Histoire of Graunde Amoure and la Bell Pucel, Called the Pastime of Plesure* (London: John Wayland, 1554), F2r–F3r.

[41] The text is a translation of Gratarolo's *De memoria reparanda*. Fulwood, *The Castle of Memorie*, A1v.

[42] Here and elsewhere in this study, I do not wish to posit that Shakespeare was singular in his approaches to the arts of memory in the *Sonnets*, given the "socially and epistemologically diffuse tendencies of the memory arts" that resist "a unitary language, single belief system, or grand narrative." Yet I do believe we see Shakespeare embracing alternatives to distinct commonplaces in the memory arts and describing discernable strategies that appeal to the speaker across the *Sonnets*. While the poet's mental images might be associated with remembered pleasures, these specific mnemonics themselves need not be shared with the public. William E. Engel, Rory Loughnane, and Grant Williams, "Introduction," in *The Memory Arts in Renaissance England* (Cambridge: Cambridge University Press, 2016), 16.

from the sonnet deny the impending change of the seasons and point to the time-defying effects of desire discussed in Chapter One. Scholars often focus on what Hester Lees-Jeffries terms "the eternizing conceit" of the *Sonnets*, which points to the promise of the poems to immortalize both Shakespeare and his beloved through fame.[43] The calculus of the poem thus relies on infinity:

> Sometime too hot the eye of heaven shines,
> And often is his gold complexion dimmed,
> And every fair from fair sometime declines,
> By chance or nature's changing course untrimmed;
> But thy eternal summer shall not fade[.] (5–9)

Carlos Eire has traced a long trajectory in western thought since Plato where "by reducing the body to a nuisance and an obstacle to the true eternal destiny of the human soul, all physical pleasure was made suspect."[44] This helps us understand why pleasure in the poems is so often tied to memory; it makes the pleasure a function of internal thoughts and of fantasy. The body, as we will see in Chapter Four, is at times invoked as a site of pleasure but so often is described in terms of a textual body. Because it offers, in Raymond Williams's words "a myth functioning as a memory," the Golden Age represents an actual past presented as a possibility that could be recaptured.[45] In its invocation of the "eternal summer," Sonnet 18 ties the beloved to cultural memory that is both recollective and anticipatory by likening him to the classical past *and* to the speculated future. However, the "eternal summer" can also operate as an analogue for death or the afterlife. Thus, this poem is tinged with the possibility that the beloved is already lost and this may explain the potentially elegiac tone of the excessive praise and wish for immortality expressed within it. In that reading of the phrase, recollection of the beloved in a perfect, timeless space constitutes a reaction to traumatic memories of loss.

Given that we retain the identity of Shakespeare as the author of the *Sonnets* but have no real idea who his objects of pleasure might have been, we might understand the unfading beauty here to refer to the author's craft and handicraft. As Adena Rosmarin acutely observes, "by expecting the future readers they find, the sonnets prefigure our retrospective confirmation of their excellence."[46] The *Sonnets* function as devices that train our pre-memory, telling us how we will feel about them after reading them as we read them. Indeed, we can see the dual operations of post-memory and pre-memory within the anaphora that occurs in the closing couplet: "So long as men can breathe or eyes can see, / So long lives this,

---

[43] Lees-Jeffries, *Shakespeare and Memory*, 137.
[44] Carlos Eire, *A Brief History of Eternity* (Princeton and Oxford: Princeton University Press, 2010), 45.
[45] Raymond Williams, *The Country and the City* (London: Chatto and Windus, 1973), 43.
[46] Rosmarin, "Hermeneutics versus Erotics," 30.

and this gives life to thee" (13–14). Aaron Kunin suggests that this couplet under-scores how, "In sonnet 18, poetry makes the image of the young man available to anyone who sees, hears, or recites the poems."[47] However, while the beloved is recreated in the recitation of the poem, it is an image-less form of the young man.[48] Thus, what this makes available to future generations is only the notion that Shakespeare had a private memory of his addressee and that now readers can delve into their own memories to imagine how such a beloved might look.

Part of what makes Shakespeare's *Sonnets* such rich ground for readers seeking pleasure or seeking distraction from displeasure involves the ways that the poems deploy transportable discourses. In his discussion of Sonnet 18, Paul Innes sug-gests that "here the friend is described as having the physical characteristics of the women of other sonnet sequences."[49] Another way to think about such parallels is to accept the proposition that we do not know the gender of the addressee of this and many other sonnets. Sonnet 20 will, of course, contemplate not just the transfer of feminine beauty to a male body but the attraction of an indeterminacy of the gender of the "master-mistress." Even more broadly, many of the sonnets (including Sonnet 18) do not contain gendered pronouns. Paul Edmondson and Stanley Wells go as far as to state,

> only twenty of the poems, all in the first group (Sonnets 1–126), can confidently be said, on the evidence of forms of address and the presence of pronouns, to be addressed to, or concern, a male, while seven, all in the second group (Sonnets 127–152) are clearly about a female. Other sonnets which might seem definite about the gender of their addressees rely on context, or subject matter, rather than pronouns.[50]

The present study does argue for several sonnets having a male addressee based on such contexts and subject matter, but I advance these only as possible interpre-tations. Perhaps various interpreters of the gendered addressees of the poems all sense how the love of the friend is by nature transferable. Indeed, the *Sonnets* offer compelling case studies for Jeffrey Masten's recent analysis of how loving discourse among same-sex friends in Shakespeare taps into language "spoken across *kinds* of relationships in early modern England, including those we would now separate into homosexual and heterosexual" and thus "represents yet more evidence for the mobile quality of desire, erotics, and affect."[51] Masten's claim can be extrapolated

---

[47] Aaron Kunin, "Shakespeare's Preservation Fantasy," *PMLA* 124, no. 1 (2009): 98.

[48] Christopher Warley suggests that the "mystery" of the young man's identity is "not simply a matter of a lack of biographical details." Rather, the question of "who is the youth?" also emerges as "a question the speaker himself asks." Christopher Warley, *Sonnet Sequences and Social Distinction in Renaissance England* (Cambridge: Cambridge University Press, 2005), 134.

[49] Innes, *Shakespeare and the English Renaissance Sonnet*, 109.

[50] Edmondson and Wells, *Shakespeare's Sonnets*, 31.

[51] Masten, *Queer Philologies*, 72.

onto the pleasurable relations between readers and a text. Sonnet 18's showcase of indescribable beauty makes its depicted pleasure more transferable.[52]

Because readers are asked to conjure their own image of what might be more lovely than a summer's day, they become enrolled in the language and situation of Sonnet 18. Barthes posits that while "pleasure can be expressed in words, bliss cannot" because "bliss is unspeakable."[53] Yet Shakespeare may admit the negative aspect to unspeakability where Barthes does not. The inability to speak or to describe in Sonnet 18 could be interpreted as the refusal to name the negative side of the beloved's refusal to reciprocate the speaker's love. Sonnet 18, unlike Barthes's *The Pleasure of the Text*, leaves open the possibility that the inability to speak might stem from inarticulable rage or sadness from loss. It is intriguing, then, that this poem—which does not actually make clear the similitude of its praised object—is so frequently performed at weddings. It is possible that it appeals because it recognizes the private nature of the feelings that bind the couple being celebrated, but it is perhaps equally possible that it reflects a desire to occlude the negative aspects of relationships for the sake of ceremony.

Desire and Eternity

Sonnet 55 is perhaps paradigmatic for the "eternizing conceit" at work in the collection, yet it still points to more complex forms of desirous memory. As noted above, we can interpret the poem's use of "your" in "your memory" to refer to not only the beloved but also the reader (8). Thus, this sonnet offers a flashpoint for what we might call "pre-memory," that dynamic where memories are already preformed before an experience. Sonnet 55's central idea that the beloved's "praise shall still find room, / Even in the eyes of all posterity / That wear this world out to the ending doom" boldly claims that the speaker can predict what future readers will find appealing (10–12). In fact, the formulation speaks directly to readers and informs them that they will be recalling the poem and the beloved just as their own future generations will. The dimensions of memory imagined here are both cultural and personal. On one level, the beloved will be recalled among later readers to a degree that exceeds the capability of "monuments" (1). At the same time, this recollection will occur "in lovers' eyes," suggesting that the words of the poem will resonate on a deeply emotional level to readers in intimate relationships (14).

The use of "lovers" also points to the erotic dimension of the operations of recollection described here. The romantic feelings associated with memorialization

---

[52] P. J. Kavanagh's recent adaptation of Sonnet 18 reads, "Our dreams can fall a grandeur and the heart / Speak languages we waking do not know" (lines 3–4). It is an apt description for what reading bliss can be. P. J. Kavanagh, "Dream," in *On Shakespeare's Sonnets: A Poet's Celebration*, ed. Hannah Crawforth and Elizabeth Scott-Baumann (London and New York: Bloomsbury, 2016), 15.

[53] Barthes, *The Pleasure of the Text*, 21.

in a sonnet is counterposed to the "sluttish time" of a monument, suggesting that modes of erotic desire cannot be disaggregated from modes of recollection (4). This pairing of sexual innuendo with the terms "Judgment" and "ending doom" calls into question the promise of pleasure offered by memory in the poem. Unlike Barthes's secular meditation on pleasure, which focuses only on earthly experience, Shakespeare's poetry should be read in the cultural context of religious belief that weighed moral behavior as a limiting factor for access to a pleasurable afterlife. The religious terms qualify the secular consolations in this poem and in other poems where such terms are invoked. They underscore that the poet may promise immortality and encourage meditations of erotic pleasures, but a Protestant viewpoint will see salvation as the only true transcendence and the divine as the ultimate arbiter of an afterlife for a soul deemed morally worthy.

Because it places the author's work, the author's beloved, and the author's envisioned reader in the time of eternity, which encompasses all future readers until the "ending doom," Sonnet 55 suggests it can productively dislodge those who encounter it from a specified time and place. However, this promise reads as a false promise of wishful thinking in yet another way. Such timeless space would have only been available to *some* readers who encountered the poem, and indeed the message about it would have excluded those who could not read. And printed love poems, as well as physical monuments, typically valorize those individuals who reflect and reinforce the racial and class hierarchies that make the creation of such paeans possible. As I discuss at length in Chapter Five, the speaker ignores the ways that power relations and privilege make some of his formulations unattainable for groups of early moderns or ignores the painful lived experience to which some of his analogies are insensitive.

Perhaps, for some readers, the sonnet form "is a moment's monument," as Dante Gabriel Rossetti once wrote.[54] However, this notion need not mean that a short poem concretizes a single moment in the past. Instead, a sonnet constitutes, as Rossetti goes on to say, a "memorial from the soul's eternity / To one dead deathless hour." That is, the moment described in the poem becomes all moments in time, as it is tethered by the space of infinite time in which the soul dwells and inhabits an hour that comes to a close. Discussing Shakespeare's *Sonnets*, Colin Burrow observes that "lyrics do not address one time or occasion, but many possible occasions."[55] The imagined timelessness described here in Sonnet 55, as well as the capacious temporal period described by Rossetti and Burrow, track to Barthes's notion that "bliss of the text is not precarious [...] it does not come in its own good time, it does not depend on any ripening. Everything is wrought to a transport at

---

[54] Dante Gabriel Rossetti, "The House of Life: A Sonnet-Sequence," in *The Pre-Raphaelites: An Anthology of Poetry by Dante Gabriel Rossetti and Others*, ed. Jerome H. Buckley (Chicago: Chicago Review Press, 2001), 96.

[55] Burrow, "Shakespeare's Sonnets as Event," 99.

one and the same moment."[56] Pleasure, in Shakespeare's *Sonnets*, occurs when one moves outside of the limits of a discrete time and place.

The focus on eternity in this sonnet ties it to Sonnet 18, which promises to immortalize the beloved in "eternal lines to time" (12).[57] Indeed, Sonnets 18 and 55 both exemplify a shift where the speaker focuses more on his own pleasure in recalling the beloved rather than the pleasure that the beloved might experience from producing a child. Such an interplay between memory and pleasure obviates the need not only for the beloved's response or presence but also his consent. Indeed, it also troubles the access to what Barthes conceives of as "bliss." By conscripting highly charged or ephemeral elements (e.g., death, sex, bodies, passion) to the controlled and much more genteel space of the sonnet form, the poet suggests a regulation of desire and experience that runs counter to what he might be encouraging. We will see a fuller exploration of this idea about the beloved's absent presence in the next chapter as well as further discussion of the speaker's tendency to place limits on the beloved in the following chapters.

While Sonnet 55 is emblematic of Shakespeare's depiction of his poems as memorializers superior to physical monuments, Sonnet 122 is one of the poems that directly express practices from the early modern memory arts. Intriguingly, it renders visible the relationship between reading and the excess that brings about bliss. The speaker promises that his own memory surpasses the ability of a notebook to contain the beloved, who should be remembered "Beyond all date even to eternity" (4). He reassures the beloved that "Nor need I tallies thy dear love to score," even while he describes his mind as if it were a writing tablet (10). In doing so, he echoes Socrates's image of our mind as a block of wax upon which memories can be inscribed.[58] Loving memory is more powerful than the regularized activity of recording memory on a wax tablet. He lets go of such "tables" in order to give into excess and "receive thee more." The final couplet, "To keep an adjunct to remember thee / Were to import forgetfulness in me," ties to another of Socrates's arguments: that writing destroys memory (13–14).[59] It may also be that the speaker seeks to avoid recording new experiences in memory that might occlude thoughts of the present beloved. Neuroscience has come to recognize how, "as time passes, we encode and store new experiences

---

[56] Barthes, *The Pleasure of the Text*, 52.

[57] As Garrett A. Sullivan notes that the "poet's 'eternal lines' [...] emerge as a model for memory that solves the problem of procreation by granting immortality to the young man (and, of course, to the poet) without having to secure his consent." I explore the cost of the speaker claiming partial ownership of the beloved's memories in much more depth in Chapter 6. Garrett A. Sullivan Jr., "Voicing the Young Man: Memory, Forgetting, and Subjectivity in the Procreation Sonnets," in *A Companion to Shakespeare's Sonnets*, ed. Michael Schoenfeldt (Malden and Oxford: Wiley-Blackwell, 2007), 339.

[58] Plato, *The Theaetetus of Plato*, trans. Myles Burnyeat and M. J. Levett (Indianapolis: Hackett Publishing Company, 1990), 100–1.

[59] Plato, *Phaedrus*, in *The Collected Dialogues of Plato*, ed. Edith Hamilton and Huntington Cairns (Princeton: Princeton University Press, 1961), 274–5. For a discussion of this ancient argument as well as its implications for users of contemporary technology, see Walter J. Ong, *Orality and Literacy: The Technologizing of the Word* (New York and London: Routledge, 2002), 78–80.

that interfere with our ability to recall previous ones."[60] It may be crucial to Shakespeare's professed process that he avoids comparisons, as he does in Sonnet 18, or avoids the distraction of written memory aids, though that claim in Sonnet 55 seems countered by the collection of poems itself. Sonnet 55 promises the beloved that Shakespeare's poems will help guarantee "The living record of your memory" (8), both because the text can outlive monuments and because, as John Michael Archer observes, memory will be instilled in "the living bodies of future readers."[61] The *Sonnets* may be necessary tools by which to transmit memories of the beloved to future readers, but Shakespeare still privileges his private and constant thoughts as the most accurate vessel to contain him.[62]

It is in Sonnet 55 that Vendler identifies an "absent center" in the *Sonnets*.[63] While Chapters 3 and 5 will address absence as an operative function in the *Sonnets*, it is worth noting here that this absence is generative not only for the poet (who writes about it) but also for the readers (who seek a space to locate themselves in the experience being described). Sonnet 55 and Sonnet 122 present us with evidence for Joel Fineman's claim that Shakespeare's *Sonnets* invented a new type of poetic subjectivity for us in epideictic poetry, in which the poetic persona praises the addressee. He asserts that Shakespeare complicates the tradition of praise poetry by rendering visible the "perjured eye" (or "I") that speaks through an invented literary self.[64] This self cannot possibly know the nature of future readers but instead invests in the fantasy that he can, just as Whitman does in "Crossing Brooklyn Ferry."[65] Shakespeare also speaks about future readers' adoration, an adoration expressed in the form of recollection, when he means to speak about his own desire not to forget the beloved. A similar claim can be made of Sonnet 126.

Making Space for Desirous Memory

While Sonnet 122 is the last poem in the collection where the word "memory" occurs, Sonnet 126 is the last to use the term "pleasure." Both intriguingly make demands on the reader's memory. The poems do more than guarantee immortality

---

[60] Daniel L. Schachter, *Searching for Memory: The Brain, the Mind, and the Past* (New York: Basic Books, 1996), 76.

[61] Michael Archer, *Technically Alive: Shakespeare's Sonnets* (London: Palgrave Macmillan, 2012), 102.

[62] Archer sees Shakespeare's *Sonnets* as "a collection of poems written on the cusp of modern technology" such that they demonstrate how "technology, life, and consciousness are tied together in an exigent knot." Archer, *Technically Alive*, 6 and 1 respectively.

[63] Helen Vendler, *The Art of Shakespeare's Sonnets* (Cambridge, MA: Harvard University Press, 1997), 518.

[64] See Fineman, *Shakespeare's Perjured Eye*, esp. 1–48.

[65] While Shakespeare speaks to his beloved in a seeming one-to-one communication, Whitman even more overtly states that his poem speaks to future generations when he exclaims, "I am with you, you men and women of a generation, or ever so many generations hence" (21–2), and "Gorgeous clouds of the sunset! drench with your splendor me, or the men and women generations after me!" Walt Whitman, "Crossing Brooklyn Ferry," in Walt Whitman, *The Complete Poems*, ed. Francis Murphy (New York: Penguin, 2005), 189–95.

for Shakespeare and his addressee. They engage the reader's private thoughts and own experiences. Sonnet 126 opens by addressing:

> O thou my lovely boy, who in thy power
> Dost hold Time's fickle glass, his sickle, hour;
> Who hast by waning grown, and therein show'st
> Thy lovers withering as thy sweet self grow'st[.] (1–4)

The "lovely boy" here could be the young man addressed in previous poems (especially Sonnet 20 where he is doted on by Nature) or could be the boy-god cupid (who will figure in the final two sonnets of the collection). We are told that this "minion of her pleasure" must answer to Nature's "audit" (9, 11). The use of "minion" here underscores a negative aspect of pleasure here as it renders a person subservient, far from the extreme pleasure of bliss and much closer to the displeasure of being reminded of being under the power of someone else or one's emotions. This term "audit" suggests the type of tallying and recounting described in Sonnet 122 and also speaks to the work of listening—as it invokes the Latin *audio, audire*—which implicitly urges the reader to partake in the work of memory. Shakespeare's use of "audit" also recalls the use of the term in Mary Herbert's memorial poem to Philip Sidney in the edition of the Psalms that she completed after his death. When she summons memory of her brother, she announces,

> When to this accompt, this cast-up sum,
> This reckoning made, this audit of my woe,
> I call my thoughts whence so strange passions flow,
> How works my heart, my senses stricken dumb?
> That would thee more than ever heart could show,
> And all too short: who knew thee best doth know
> There lives no wit that may thy praise become.[66]

Andrew Hiscock describes Herbert's lines as "a memorial discourse that [...] relies upon the lexis of obligation and debt."[67] The obligation here explicitly involves her own desire to recollect her brother properly in the public space of the dedicatory verse and implicitly urges the reader to partake in that work of memory. Yet it also reminds us that the work of memory, especially in its public dimension of performed mourning, can be a duty or burden rather than a chosen, pleasurable activity.

---

[66] Mary Herbert, "To the Angell Spirit of the Most Excellent Phillip Sidney," in *The Collected Works of Mary Sidney Herbert, Countess of Pembroke*, Vol. 1: *Poems, Translations, and Correspondence*, ed. Margaret P. Hannay, Noel J. Kinnamon, and Michael G. Brennan (Oxford: Oxford University Press, 1998), 111, lines 57–62.
[67] Hiscock, *Reading Memory in Early Modern Literature*, 145.

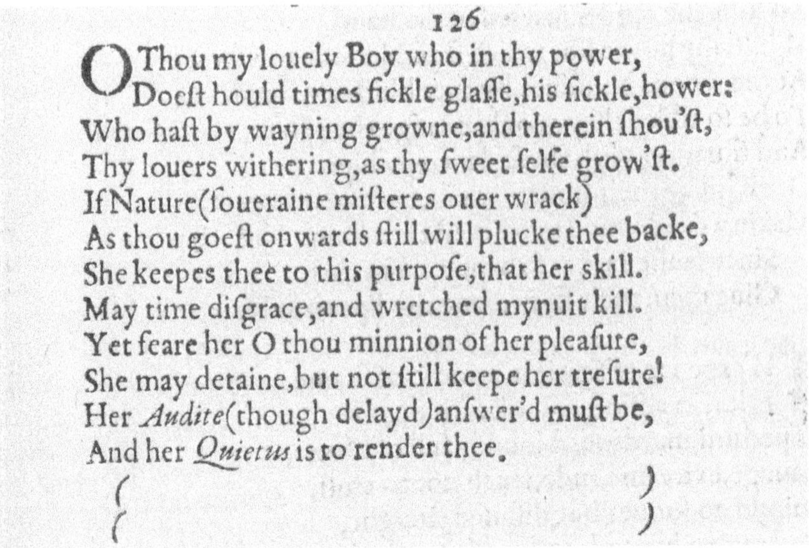
126

O Thou my louely Boy who in thy power,
Doeſt hould times fickle glaſſe,his ſickle,hower:
Who haſt by wayning growne,and therein ſhou'ſt,
Thy louers withering,as thy ſweet ſelfe grow'ſt.
If Nature(ſoueraine miſteres ouer wrack)
As thou goeſt onwards ſtill will plucke thee backe,
She keepes thee to this purpoſe,that her skill.
May time diſgrace,and wretched mynuit kill.
Yet feare her O thou minnion of her pleaſure,
She may detaine,but not ſtill keepe her treſure!
Her *Audite*(though delayd)anſwer'd muſt be,
And her *Quietus* is to render thee.
( )
( )

Fig. 2.1. Sonnet 126. William Shakespeare, *Sonnets* (1609).

Sonnet 126 has fascinated readers as the version in the 1609 quarto contains a pair of empty brackets after the phrase "And her quietus [that is, her 'quiting' or settling of accounts] is to render thee" (Fig. 2.1). The bracketed, empty lines in Sonnet 126 have been variously interpreted as a printer's error (where either the two lines were left out or Shakespeare intended the poem to only be twelve lines) or a placeholder for missing text. They may also represent that which is held in memory but not articulated in spoken speech. The missing lines might signal the death or loss of the addressee, just as the eternal summer might. Or they might signify the speaker censoring his own anger, remembering it but not stating it. Another way to think of them is as an indication that readers might insert their own couplet in the space. Perhaps the empty brackets demarcate the space of bliss, especially as that poem grapples with the intense "pleasure" noted in line 9. Indeed, the brackets constitute a space where memory and desire intersect. One might imagine that the reader can insert a new couplet based on personal memory or memories of preceding sonnets. The author has given us his pattern for 121 sonnets and, in many examples beyond those discussed here today, withholds his own individual memory in order to invite readers to contribute theirs in the project of sense making. Another way in which the sonnets are a memory of each other is that the book appears, as Colin Burrow puts it, "sourced in itself, and to be made up of readings and re-readings of its own poems."[68] If reading them in the order presented in the

[68] Colin Burrow, "Introduction," in William Shakespeare, *The Complete Sonnets and Poems*, ed. Colin Burrow (Oxford: Oxford University Press, 2003), 116.

1609 quarto, we encounter sonnets with recollection of specific previous sonnets. It is evocative to imagine that Shakespeare even imagines that the reader will help him remember lines. Lemnius's *The Touchstone of Complexions* (1576) suggests that "venery" can be "very hurtful to memory."[69] Perhaps the speaker's own excessive dwelling on sexual activity has made it difficult to remember things, and now it falls upon the reader to share his burden.

The notion that the lacuna in Sonnet 126 is meant to be filled by the reader finds support in early modern discussions of reading. For example, Francis Meres's *Palladis Tamia: Wit's Treasury* gives us an intriguing glimpse into such reading practices. While Meres is well known for his commentary on Shakespeare's early career, Catherine Nicholson has recently observed that "few have ventured beyond his comments on Shakespeare."[70] Sonnet 126 makes manifest Meres's advice given within a section titled "The Use of Reading," which explains "what thou read is to be transposed to thine own use."[71] Meres nods toward discourses of sweetness and pleasure when he chooses the analogy of bees to explain the role of the reader in creating meaning: "Bees out of diverse flowers draw diverse juices, but they temper and digest them by their own virtue, otherwise they would make no honey."[72] Richard Barnfield senses the sweetness of Shakespeare's lyric when he describes him in the 1598 poem entitled "A Remembrance of Some English Poets": "And Shakespeare thou, whose honey-flowing vein, / Pleasing the world, the praises doth obtain."[73] The poet here describes *Venus and Adonis*, yet the sentiment might as well apply to the *Sonnets*. The language closely echoes that of Frances Meres, whose *Palladis Tamia* claimed in the same year, "the sweet witty soul of Ovid lives in mellifluous and honey-tongued Shakespeare, witness his Venus and Adonis, his Lucrece his sugared *Sonnets* among his private friends, etc." Once more, sweetness and the love of friends seems to be associated with transportable discourses. Indeed, bees seem an especially apt metaphor for describing the transmission of sweetness.

In a section titled "Reading of Books," Meres observes that "as we see ourselves in other men's eyes, so in other men's writings we may see what becomes us and becomes us not."[74] Achilles makes a similar point in *Troilus and Cressida* when he tells Ulysses "speculation turns not to itself / Till it hath travelled and is mirrored there / Where it may see itself" (3.3.104–6). Achilles may refer to the ancient idea that the eye can only see itself accurately when reflected in another person's eye, just as a soul can only see itself accurately reflected in another soul. The notion

---

[69] Levinus Lemnius, *The Touchstone of Complexions* (London, 1576), P8r.

[70] Catherine Nicholson, "Algorithm and Analogy: Distant Reading in 1598," *PMLA* 132, no. 3 (May 2017): 643.

[71] Nicholson, "Algorithm and Analogy," 643.

[72] Meres, *Wit's Treasury*, 268v.

[73] Richard Barnfield, *The Complete Poems*, ed. George Klawitter (Selinsgrove: Susquehanna University Press, 1990), 182.

[74] Meres, *Wit's Treasury*, 266v.

that reading a poem might make us realize our own desires is nicely described in Richard Barnfield's Sonnet 11, "He opened it, and taking off the cover, / He straight perceived himself to be my lover." Reading a book or a poem (here framed as if a glass) can incite desire and make one realize their own desires. Barthes suggests, "the text you write must prove to me *that it desires me*."[75] His claim illuminates how a poem might be thought of as a body itself. In turn, that poem may constitute contact for intimacy between the writer and the reader. We find an example of how lyrical language might enable bodily connection in *The Winter's Tale*, when Cloten says to the musicians, "Come on, tune. If you can penetrate her with your fingering, so; we'll try with tongue too" (2.3.13–14). We find a more overt conception of the text as body in William Percy's Sonnet 20, the last poem in his *Sonnets to the Fairest Coelia*: "Receive these writs, my sweet and dearest friend, / The lively patterns of my lifeless body" (1–2).[76] Percy supposes, as we will find the speaker of Shakespeare's *Sonnets* supposing in subsequent chapters, that the textual encounter might prove even more exciting than the encounter between two physical bodies.

The Sonnet Form and the Memory of Desire

Barthes tantalizes his readers with the idea that they might recognize themselves within a literary text and, surprisingly, delightfully experience that reflection as erotic pleasure. Shakespeare and his *Sonnets* seem particularly aware of the possibility of this dynamic but go even further to assume the reader's association with the pleasures described, even obtusely, in the text. The earlier writer seems more prone to ignore the distance between the reader and the writer, disregarding the fact that, as Roger Chartier puts it, "authors do not write books; they write texts that become written objects."[77] In the case of the *Sonnets*, the written objects could be manuscript versions of the poems—copied and recopied, then circulated among private friends—or the printed 1609 quarto or a later volume. A commendatory poem in the 1623 First Folio laments that the engraver of the frontispiece "O, could have drawn his wit / As well in brasse, as he hath hit / His face"; instead, "since he cannot, Reader, look / Not on his picture but on his book" (Fig. 2.2). The author of this commendatory poem seemed to know, long before Barthes announced it, that the deceased author gives prominence to the reader.[78]

---

[75] Barthes, *The Pleasure of the Text*, 6.

[76] William Percy, *Sonnets to the Fairest Coelia* (London: Printed by Adam Islip, for W. P., 1594), Lvi.

[77] Roger Chartier, *The Order of Books: Readers, Authors, and Libraries in Europe Between the 14th and 18th Centuries*, trans. Lydia G. Cochrane (Palo Alto: Stanford University Press, 1994), 10.

[78] I refer here to Roland Barthes's announcement, in "The Death of the Author," that "to give writing its future, it is necessary to overthrow the myth: the birth of the reader must be at the cost of the death of the author." While certainly vital to my opening discussion of this book, I freely acknowledge that not all of Barthes's thinking was as radical as he might have framed it to be. Roland Barthes, "The

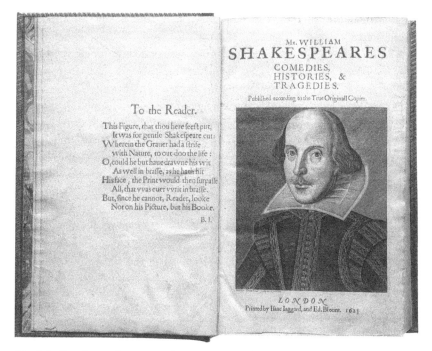

Fig. 2.2. Ben Jonson's commendatory poem in the First Folio, William Shakespeare, *Comedies, Histories, and Tragedies* (1623).

Thus we can understand this counsel in Jonson's prefatory poem to emphasize how the book becomes the object with which readers engage in order to derive their own pleasure, even if that gives them permission to sometimes disregard the writer's own insistence on what might be pleasurable.

As we have seen above, part of what fuels the pleasure of reading depicted in the *Sonnets* is the dynamic by which Shakespeare's memory and the reader's memory intermingle. Because these poems are at times so private, they might all the more invite the reader to engage with them or they might exclude the reader. Lynne Magnussen has observed that the *Sonnets* "invent or give language to mental experiences their readers could not have described but nonetheless recognize, or feel they inhabit, and then appropriate and quote the words almost as their own thoughts."[79] Her argument dovetails with how neuroscience understands the

Death of the Author," in Roland Barthes, *Image—Music—Text*, trans. Stephen Heath (New York: Hill and Wang, 1978), 148.

[79] She adds that "the lyric 'I' of these poems seems to summon these identifications." Perhaps this explains the popularity of Shakespeare's poems such as Sonnet 18 or 116 at weddings, regardless of the gender of the original addressee to whom Shakespeare may have intended them. Wells notes that the opening of Sonnet 125 ("Were't aught to me I bore the canopy, / With my extern the outward honouring, / Or laid great bases for eternity / Which proves more short than waste or ruining?") "reads to me more like a private allusion than anything that a general reader could ever have been expected to

brain to generate "feelings," which Damasio tellingly describes as "mental sensors of the organism's interior, witnesses of life on the fly."[80] Taken together, the literary scholar's insight and the neuroscientist's understanding of emotion nicely capture how even the briefest encounter with life experience, even that which is only depicted on paper, can generate an internal reaction that binds the reader or witness to others based on shared experience of a feeling. And by this operation the experience of reading becomes dialogic, even if that dialogue excludes the author when a reader instead connects with other readers or even just with oneself.

Jorge Luis Borges seems to have sensed this to be true. In his short story entitled "Shakespeare's Memory," a character who has inherited Shakespeare's memory relates:

> *Tengo, aún, dos memorias. La mía personal y la de aquel Shakespeare que parcialmente soy. Mejor dicho, dos memorias me tienen. Hay una zona en que se confunden. Hay una cara de mujer que no sé a qué siglo atribuir.*

> (Yet now I have two memories. My own personal memory and that of Shakespeare who I partially am. More accurately, two memories possess me. There is a zone where they intermix. There is a face of a woman to which century I do not know to attribute.)[81]

Borges renders fantastical that which is the normative experience of reading Shakespeare's poetry. The result is a dynamic which mirrors the operations of the *Sonnets* themselves. The poet's memory and his objects of desire (here pinpointed as the face of a woman) blur into those of the reader. Borges leaves uncertain, then, whether his protagonist connects deeply with Shakespeare and the poet's experience, or whether the protagonist's encounter with Shakespeare enables him to realize the very division between two memories. In this latter interpretation, the encounter with claims to universal or communal memory can drive one to acknowledge how recollection, like pleasure, might necessarily be a largely private experience. Encountering Shakespeare's collection thus intermingles while it also separates cultural and personal memory, public and private experience, erotic and intellectual pleasure. This might just be the pleasure of the *Sonnets*.

---

understand." Lynne Magnusson, "Non-Dramatic Poetry," in *Shakespeare: An Oxford Guide*, ed. Stanley Wells and Lena Cowen Orlin (Oxford: Oxford University Press, 2003), 297, and Wells, *Looking for Sex in Shakespeare*, 49.

[80] Damasio, *Looking for Spinoza*, 139.

[81] Jorge Luis Borges, *Obras Completas, Tomo 3* (Buenos Aires: Emecé Editores, 2005), 433. The translation is my own.

3
Embracing Absence

While much Petrarchan poetry is driven by the absence of a beloved, Shake-speare's *Sonnets* deploy this convention to unusual ends, especially in terms of how recollection is framed as compensation for such absence. Yet perhaps the most surprising presence of absence in the collection can be found in an apostrophe within Sonnet 39. In the third quatrain, the speaker pivots away from praising the absent friend in order to address a seemingly abstract concept when he says, "O absence." This strange apostrophe, rather than following the tradition of address-ing something missing, addresses the concept of missingness itself. This chapter begins with this peculiar moment before examining other flashpoints for absence in the *Sonnets*. What emerges is a pattern where the absent beloved becomes a figure of pleasure because the speaker can manipulate the operations of memory in order to realize new forms of erotic experience impossible when the beloved is physically present.[1]

Before it deploys its unusual apostrophe, Sonnet 39 begins like many other son-nets addressed to the friend, with praise of his positive qualities: "O, how thy worth with manners may I sing" (1). Note how the inverted syntax places the friend's "worth" before the verb and the speaking subject. The structure of the sentence mirrors the operations of memory as the friend's outstanding qualities are recalled into the mind before the speaker can articulate them in song. Placing the "I" at the end of the sentence locates the beloved before the speaker in order to under-score the addressee's higher standing and to echo the formulaic opening of the epic genre.[2] Thus even at the level of the poem's generic markers, adulation raises the friend far above the speaker, yet such genuflection does not entirely separate the two men. The subsequent line emphasizes that they remain conjoined by the notion at the heart of the Renaissance friendship ideal: the friend-as-another-self.[3] When the speaker declares, "thou art all the better part of me," we hear echoes of

---

[1] Some sections of this chapter draw from earlier thinking and articulation in my essay "Recollec-tion and Preemptive Recollection in Shakespeare's Sonnets," which appears in *Memory and Mortality in Renaissance England*, ed. William E. Engel, Rory Loughnane, and Grant Williams (Cambridge: Cambridge University Press, 2022), 61–77.

[2] Certainly this opening is not exclusive to the epic, but early modern readers would recognize echoes of the genre in the choice of the verb-phrase "I sing" and in the syntax as the *Iliad*, *Odyssey*, *and Aeneid* all start with the object then the verb.

[3] This formulation can be found across ancient descriptions of the classical ideal upon which the Renaissance one is based. For example, Cicero reiterates this notion (*"verus amicus est* [...] *alter idem"*) from Aristotle because it captures the way a man "looks for another whose mind he may, so to speak, mingle with his own so as to turn the two into one" (*"alterum anquirit cuius animum ita cum suo*

The Pleasures of Memory in Shakespeare's Sonnets. John S. Garrison, Oxford University Press. © John S. Garrison (2023).
DOI: 10.1093/oso/9780198857716.003.0004

Michel de Montaigne's famous formulation where friends "intermix and confound themselves one in the other, with so universal a commixture, that they wear out, and can no more find the seam that had conjoined them together."[4] Shakespeare's articulation of the two men's bond does not fully realize the ideal described by Montaigne as the speaker notes that the friend is still a divisible "part" of him. However, the sonnet still seizes upon the logics that define such perfect amity when the poet describes himself as co-constituted with his beloved.

In line 4's question, "What is't but mine own when I praise thee?," we hear the speaker both hesitate around the narcissism inherent in praising the beloved and claim ownership over the beloved through intimate description. For the poet, to love himself at the level at which he praises the addressee is to risk the sin of self-love for which he admonishes himself in Sonnet 62 ("Sin of self-love posses-seth all mine eye"). Yet, as Laurie Shannon has demonstrated, in the Renaissance friendship ideal, "likeness, parity, equality, and consent present a thoroughgoing antidote to hierarchies."[5] Thus, we might understand the discourses being deployed by the speaker to aspire toward this dynamic where "likeness between friends radically cancels vertical difference."[6] The lack of parity between the two men may not inhibit the speaker from claiming that he and his beloved share "one mind and one heart" across two bodies as the friendship model entails.[7]

In fact, the friend-as-absent plays a crucial role in the claims to intimacy made in early modern ideals of friendship, and this helps the speaker build his fantasy of the presence of the friend even in absence. Consider, for example, the story of the paradigmatic friends Damon and Pythias from classical antiquity. One of them is confined at court yet needs to travel abroad to put his affairs in order. The other takes his place in order to allow the friend to travel. Witnessing such dedication, the ruler who had imprisoned the one friend absolves him and asks to join in Damon and Pythias's friendship.[8] Such examples suggest that a friend best proves their likeness to, as well as their use to, the other friend when separated. These instances also underscore that one friend's physical presence is not needed when the other friend is present. We hear resonances of this surprising relationship

---

misceat ut efficiat paene unum ex duobus"). Cicero, *De amicitia*, Section 21. Aristotle, *Nicomachean Ethics*, Book IX, 1166a32.

[4] Montaigne, *Essayes*, 92.

[5] Laurie Shannon, *Sovereign Amity: Figures of Friendship in Shakespearean Contexts* (Chicago: University of Chicago Press, 2002), 11.

[6] Shannon, *Sovereign Amity*, 11.

[7] I explore the limitations of such commonplace claims to parity, especially as they are used in the *Sonnets* to undergird some of the more surprising claims about memory, in Chapter 5. The early modern commonplace takes up a classical definition of ideal friendship seen in, for example, Cicero, *De Amicitia*, sec. 1.25.

[8] For a history of the reception of this story in early modern contexts, see Robert Stretter, "Cicero on Stage: *Damon and Pithias* and the Fate of Classical Friendship in English Renaissance Drama," *Texas Studies in Literature and Language* 47, no. 4 (Winter 2005): 345–65. For a broader discussion of the early modern notion that one friend could act as the other's proxy, see John Garrison, *Friendship and Queer Theory in the Renaissance* (New York: Routledge, 2014), 1–22, esp. 17–22.

between friendship and absence on the title page of Charles Goldwell's treatise on friendship, *The True Choice of a Friend: Showing the Comfort of a Faithful Friend* (1625). The aphorism that appears just below the title, "a friend is nearer than a brother," reminds us how the terms of physical location intertwine with the terms of emotional intimacy. Such entanglements make possible the sense that a dear friend is always close by, even when separated from us by time and distance.

Given how the speaker claims his beloved is "part" of him, we can understand the poet's recollection of his positive qualities to have a bodily dimension. To *remember* the absent friend is also to *re-member* him as the ego-collapsing formulation for idealized friendship means the two men cannot be fully disaggregated. As we have begun to see through this volume, the *Sonnets'* repeated formulations of loving memory complicate Adam Phillips's claim that "to desire is to remember the one thing we are trying to forget."[9] In Phillips's formulation (which paraphrases Lacan), our longing for something or someone makes us aware of an area of lack that we have previously tried to ignore. Shakespeare, however, repeatedly returns to the topic of the absent beloved and does so with such frequency that it implies that he derives pleasure from recollection in isolation. And it is not just that he pleasantly remembers his beloved but also that he enhances his own sense of self-worth, despite his gestures of self-abnegation. He can allow himself to forget his own more negative aspects when he asks the beloved to remember that "better part" of him that mirrors the addressee. To lose or forget the beloved might involve losing the reinforcement that the best parts of him exist.[10] Such a dynamic finds expression in other Renaissance poetry. For example, in Donne's elegy "Sappho to Philaenis," the beloved "dwells with me still mine irksome memory / Which, both to keep and lose, grieves equally."[11] These lines from Donne's poem capture the dialectic energies that link memory, loss, and desire. In mourning, to forget the lost object is to finally acknowledge its permanent absence and begin to move toward acceptance of a world without the deceased or departed.

To keep the lost object in the mind, though, acts as a constant reminder of the object's absence and may inhibit completion of the mourning process. Freud suggests that we complete the process of mourning when we transfer our affection from a lost beloved to a new individual. However, this formulation overlooks the ways that we may still possess a version of the beloved lingering in our memories

---

[9] Phillips, *Side Effects*, 59.

[10] Studies in cognitive psychology have found that "by distancing negative past selves, people can avoid deprecating their present selves. In contrast, people can enhance the present self by perceiving successful past selves to be close." This may help explain why the speaker at once stresses the distance of the actual friend (who might remind him of his inadequacy) but enjoys the presence of the recollected friend (who reflects back his best self but cannot actively criticize him). I engage in an extended discussion of the multiple selves generated through memory in Chapter Five. Michael Ross and Anne E. Wilson, "Constructing and Appraising Past Selves," in *Memory, Brain, and Belief*, ed. Elaine Scarry and Daniel L. Schacter (Cambridge, MA: Harvard University Press, 2000), 245.

[11] John Donne, *The Complete English Poems*, ed. A. J. Smith (London and New York: Penguin, 1996), 127, lines 13–14.

or how we ourselves might change to resemble the lost beloved. This is surely only part of the story of how we are affected by our relations with the dead. Judith Butler argues that while Freud "suggested that successful mourning meant being able to exchange one object for another [...] Perhaps, rather, one mourns when one accepts that by the loss one undergoes one will be changed, possibly forever."[12] As discussed in the first chapter, it is possible that Sonnet 30 and other instances of the speaker addressing previous loss demonstrate how he has been changed by previous mourning. In either dynamic, recollection and forgetting operate in tandem to manage the catastrophic effects of loss.[13]

Because the love between friends depicted in Sonnet 39 comes short of idealized friendship, it showcases the shortcomings of romantic relations more typically based in longing. Roland Barthes observes,

> Love illuminates for us our imperfection. It is nothing other than the uncanny movement of our consciousness comparing two unequal terms—on the one hand, all the perfection and plentitude of the beloved; one the other hand, all the misery, thirst, and destitution of ourselves—and the fierce desire to unite these two such disparate terms.[14]

Sonnet 39 and others that dwell on the missing beloved seem to follow Barthes's logic: the very act of loving induces an impulse to question one's own appeal while exaggerating the tantalizing qualities of the beloved. At first, the poet in Sonnet 39 appears to struggle with a conflict that courses through the entire collection. Self-abnegation, which is at the heart of the Petrarchan tradition, conflicts with the logic of idealized friendship that might compel the beloved to reciprocate the speaker's love. Resolving this conflict requires rethinking the problem of separation, and this perhaps spurs the poem's peculiar apostrophe:

> O absence, what a torment wouldst thou prove,
> Were it not thy sour leisure gave sweet leave
> To entertain the time with thoughts of love,
> Which time and thoughts so sweetly dost deceive[.] (9–12)

---

[12] Judith Butler, *Undoing Gender* (New York and London: Routledge, 2004), 20–1.

[13] For his memorialization of Paul de Man, Derrida chooses not to engage in a mode he terms "possible mourning, which would interiorize within us the image, idol, or ideal of the other who is dead and lives only in us" and instead chooses an "impossible mourning, which, leaving the other his alterity, respecting thus his infinite remove, either refuses to take or is incapable of taking the other within oneself, as in the tomb or the vault of some narcissism." What Shakespeare does, though, falls into this category of "possible mourning." It may not recognize the alterity and independence of the Other, but the poet attempts to balance the power relations with his beloved while striving to manage his own narcissism. Jacques Derrida, *Memoires for Paul de Man*, trans. Cecile Lindsay, Jonathan Culler, and Eduardo Cadava (New York: Columbia University Press, 1986), 6.

[14] Roland Barthes, "Letter to Robert David, December 8, 1944," in *Album: Unpublished Correspondence and Texts*, trans. Jody Gladding (New York: Columbia University Press, 2018), 53.

While "absence" is admonished for causing torment, it is ultimately praised for the dialectical tension it fuels. The "sour leisure" collides with "sweet leave," and the intermingling of these unlike elements generates pleasurable "thoughts of love."[15] These thoughts do not unite the two men physically. Instead, they ignite a creative process wherein the speaker conjures memories of past encounters or fantasies of future ones in order to derive erotic pleasure from the presence of absence. By contemplating such an operation, Sonnet 39 links to Sonnet 45, where the speaker describes "my thought" and "my desire" as "present-absent" (3–4).

Sonnet 39's shift from "sour" to "sweet" in line 7 hinges on the shift from "leisure" to "leave." The *Oxford English Dictionary* informs us that, in Shakespeare's time as in our own, "leisure" denoted "the state of having time at one's own disposal; time which one can spend as one pleases; free or unoccupied time." In fact, the entry uses this line from Sonnet 39 as one of its examples for this definition. In contrast, "leave," in its noun form, has had a primary meaning of "permission asked for or granted to do something; authorization" since the thirteenth century and has denoted "a period of time when a person has permission to be absent" since the middle of the sixteenth century. Intriguingly, then, it is not unencumbered free time but rather absence—bound by agreement and implied to be limited in duration—that makes possible the pleasurably sweet experience. The use of the noun "leave" suggests that the beloved is expected to return and (when we consider its connotations as a verb) points to the fact that the beloved has left the speaker alone. So to recall the beloved into present thoughts is to engage both anticipatory memory and recollective memory. Each of these forms of memory have their own pleasures. Recall from the Introduction how two forms of memory-inflected eros were pinpointed by Foucault's response to Casanova's notion that "the best moment of love is when one is climbing the stairs." Rather, he said, "the best moment of love is likely to be when the lover leaves in the taxi."[16] In either formulation, the actual encounter does not take primacy. Desirous memory offers a compelling alternative to lived experience, which threatens disappointment. Foucault's and Casanova's remarks, though seemingly in opposition at first, both suggest that our best moments of erotic experience lie in anticipation or recollection, when the power of fantasy begins to assert its narrative over the material provided by memory.[17]

---

[15] Many editors emend the quarto edition's "dost" in line 12 to read either "doth" or "do." These changes shift the subject from "absence" to "love" or "time and thoughts" (respectively). Maintaining the original spelling supports a reading where absence instigates the pleasure experienced by the speaker. For more detail on the history of this line's emendation, see Burrow's discussion in *The Complete Sonnets and Poems*, 458n12.

[16] Foucault, "Sexual Choice, Sexual Act," 330.

[17] Reacting to Anna Freud's claim that "In your dreams you can have your eggs cooked the way you want them, but you can't eat them," Adam Phillips claims, "We could reverse Anna Freud's formulation and say that when it comes to sexuality it is the fact that you can't eat the eggs that make them so satisfying," I believe that taking into account Casanova's and Foucault's formulations, we can see how memory complicates such claims. Shakespeare, in the same vein, suggests not that *we want the one we*

In the case of Shakespeare's speaker and his beloved, we know nothing concrete about the time they have spent together or whether they will spend time together in the future. The "thoughts of love" may be left intentionally ambiguous because these thoughts' relationship to lived experience is largely irrelevant. Memory can generate positive—even idealized—experiences that never occurred.[18] In his discussion of Sonnet 35 (a poem to which I turn in detail in Chapter 6), Stephen Guy-Bray has remarked that "love is a particularly intense form of memory," and we can extend this formulation to apply to Sonnet 39 as well as to other moments in the collection which lament the beloved's absence. The poems dramatize how to love someone is to frequently recall them into the mind. And this recall—motivated by a state of missing the friend and generative of fantasy—involves not only retrospective but also prospective memory. Shakespeare's beloved is continually reconstituted in imagined scenes of union, parting, and subsequent reunion.[19] And our desire for initial or repeated coupling with someone relies on first conjuring an interaction in fantasy. Derrida nicely captures how fantasy pre-forms lived experience: "it has never been possible to desire the presence 'in person,' before this play of substitution and the symbolic experience of auto-affection."[20] In other words, desire arises when we take material from memory and shape it to imagine what an erotic experience with someone might look like. After the actual physical encounter, we might long for a reunion as we charge the lived experience with meaning and renarrate it in recollection.[21] A romantic relationship thus might be considered an ongoing process of forgetting and remembering someone. Such a process is imbued with an elegiac strain, captured nicely in Arthur Schopenhauer's notion that "Every parting gives a foretaste of death, every coming together again a foretaste of the resurrection."[22] Such a commixture of death and love would be familiar to early modern writers, whose formulations of erotic experience were so often tinged with thoughts of death.

Indeed, when Juliet tells Romeo that "parting is such sweet sorrow," we hear a nod to the way that separation between lovers gives access to the pleasurable

---

can't have but rather that *the one we actually want is only a remembered version of the one we might want to have.* Phillips, *Side Effects*, 64.

[18] By not revealing the details of his fantasies about the beloved, the speaker underscores the intimacy of whatever interaction he imagines. "Sex may be good to think with," Valerie Traub remarks, "Not because it permits access, but because it doesn't." Traub, *Thinking Sex with the Early Moderns*, 4.

[19] Stephen Guy-Bray, "Remembering to Forget: Shakespeare's Sonnet 35 and Sigo's 'XXXV,'" in *Sexuality and Memory in Early Modern England: Literature and the Erotics of Recollection*, ed. John S. Garrison and Kyle Pivetti (London and New York: Routledge, 2015), 43.

[20] Jacques Derrida, *Of Grammatology*, trans. Gayatri Spivak (Baltimore: Johns Hopkins University Press, 1976), 154.

[21] This operation resembles the one articulated by the speaker in Barthes's *A Lover's Discourse*, who states that "the being I am waiting for is not real. [...] 'I create and re-create it over and over, starting from my capacity to love, starting from my need for it': the other comes here where I am waiting, here where I have already created him/her." Barthes, *A Lover's Discourse*, 39.

[22] Arthur Schopenhauer, *Studies in Pessimism*, trans. T. Bailey Saunders (Whitefish, MT: Kessinger Publishing, 2010), 65.

longing that marks separation until reunion (2.1.229). Jeffrey Masten has usefully traced how the "sweet," used across personal letters in the early modern period, carried an erotic charge, including when used to describe same-sex friendship. At the end of his discussion of the term, Masten sketches out "one of several directions in which an understanding of early modern male-male sweetness might pro-ceed."[23] He suggests that further scholarship might explore how "*sweet* indicates the fungibility of male friends" on an embodied level.[24] Such fungibility mani-fests itself in Shakespeare's apostrophic pining for the absent beloved and opining to the concept of absence. Sweetness not only may capture the shared affection between friends, as Masten reveals, but also may describe an affective operation that allows the friend to inhabit the space where he is not. Sonnet 30 overtly posi-tions "sessions of sweet silent thought / [that] summon up remembrance of things past" as capable of revivifying dead friends and bringing the living (but missing) beloved into the bleak moment of the present. Given the clear absence of both liv-ing and deceased beloveds, these silent thoughts must necessarily draw upon the past or be longing for love in the future. As George Wright observes, "Hardly any of the first 126 sonnets seem likely to have been written in the friend's presence."[25] So, absence becomes the normative mode of relation with the beloved. Yet these sweet moments of connection seem to stem from moments of isolation that make possible intense engagement with recollection of the past.

Absence takes on a positive quality in the *Sonnets* as it is transformed through the power of memory. And Sonnet 39's apostrophe to "absence" leads to a cul-minating couplet where the speaker announces that the concept of absence has taught him how to obviate the problem of physical separation from the one he loves: "And that thou teachest how to make one twain, / By praising him here who doth hence remain" (13–14). Although absence is the final addressee of the poem, the final thought is that the beloved is "here" and will "remain." The adver-sarial relationship with absence as a tormentor in line 9 has given way to absence as a teacher in line 13. The heuristic power of the concept of absence is that it instructs the speaker how to split the addressee into two parts, and one of those parts can remain there with him. The dualities at the end of the poem echo lan-guage in Donne's poem quoted above where "still mine" ambiguously may point to the memory of the beloved that lingers in the speaker or to the beloved as still belonging to the speaker through claims of remembering her. Odd as this dynamic might seem at first, we can understand it as an extension of a normative response to the demands of a romantic relationship where, as Lauren Berlant puts it, "love is one of the few situations where we desire to have patience for what isn't working, an affective binding that allows us to iron things out, or to be elastic, or to try a

[23] Masten, *Queer Philologies*, 78.
[24] Masten, *Queer Philologies*, 78.
[25] George T. Wright, "The Silent Speech of Shakespeare's Sonnets," in *Shakespeare's Sonnets: Critical Essays*, ed. James Schiffer (New York and London: Garland, 2000), 137.

new incoherence."[26] Love demands that we create new forms of relating in order to sustain the love relation. In Shakespeare's *Sonnets*, such forms rely on extensive play with memory.

The use of "one twain" in this sonnet's closing couplet nods once more to the friendship ideal, invoking a formulation from Aristotle and Cicero in the classical tradition and repeated by early modern essayists such as Bacon and Montaigne.[27] For example, a poem appearing in Richard Tottell's *Miscellany* (1557) contains the formulation: "Behold thy friend, and of thyself the pattern see / One soul, a wonder shall it seem in bodies twain to be."[28] It is this notion adapted from idealized friendship that allows Shakespeare's speaker to reconstitute the friend even when he is missing. "Twain" is a particularly charged word here, as it functioned as a contranym in the early modern period denoting both "separate, parted asunder; disunited, estranged, at variance" and "consisting of two parts or elements; double, twofold." This curious play of meaning signals the fracture, the lack of agreed-upon meaning of the outcomes of the very act of twinning. The friend, like absence itself in this cryptic poem, seems to be neither absent nor present. Rather he seems to occupy both states at once. This dynamic at the heart of desire is captured nicely when Barthes remarks: "But isn't desire always the same, whether the object is present or absent? Isn't the object *always* absent?"[29] If Shakespeare's friend were present, we can imagine that the friendship would still feel incomplete as the speaker fixates on their inequality. As the remembered friend, the absent friend then is one with whom the speaker can realize closer intimacy.

Absence remains the addressee of Sonnet 39 through the final couplet. Consequently, we realize that not only has the beloved been doubled but, evocatively, so has absence. There are now two absences: the abstract one that the speaker addresses at a distance and the absence that is palpably present with him in the moment of speaking. In his treatise on rhetoric entitled *The Garden of Eloquence* (1577), Henry Peacham describes apostrophe as "a form of speech by which the orator turn suddenly from the former frame of his speech to another."[30] Shakespeare does not follow the strict formal rules of address that Peacham avers, where this turning away is "no other thing than a sudden removing from third person to the second."[31] Shakespeare gives us a nuanced version of this, signaled by the use of second-person address for both the friend and absence. As we begin to see

---

[26] Lauren Berlant, "A Properly Political Concept of Love: Three Approaches in Ten Pages," *Cultural Anthropology* 26, no. 4 (November 2011): 685.

[27] For a brief overview of classical and early modern ideals in Shakespeare's work, see John S. Garrison, "Shakespeare and Friendship: An Intersection of Interest," *Literature Compass* 9, no. 5 (May 2012): 371–9.

[28] Nicolas Grimald, "Of Friendship," in *Tottel's Miscellany*, ed. Richard Tottel (London, s.n., 1867), 145.

[29] Barthes, *A Lover's Discourse*, 15.

[30] Henry Peacham, *The Garden of Eloquence* (London, 1593), 116.

[31] Peacham, *The Garden of Eloquence*, 116.

the ambiguous way that absence itself is arguably present in this and other sonnets, the collection stands out as a case study for Derrida's notion of "hauntology,"
where the "element itself is neither living nor dead, present nor absent: it spectral-
izes."[32] In the poet's cry, "O absence," the missing element is missingness itself and
thus is present when addressed. Derrida suggests that hauntological states have
direct ties to remembrance as the French term he uses repeatedly in his book,
hauntise, is translated in the standard English version as "haunting" but more
broadly means "an obsession, a constant fear, a fixed idea, or a nagging memory."[33]
Sonnet 39 deploys apostrophe to render visible the hauntological underpinning of
the speaker's desirous memory.

    The turn in this poem to see the friend and absence together occurs at the volta
(a term itself that indicates a turning point in a sonnet), and indeed George Puttenham's 1589 *The Arte of English Poesie* entry on the apostrophe notes that "the
Greeks call such figure (as we do) the Turn-Way or Turn-Tale."[34] Though the poem
does celebrate the friend at the end, it does not turn the speech back to him as,
for example, Sonnet 29 does ("Haply I think on thee"). Elizabeth Harris Sagaser
argues that Sonnet 29 "does not anticipate a particular reunion with the beloved";
instead "it demonstrates how an act of memory can procure at least momentary
happiness."[35] However, I would argue that such turns to memory offer more than
a momentary experience of joy. Instead, memory offers the guarantee of repeated
reunion with a possibly more perfected version of the beloved. Sonnet 39 (and, as
we will see, other sonnets) offers an overt expression of what is alluded to in Sonnet 29.[36] The speaker of Sonnet 39 turns away from the missing friend to consider
the friend that is present, the one in his memory now taking on palpable presence.
Puttenham goes on to say that an apostrophe "breedeth by such exchange a certain
recreation to the hearers' minds."[37] So, as we have begun to see across the chapters
of my study, Shakespeare's *Sonnets* are consistently interpolating the reader into
their dialogic machinations. In Sonnet 39, the apostrophe invites the reader to
consider themselves as either of the second-person addressees, for the reader is
absent from the moment of writing yet still hearing the plea. Sonnet 30, when it
"summon[s] up remembrance of things past," too invites readers to summon up
their own memories, even if those are just recollections of their own moments

---

[32] Jacques Derrida, *Specters of Marx*, trans. Peggy Kamuf (London and New York: Routledge, 1994),
63.

[33] Derrida, *Spectres of Marx*, 224n2.

[34] Puttenham, *The Art of English Poesy*, 323.

[35] Elizabeth Harris Sagaser, "Shakespeare's Sweet Leaves: Mourning, Pleasure, and the Triumph of
Thought in the Renaissance Love Lyric," *ELH* 61, no. 1 (1994): 12.

[36] Stephen Booth locates a "sound of final defeat" in Sonnet 29's "oxymoron of *most* and *least*" in the
lines "Desiring this man's art, and that man's scope, / With what I most enjoy contented least" (7–8). As
we will see in the next chapter, it may be these extreme low moments that trigger the speaker's turn to
memory and expressions of abject devotion to the beloved. Stephen Booth, *An Essay on Shakespeare's
Sonnets* (New Haven and London: Yale University Press, 1969), 48.

[37] Sagaser, "Shakespeare's Sweet Leaves," 12.

of remembrance. Adding further dimension to the discussion in the first chapter, I find that the apostrophe represents another way in which the reader becomes interpolated into the conversation between the speaker and the addressees of the *Sonnets*.

Absence and the Elegiac Mode

Acknowledging the states of absence dwelt upon by Shakespeare's poems helps us see how they recall an earlier genre of poetry. We saw how these *Sonnets* engage cultural memory, both innovating the Petrarchan tradition and acknowledging their status as out of fashion. True to genre, the *Sonnets* long for a beloved and the address to absence in Sonnet 39 throws into relief how central memory is to Shakespeare's poetic project. Jonathan Culler goes as far as to contend that we should "identify apostrophe with lyric itself."[38] If so, the missing is at the heart of the poetic project, and poetry is the genre most appropriate for articulating and wrestling with the state of being absence from the desired interlocutor.[39] Yet the sonnet is a poem of praise and, as such, entails mimetic dimensions. As Fineman notes, "praise is not simply one among the many kinds of poetry but it is instead the ideal kind to which all other kinds aspire to be like"; that is "praise is the noblest form of poetry because it imitates the noblest things."[40] So, if we understand the objective of the poems to be the reproduction of the beloved in the presence of the lover through memory and through the operations of the friendship model where one man is at least part of the other, we can see this occurring on the level of the choice of genre. Because they can only gesture toward the situations and feelings being described, short poems are perhaps necessarily about absence.[41] As we saw

[38] Jonathan Culler, "Apostrophe," in *The Pursuit of Signs: Semiotics, Literature, Deconstruction* (Ithaca, NY: Cornell University Press, 1981), 152. The essay first appeared in a 1977 issue of *Diacritics*.

[39] Culler's claims regarding the apostrophe have drawn interlocutors who have helped tease out the nuances of this poetic technique. For an excellent essay that challenges Culler's claims and also builds upon them, see Barbara Johnson, "Apostrophe, Animation, and Abortion," *Diacritics* 16, no. 1 (Spring 1986): 28–47. For a starting point on the use of apostrophe in the early modern period, see Paul Alpers, "Apostrophe and the Rhetoric of Renaissance Lyric," *Representations* 122, no. 1 (Spring 2013): 1–22. Lauren Berlant argues that apostrophe appears to be someone reaching out to a desired interlocutor, but it is "actually a turning back, an animating of a receiver on behalf of the desire to make something happen *now* that realizes something *in the speaker*, makes the speaker more or differently possible, because she has admitted, in a sense, the importance of speaking for, as, and to, two—but only under the condition, and illusion, that the two are really (in) one." She goes on, "Apostrophe is thus an indirect, unstable, physically impossible but phenomenologically vitalizing movement of rhetorical animation that permits subjects to suspend themselves in the optimism of a potential occupation of the same psychic space of others, the objects of desire who make you possible (by having some promising qualities, but also by not being there)." Berlant, *Cruel Optimism*, 26.

[40] Fineman, *Shakespeare's Perjured Eye*, 89.

[41] Those looking for throughlines and plot lines in the *Sonnets* will find themselves charting even more of what is missing. Stephen Orgel notes how "the several narratives of the Sonnets are notoriously, maddeningly, incomplete, withholding the name of the beloved youth whose name is to be celebrated for eternity, concealing the identity of the dark mistress, and identifying the rival and the mistress's

in the first chapter, the collection also laments the waning of the sonnet genre itself and its absence from the contemporaneous literary landscape. So, at the level of cultural memory, the collection registers as a project of looking backward. As we saw in the previous chapter, tracing the prominent and multivalent role of memory in Shakespeare's *Sonnets* helps us see not only how they represent memory for their most overt genre but also how they recall another genre where loss and desire collide: the love elegy.

Adding Sonnet 31 to this discussion helps us see even more clearly the intermingled erotic and funereal sentiments in these elegiac lyrics. Barbara Correll notes that "In Sonnet 31, Shakespeare significantly departs from 29 and 30 in that he explores and ardently commits his speaker to loss."[42] We can see strands of such commitment in the third quatrain,

> Thou art the grave where buried love doth live,
> Hung with the trophies of my lovers gone,
> Who all their parts of me to thee did give;
> That due of many, now is thine alone. (9–12)

It does seem at first to articulate a negative view of the friend's ability to be co-constituted as both the speaker and his missing friends. If the current beloved rejects the poet, then all his attempts at love will be cast as failure. However, we can consider an alternate reading if we extend J. K. Barret's reading of the previous two sonnets. She remarks, "the removal of the young man does not hamper his restorative potential" because "Sonnets 29 and 30 rely on that lack; the absent youth, once invoked, provides relief and resolution."[43] Correll incisively notes that in Sonnet 31 "The young man is the container, the record, reminder and remainder of loss; he replays rather than repays it," yet we might interpret this fact as yet playing a restorative role.[44] Friends were thought to represent "one soul to quicken two bodies," as Goldwell puts it in *The True Choice of a Friend*.[45] Yet the dialectic is in operation here as the speaker is able to experience a premature and pleasurable experience of death by associating the friend with lost loves of the past. Fineman gives us another way to reassess Correll's claim, as he argues that Sonnet 31's claim "is not that the young man brings the dead to life, but, rather, that the poet sees

husband only with the least specific of the poet's own names, Will." Stephen Orgel, "The Desire and Pursuit of the Whole," *Shakespeare Quarterly* 58, no. 3 (Fall 2007): 293.

[42] Barbara Correll, "'Terms of 'Indearment': Lyric and General Economy in Shakespeare and Donne," *ELH* 75, no. 2 (2008): 253.

[43] J. K. Barret, "Enduring 'Injurious Time': Alternatives to Immortality and Proleptic Loss in Shakespeare's Sonnets," in *The Sonnets: The State of Play*, ed. Hannah Crawforth, Elizabeth Scott-Baumann, and Clare Whitehead (London and New York: Bloomsbury Arden Shakespeare, 2017), 143.

[44] Correll, "Lyric and General Economy," 254.

[45] Charles Goldwell, "My Friend," in *The True Choice of a Friend* (London: 1625), N7v.

the young man is a kind of death *in* life."[46] In this way, the friend can be thought of as the embodiment of memory, a manifestation of the erotohistoriographical process that hybridizes the past and the present during states of erotic pleasure.

Such an experience is fleeting yet deeply pleasure-inducing. By placing him in a grave or otherwise associating him with deceased friends, Sonnets 30 and 31 openly recognize the failure of any project to immortalize the actual beloved. Yet Sonnet 31 emphasizes that loss is very much a question of the subjectivity when it describes the "hearts" embedded in the beloved as only "supposèd dead" (1–2). This recalls the formulation in the previous sonnets, where it is "when *I think* on thee" (emphasis mine) that all losses are restored. In other words, the subject can and does constitute himself and his beloved in the private interiority of his own mind in order to revivify the past and realize the pleasures of memory. Perhaps this is true of every desiring subject, but it seems to be particularly the preoccupation of the *Sonnets* as Shakespeare explores and attempts to explain this process. Cynthia Marshall finds in her study of the theme of self-shattering in early modern lyric, "love decenters the subject by involving emotional investment in another person and perhaps identification with that other."[47] Yet this is not the whole story. We see a reconstruction of the shattered, desiring self in the final couplet of Sonnet 31, which informs us, "Their images I loved I view in thee, / And thou (all they) has all the all of me." In the doubling of the "I/I" and the "thee/thou," as well as in the tripling of the "all," we can recognize this site of desirous memory as one of multiplication, however fracturing that multiplication might be. As I have been arguing here, in Shakespeare's *Sonnets* the subject seems less interested in a project of inhabiting the other but rather a project to claim the other (and others) as a part of himself.

A World of Recall

While there are numerous instances when the speaker overcomes separation by conjuring memories of the beloved into the interior of the mind, the triptych of Sonnets 97–9 depicts a particularly intriguing strategy for addressing the problem of the absent beloved that involves instead the exterior world. These three poems connect to each other in theme and formulation, so much so that John Benson, in his 1640 volume of Shakespeare's poems, presents them as a single poem with the title "Complaint for his Love's Absence."[48] Benson makes a series of changes

---

[46] Joel Fineman, *Shakespeare's Perjured Eye: The Invention of Poetic Subjectivity in the Sonnets* (Berkeley, Los Angeles, and London: University of California Press, 1986), 158.

[47] Cynthia Marshall, *The Shattering of the Self: Violence, Subjectivity, and Early Modern Texts* (Baltimore: Johns Hopkins University Press, 2002), 57.

[48] While presented as a single poem, the indentation of the rhymed couplets makes visible the embedded sonnets. William Shakespeare, *Poems: Written by Wil. Shake-speare. Gent.* (London: Thomas Cotes for John Benson, 1640), D8v–E1r.

to Shakespeare's poems when he compiles his volume, including clustering some sonnets with descriptive titles, combining some into longer poems, and changing the pronouns in some to suggest a female rather than male addressee. Yet, while not accurate to the original presentation of the 1609 collection, the book does give us a sense of how early consumers of Shakespeare's work would encounter the poems. As Faith Acker observes, "most seventeenth-century and eighteenth-century readers would have experienced Shakespeare's Sonnets not in their sequence from 1609 but in Benson's title arrangement."[49] Indeed, the titles function to frame the poem(s) because they introduce themes or meanings before the reader's encounter with Shakespeare's actual lyric. Cathy Shrank notes that the titles in the volume "offer a record of how someone has read—and how contemporary readers were being invited to read—the verses beneath."[50] In this case, the triptych of poems gathered under the keyword "absence" do not simply resemble each other but rather articulate a progression of thought.[51] As the speaker fantasizes about the changing of the seasons while separated from his beloved, he comes to seize upon memory as a way to parse the beloved into constant pleasing reminders present within the natural world.

Sonnet 97 opens what Benson presents as a conflated poem, and this particular sonnet is itself engaged in the operations of conflation. The present, past, and future collapse into each other within the speaker's memory, exemplifying Dinshaw's notion of "a fuller, denser, more crowded *now*" that I discussed in Chapter One.[52] The first quatrain reads:

> How like a winter hath my absence been
> From thee, the pleasure of the fleeting year?
> What freezings have I felt, what dark days seen?
> What old December's bareness everywhere? (1–4)

The use of past tense in line 3 puts us in the space of memory as the speaker recalls cold and darkness he has experienced, and the present-perfect tense in the first line informs us that these cold states in the past continue into the *now* of speaking. The speaker will later reveal that this viscerally felt winter is in fact only a resurgence

---

[49] To emphasize how widely Benson's versions would have shaped readers' receptions of the *Sonnets*, Acker notes that Benson's versions of the poems were reprinted in 1710, 1714, 1725, 1726, 1728, 1760, 1771, 1774, and 1775. Acker, "John Benson's *Poems* and Its Literary Precedents," 91.

[50] Cathy Shrank, "Reading Shakespeare's *Sonnets*: John Benson and the 1640 Poems," *Shakespeare* 5, no. 3 (September 2009): 279.

[51] Another important keyword in the title here is "complaint," a charged genre term in the seventeenth century. Lauren Berlant also notes a double action in the genre of the complaint as the text represents the speaker's public expression of lament over the beloved while the utterance "implicitly marks the conditions and the probability of its failure to persuade the addressed subject." This only makes even more urgent the need to create a version of the responsive beloved in private thoughts. Lauren Berlant, "The Female Complaint," *Social Text* 19/20 (Autumn 1988): 243.

[52] Dinshaw, *How Soon Is Now?*, 4.

of memory as the time of speaking is summer. In "old December's bareness every-where?" we hear the desolation that the speaker experiences in the "crowded now" of the poem. It is not simply that his internal emotional state resembles winter. Rather, he sees the world as a barren winter landscape which mirrors his feelings of despair. The use of the adjective "old" to describe December points both to this being the recollection of a previous winter and to the present isolation fulfilling his own fears about his pending old age.

These opening lines also function as a recollection of previous poems. In them, we hear echoes of Sonnet 2 where the poet anticipates the young man's aging ("When forty winters shall besiege thy brow, / And dig deep trenches in thy beauty's field" [1–2]), lines which invite the beloved to imagine himself looking back on his life at some point in the future. In Sonnet 6, we see a contrast simi-lar to 97's conflict between the present season and the internal perceptions of the mind. Sonnet 6's opening plea, "Then let not winter's ragged hand deface / In thee thy summer," suggests that the beloved embodies a season other than the impend-ing one. The subsequent fantasy that the friend's essence can be "distilled" into a "vial" and released with summer's scent in the height of winter suggests further that memory can overpower the reality of one's current physical surroundings (2–3). More evocatively, and important for the discussion of Sonnets 98 and 99 below, this fantasy suggests that memory of the friend can be transferred from his human body to a material substance. In Sonnet 6, the beloved can become glass; in Sonnet 2, the lover can embody leaves. Sonnet 97's reference to December as analogous to the speaker's aging further recalls Sonnet 73 ("That time of year thou mayst in me behold / When yellow leaves, or none, or few, do hang / Upon those boughs which shake against the cold" [1–3]).[53] Across these examples, in order to make sense of loss, the speaker understands the world reflecting his emotional state and uses the metaphor of the natural world to describe this state.

The temporality of Sonnet 97 is unmoored as the speaker finds himself in a "time removed" both from the beloved and from "summer's time" (5). Like Sonnet 39, this poem contains a dual apostrophe. "The pleasure of the fleeting year" functions as a possible appositive for "thee," offering yet another instance where the speaker addresses an absent element that still resides in present mem-ory. The poem is simultaneously also addressed to the beloved, as Benson's title suggests. The beloved, the source of pleasure, is associated with the absent (but, in reality present) summertime. This association can be found throughout the collection, including in Sonnets 5, 6, and 18. It is possible that the speaker can only see this optimal version of the beloved when distilled in memory and con-sidered while he seeks to master those memories. As cognitive psychology has

[53] Maurice Charney notes that this sonnet's image of a tree in winter resonates with Cymbeline's description of his state after the departure of his beloved Belarius, a separation which "shook down my mellow hangings, nay, my leaves, / And left me bare to weather" (3.3.63–4). Maurice Charney, *Wrinkled Deep in Time: Aging in Shakespeare* (New York: Columbia University Press, 2009), 17.

found, "development—movement in the direction of the good, inspired by what is Other—is intimately and necessarily linked to hindsight, that is, the capacity to look back on an earlier mode of knowing or being and to realize its poverty."[54]

As we hear about the speaker's "hope" and "dread," we find present anxiety about the future being shaped by memory of past experience. That is, anticipatory memory informs emotion in the present.[55] Edmondson and Wells link this line to the sentiment found in Amiens's song in *As You Like It* that pines, "Most friendship is feigning, most loving mere folly" (2.7.182).[56] Amiens's claim can refer either to retrospective assessment once these relations have ended or to anticipation if one needs to be warned when currently in such a relationship. If loving friendship is simply fleeting fantasy, then this only adds more importance to pre-memory and post-memory in terms of bringing the lover any tangible joy. If our actual experience of rewarding intimacy is brief and largely foolish, we need to reconstruct those experiences as more robust and more meaningful when we anticipate or recall them. As the poem closes, the speaker re-emphasizes that the natural world resembles his external state of lament, "And thou away, the very birds are mute. / Or if they sing, 'tis with so dull a cheer" (12–13). We find that the lack of birdsong concerns not the present but rather anticipation of the return of a recalled season as "leaves look pale, dreading the winter's near" (14). The multiple meanings of "leaves"—including the undetermined amount of time that the beloved will be absent, the pages upon which the speaker writes, and the poet's lament about having been *left* alone—locates readers in a place that leaves us with a lack of resolution at the end of the poem. Perhaps that is why Benson senses that two more poems were needed to complete the arc and leave the speaker (and the reader) with a more positive revelation.

Sonnet 98 locates the speaker in springtime, and Colin Burrow notes that it is unclear whether this is the spring previous to the season described in Sonnet 97 or the spring that follows it.[57] Given the way that this sonnet shifts from one season to another, we can see why Benson would interpret a narrative arc to connect it to

---

[54] Freeman, *Hindsight*, 218.

[55] The focus on the future, and its seemingly unpredictable outcomes, resonates with what Lauren Berlant has termed "cruel optimism," an experience where one hopes that romantic relationships might bring about positive experiences while the subject is in denial that it will only be a return to the failures that characterized past sites of failed love. In this way, the future is always a self-reinforcing rehearsal of memories of the past yet remains attractive as subjects, such as Shakespeare's speaker, are drawn to "a concept of the *later* to suspend questions about the cruelty of the *now*." Berlant, *Cruel Optimism*, 28.

[56] Edmondson and Wells, *Shakespeare's Sonnets*, 88.

[57] When we see the play of temporality in the poems, we can extend Stephen Booth's claim about Sonnet 73, that "the mind of the beholder is presented with related but not yet strictly ordered objects— objects that have not yet undergone the process of being sorted and organized into an experience, something shaped into usefulness so that it can be carried as a conscious memory and reported." Booth finds Sonnet 73 to involve an intentional confusion of the order of seasons toward the end that confuses memory. Here, too, we see such a process to align the passage of time with the shifting of emotions. Burrows, *The Complete Sonnets and Poems*, 576n1, and Booth, *An Essay on Shakespeare's Sonnets*, 122.

the previous one.[58] The natural world observed in this sonnet reflects the speaker's somewhat ameliorated state because he can now acknowledge its beauty. However, the external world's bucolic pleasures only function to evoke recollections of the addressee: "From you have I been absent in the spring, / When proud-pied April (dressed in all his trim) / Hath put a spirit of youth in every thing" (98.1–3) Yet neither "the lays of birds" nor "the sweet smell / Of different flowers" can excite the speaker enough to tell "summer's story" (5–7). In a narrative universe where the beloved embodies summer, the speaker cannot generate enough optimism to imagine his return.

At its volta, the sonnet begins to tease out an increasingly complex relationship between the beloved and the natural world. The flowers "were but sweet, but figures of delight / Drawn after you, you pattern of all those" (11–12). In the early modern period, the verb "pattern" carried now-obsolete meanings of "To match, parallel, equal" or "To be a pattern, example, or precedent for; to prefigure."[59] Thus, we can begin to see the external, natural world as not just a reflection of the speaker's emotional state but also a double of the absent beloved.[60] Matthew Harrison points to Sonnet 98 as a key example of how the *Sonnets* as a whole seek to "interrogate the relation of desire to pattern, repeatedly finding a type of loving anachronism in which desire transforms the meanings we make of the world."[61] Early modern readers would especially have seen such connotations in Shakespeare's choice of the word "pattern," which resonates with the notion that one entity can be copied into other like forms.

Vendler describes Sonnet 98 as a "simpler version" of Sonnet 97, a claim that perhaps holds true in terms of the formalistic operations of the sonnet. However, a focus on the shifting uses of memory across these poems suggests an increasingly complex exploration of the relationship between longing and absence. Burrow suggests that the 1609 collection overall is "made up of readings and rereadings of its own poems."[62] Memory itself relies on the same operations of continually returning to a particular scene and reconsidering it or trying to see it with new clarity. Lauren Berlant notes that "desire tends to be associated with specific places,"

---

[58] Edmondson and Wells similarly see these three as a linked sequence around the theme of seasons. Edmondson and Wells, *Shakespeare's Sonnets*, 33.

[59] The *OED* notes that two other instances of the word used in this way are in *The Rape of Lucrece* and *The Merchant of Venice*. "Prefigure, v.3," OED online.

[60] We see flashes here of Orlando's desire to place his love in trees: "tongues in trees, books in the running brooks, / Sermons in stones, and good in everything," which I explored in my longer discussion of the elegy in Chapter One (2.1.16–17). Marjorie Swann has traced how "seventeenth-century people and plants were yoked together by an intricate set of correspondences," and this sonnet shows how such correspondences ignite an affective transference of the beloved's human qualities and the flowers' beauty in a way that speaks to the depictions in both the *Sonnets* and in *As You Like It*. Marjorie Swann, "Vegetable Love: Botany and Sexuality in Seventeenth-Century England," in *The Indistinct Human in Renaissance Literature*, ed. Jean E. Feerick and Vin Nardizzi (New York: Palgrave Macmillan, 2012), 141.

[61] Harrison, "Desire Is Pattern," 194.

[62] Shakespeare, *The Complete Sonnets and Poems*, 116.

but such associations are by no means static. Sonnet 98 is striking for the way that it begins to reimagine the possibilities for the physical landscape that once only reminded the poet of the lack of this beloved.[63] As it closes, the poem makes clear that it is still very much the desolate landscape without a beloved but now that desolation is giving way to pleasurable interaction: "Yet seemed it winter still, and, you away, / As with your shadow I with these did play" (13–14). The flowers, patterned after the beloved, now become playmates. Given how "shadow" in the early modern period denoted both an outline created by light and also a ghost, we hear echoes of the elegiac mood that was made explicit in Sonnets 30 and 31. In the same breath, the use of the term "play," punctuated by its placement as the final word, locates us in an erotically charged space. In Shakespeare's time, the term carried connotations of "movement, exercise, and activity" as well as a now-obsolete meaning of "to engage in amorous play, to make love; to have sexual intercourse *with*."[64] The absence of the beloved, made palpable in the figure of the shadow, has now become not only an object to be imagined but another subject with whom erotic activity is possible.

Sonnet 99 completes both Benson's conflated poem and a triptych on loss and doubling. It opens,

> The forward violet thus did I chide:
> 'Sweet thief, whence didst thou steal thy sweet that smells,
> If not from my love's breath? The purple pride,
> Which on thy soft cheek for complexion dwells,
> In my love's veins thou hast too grossly dyed.' (1–5)

Here, the invocation of "sweet" twice in the second line signals how, as Masten suggests above, "*sweet* indicates the fungibility of male friends." Here, though, the term is not used to suggest a trans-subjective bond between two loving individuals. Instead, the poet's desire for his friend allows him to transfer the other man's qualities to the surrounding flowers. That is, the terms of early modern friendship allow the speaker to locate his friend already as part of him (as we saw in the discussion of Sonnet 39), and this gives the lover the power to project the beloved where he likes: in the mind, in a shadow, in flowers. *Twelfth Night*'s Orsino, too, suggests that violets can facilitate the transmutation of elements. For this lover for whom love fuels intense fantasy, sound becomes breath that becomes confused with flowers: "That strain again, it had a dying fall. / O, it came o'er my ear like the sweet sound / That breathes upon a bank of violets, / Stealing and giving odour" (1.1.4–7).[65] In his speech, we see another instance where the sweetness enables an

---

[63] Lauren Berlant, *Desire/Love* (Brooklyn, NY: Punctum Books, 2012), 14.

[64] *Oxford English Dictionary*, "play," n. I and 11b.

[65] The transfer of the beloved's qualities to flowers is not an attempt to secure immortality but instead an attempt to bring him into the fleeting present moment. *Hamlet* emphasizes the transient nature

affective operation where the lover's internal feelings of love become externalized. Dympna Callaghan chooses the intriguing term "plagiarism" to describe the "theft of the friend's beauty" in Sonnet 99.[66] While my focus on memory places the active work in the poet's mind, I like how this term points to the *copying* at work here and recalls how important such action was to memorization in the early modern classroom.

Sonnet 99 evocatively reconceives one of the common techniques in the early modern memory arts, one that Mary Carruthers helpfully terms "the architectural mnemonic."[67] In this technique, the practitioner memorizes an inventory of items by associating each of them with a separate room in an imagined building through which one walks in the mind. Rather than an internal, fantasized architectural space, Shakespeare uses an external, real-world sensorium. By experimenting with this alternate model, Sonnets 97–9 parse elements of the beloved into living things whose lifetimes are fleeting yet whose essences evoke richly erotic bodily responses.[68] The violets' "sweet" smell here both recalls the distillation of the beloved into glass where he will "sweet some vial" in Sonnet 6 and points to what Holly Dugan has found to be "perfume's 'curious' materiality."[69] Dugan observes that smell connects to embodied erotic experience in these sonnets given that perfume is derived from flower essences (which are likened to the beloved) and is also a means by which to attract a beloved. As discussed in Chapter One, smell clearly links to erotic memory for Shakespeare.[70] The notion that smell links to powerful internal thoughts would not be surprising to early modern readers. Henry Peacham's *The Garden of Eloquence* (1593) specifically notes that smell "is commonly used to signify the pleasure of the mind."[71]

of the violet. Laertes says, "A violet in the youth of primy nature, / Forward not permanent, sweet not lasting, / The perfume and suppliance of a minute, / No more" (1.3.7–10), as does Ophelia when she remarks, "I would give you some violets, but they withered all when my father died" (4.5.182–4). Perhaps the transference from one form to another offers a means of forestalling such short-livedness.

[66] Callaghan, *Shakespeare's Sonnets*, 134.

[67] For a description of how this ancient practice was reintroduced in the late medieval period as part of the memory arts, see Mary Carruthers, *The Book of Memory: A Study of Memory in Medieval Culture*, 2nd edition (Cambridge: Cambridge University Press, 2008), 43–7. For an example of an early modern text that describes the technique in terms of a contemporaneous "large edifice or building," see Hugh Plat, *The Jewell House of Art and Nature* (London, 1594), N1r.

[68] This is not to say that the male beloved is the only object of desire who the poet memorializes. Joyce Sutphen finds that "memorial metaphors having to do with imprinting and and inscribing" are limited to the poems addressed to a male beloved, while memory-related metaphors "having to do with keeping and holding (the 'storehouse' family) continue to be present" across the entire collection. As we will see in subsequent chapters, Shakespeare further innovates the early modern memory arts when committing the female beloved to memory (though with different tactics). Joyce Sutphen, "'A dateless, lively heat': Storing Loss in the Sonnets," in *Shakespeare's Sonnets: Critical Essays*, ed. James Schiffer (London and New York: Routledge, 2000), 201.

[69] Dugan, *The Ephemeral History of Perfume*, 58.

[70] Jonathan Gil Harris has traced the "the time-traveling effects of smell in the Sonnets" where "smell can conjure up for 'remembrance' an otherwise-inaccessible past experience and make it crash into the present with exceptional vividness." Jonathan Gil Harris, "The Smell of *Macbeth*," *Shakespeare Quarterly* 58, no. 4 (2007): 469.

[71] Peacham, *The Garden of Eloquence*, 6.

Another component of the strategy depicted in Sonnets 97–9 suggests an innovation regarding the early modern memory arts, especially in terms of how recollection was typically associated with sexuality. Several early modern memory handbooks suggest that interpolating sexual fantasies into the work of recollection can increase the retention of memories. Peter (Petrus) of Ravenna, in the popular and subsequently reprinted *Memoriae ars quae Phoenix inscribitur* (1491), describes how instead of rooms in his mind he "put beautiful women since they greatly excite my memory." Giovan Battista della Porta's *L'arte del ricordare* (1566) similarly describes using the details of a beautiful woman's body or images of "ten to twenty beautiful women whom we have enjoyed, loved, or revered" as powerful visual associations with facts to be memorized.[72] Shakespeare deploys the obverse of the system delineated in such examples. Rather than using desirable bodies to remember a series of names or qualities in the plant kingdom, he uses the details of the natural world to remember the elements of the beloved. In this way, his strategy ties to poetic creation as it takes the blazon and utilizes it not just to praise the addressee but to assuage his own separation from the addressee. Amanda Watson suggests that, because "to use physical objects as repositories of memory is to risk forgetting," Shakespeare places "increasing emphasis on the poems themselves as a means of preserving memory."[73] Sonnet 99 and other poems analyzed in this chapter suggest that he also seriously considered other means within the collection.

The sonnet's speaker goes on to liken the lily to the beloved's hand and the marjoram to his hair, thereby *re-membering* him by parsing the most desirable body parts into surrounding nature. The rich homoeroticism of the memory in these sonnets breaks with Ravenna's assertion that his method will be of no use to those men who spurn women because "*sed isti fructus difficilius consequentur*" ("they will have much more difficulty in obtaining good results").[74] The focus on same-sex desire thus constitutes another way that we might describe the poet as innovating the early modern memory arts, just as addressing a male beloved is often described as one of his innovations of the sonnet tradition.[75]

At the poem's end, it is left interestingly ambiguous just how successful this strategy has been for overcoming absence. The final couplet could imply that the poet is sated or that he is overwhelmed when the world becomes engulfed in memories of

---

[72] Giovan Battista della Porta, *L'Arte del ricordare* [The Art of Remembering] (Naples: Marco Antonio Passaro, 1566) and Peter (Petrus) of Ravenna, *Memoriae ars quae Phoenix inscribitur* [The Art of Memory also Called the Phoenix] (Vienna: Mathias Bonhome, 1541). These and other examples are quoted and described in Lina Bolzoni, *The Gallery of Memory: Literary and Iconographic Models in the Age of the Printing Press*, trans. Jeremy Parzen (Toronto: University of Toronto Press, 2001), 146–9.

[73] Watson, "'Full character'd': Competing Forms of Memory in Shakespeare's Sonnets," 355.

[74] Qtd in Bolzoni, *The Gallery of Memory*, 147.

[75] Shakespeare was, of course, not the first author to pen a homoerotic sonnet, as the case of earlier authors such as Richard Barnfield demonstrates. This is, nonetheless, often one of the innovations attributed to him.

the beloved: "More flowers I noted, yet I none could see / But sweet or colour it had stol'n from thee" (14–15). This is the sole poem in the collection with fifteen lines and thus signals a site of excess, perhaps connected to the states of bliss discussed in the previous chapter.[76] Lina Bolzoni notes that in the early modern period it was "commonly believed that the intensity of amorous desire causes the *phantasma*— that is, the image of the beloved—to concentrate within itself all the vital forces of the lover [because] it feeds on recollection."[77] She goes on to describe rather unpleasant sounding medical treatments, which include applying hot substances to the areas of the brain associated with memory in order to disperse the persistent image of the beloved. It is thus open to interpretation whether the incessant recollection in the *Sonnets* is a situation that seems to be demanding intervention or is a situation designed as an intervention for the beloved's absence. However, if the goal of the poet is to keep the beloved in his memories, he does seem to be adapting a variety of tactics lionized by the memory arts. Thomas Wilson, in a section titled "The Division of Memorie" in his sixteenth-century treatise on rhetoric, writes "the best art of memorie that can be, is to heare much, to speak much, to reade much, and to write much."[78] This list could certainly describe Shakespeare's project in writing the *Sonnets* both in terms of how they serve his memory and attempt to influence the memory of others. Bradin Cormack has posited that "Shakespeare's representation of desire and the failed promise of love" suggests that "repetition might be thought to emerge from desire's incompleteness."[79] The analysis presented in the present chapter would support this claim, and I would suggest that Shakespeare uses repetition to stir his memory—rather than summon a response from the beloved—in order to satisfy his own desires.

In fact, Shakespeare's chosen genre for his meditation on memory may simply obviate the possibility of a response. The poems are written not in an epistolary form but rather as a sonnet and one seemingly always composed in the absence of the beloved.[80] The lack of depicted dialogue with the beloved, as well as the constant celebration of romantic love even in its absence, may indeed call into

[76] This may not be the only implication of the extra line. Edmondson and Wells suggest that the extra line conveys the poem's "conceit that the 'forward violet' and other flowers have stolen their 'sweet and colour' from the lover." However, I would argue that the excess here is reminiscent of how Constance manages her grief in *King John* where "Grief fills the room up of my absent child, / Lies in his bed, walks up and down with me, / Puts on his pretty looks, repeats his words / [...] / Stuffs out his vacant garments with his form; / Then have I reason to be fond of grief" (3.4.93–8). Her grief for her lost child seems to occupy so much more space than the embodied child would, so much so that she seems to favor grief just as much as loving the present child. Edmondson and Wells, *Shakespeare's Sonnets*, 9.
[77] I return to the notion of the phantasma in Chapter Four. Bolzoni, *The Gallery of Memory*, 146.
[78] Wilson, *The Arte of Rhetorique*, 217.
[79] In Chapter Six, I provide an extended discussion of the relationship between repetition, pleasure, and memory in the *Sonnets*. Bradin Cormack, "Shakespeare's Narcissus, Sonnet's Echo," in *The Forms of Renaissance Thought: New Essays on Literature and Culture*, ed. Leonard Barkan, Bradin Cormack, and Sean Keilen (New York: Palgrave Macmillan, 2009), 137.
[80] Vendler argues, "Since the person uttering a lyric is always represented as alone with his thoughts, his imagined addressee can by definition never be present. The lyric (in contrast to the dramatic monologue, where there is always a listener present in the room), gives us the mind alone with itself."

question the confidence the speaker may have in his claims across the collection. Such a reading of the poems would support Grant Williams's assertion that "the sonnets enshrine doubt concerning love's noble code over and over again to the point that they lay bare its flimsy pretence and arbitrariness."[81] Agreeing with this claim need not necessarily lead us to assess the *Sonnets* as a sustained contemplation of the speaker's failure to fulfill his desires or as a sequence about an increasingly pessimistic outlook on love. Rather, we can think of this sometimes-clustered collection as thought experiments, ones that variously fail or succeed in imagining new possibilities both for love and for memory, especially at those points of intersection where we find love and memory co-constituted.

Helen Vendler, "Formal Pleasure in the Sonnets," in *A Companion to Shakespeare's Sonnets*, ed. Michael Schoenfeldt (New York: John Wiley & Sons, 2006), 28.

[81] Grant Williams, "Monumental Memory and Little Reminders: The Fantasy of Being Remembered by Posterity," in *The Routledge Handbook of Shakespeare and Memory*, ed. Andrew Hiscock and Lina Perkins Wilder (London and New York: Routledge, 2017), 298.

4

Body, Remember

When recollection occurs in the *Sonnets*, it might seem as if it is a *disembodied* experience. Memory, or what Sonnet 30 describes as "sessions of sweet silent thought" (1), is so often characterized as a turn inward to the mind and the conjuration of images and other sensoria with which to realize past moments. But for this same reason, the recollections might be described as *embodied*. They are embellished with detail to materialize them in the mind, and they are enfleshed in the sense that past experiences are often imagined in terms of the presence of other bodies—or even the rememberer's own body at a previous age. Little is said directly about any of the beloveds' bodily attributes, and physical interactions with or among the beloveds can only be teased out by implication. In poems that seem to be addressed to a woman, we only receive the occasional information that she has dark hair and dark eyes as well as that she does not match traditional white European ideals of beauty. About a male beloved, we know very little except that he may be young, somewhat gender-fluid, and deserving to be reproduced.[1] Yet the collection of poems does ponder the body at various points, and the relationship between the body and memory offers an intriguing focal point for determining what the poems might tell us about embodied recollection.[2] As we begin to trace Shakespeare's poetic expression of embodied memory, we see that the body itself can be a limiting factor in making memories pleasing or it can be a tool in obtaining mastery over memory. Further, the body can be a conduit to intimacy as the subject who remembers does so in tandem with the bodies of those featured in the recollected experience.

---

[1] It might be fruitful, also, to say that one beloved is a memory of the other. Simone Chess observes that the male beloved in the poems is not described just as feminine but as an object of "genderqueer attraction," especially in the case of Sonnet 20 that "eroticizes and admires male effeminacy and androgyny." Simone Chess, "Male Femininity and Male-to-Female Crossdressing in Shakespeare's Plays and Poems," in *Queer Shakespeare: Desire and Sexuality*, ed. Goran Stanivukovic (London: Bloomsbury, 2017), esp. 230–1.

[2] I would echo Judith Butler by reiterating "This is not to say that the materiality of bodies is simply and only a linguistic effect that is reducible to signifiers." The bodies in the *Sonnets* may be constructions of the poet's imaginations, and bodies themselves are in part fictions informed by cultural norms and ways of seeing. Yet the poems will insist upon the body's sensorial inputs and reactions. With this perspective, I would extend Colby Gordon's claim about the body in Sonnet 20 to other bodies across the collection: "In the giddy, giggly pleasures of Sonnet 20, Shakespeare invokes a different creation, one governed by an infatuated Nature who crafts a world teeming with animate life in which all bodies are artificial and all genders are prosthetic." Judith Butler, *Bodies That Matter: On the Discursive Limits of Sex* (New York: Routledge, 2015), 6, and Colby Gordon, "A Woman's Prick: Trans Technogenesis in Sonnet 20," in *Shakespeare / Sex: Contemporary Readings in Gender and Sexuality*, ed. Jennifer Drouin (New York: Bloomsbury Arden Shakespeare, 2020), 283.

The Pleasures of Memory in Shakespeare's Sonnets. John S. Garrison, Oxford University Press. © John S. Garrison (2023).
DOI: 10.1093/oso/9780198857716.003.0005

For the concerns of the present volume, perhaps the most visceral form of embodied erotic memory to look for in the *Sonnets* would be orgasm. This physical outburst of emotion and sensation can sometimes be an instance where pleasure-seekers might find themselves, in expressions similar to those of Sonnet 30's speaker, moaning and wailing in the throes of thoughts about the past. Orgasms, especially those brought on by solitary sex but even those occurring in the company of others, can be driven by memory as one revisits a scene from the past or constructs a fantasy based on variations of what has happened or what might have happened.[3] The orgasm helps us see the contours of pleasure derived from the past: it evokes memories, suspends memory-making, and is forgotten because we have no real language to capture it. That wonderfully enigmatic phrase from Sonnet 129, "Before, a joy proposed; behind, a dream" (12) is demonstrative here. Despite all of the work to construct the fantasy to fuel the orgasm, the speaker seems to forget immediately how good the orgasm actually was. The promise of physical climax is that it might allow him to re-experience the past joys associated with an earlier climax in order to resurrect memories of both the sexual encounter and the pleasure associated with it, to have it recur as though for the first time or even better than the first time. Regardless of whether an orgasm is depicted in a poem, the operations of the experience point to its broader implications for how pleasure is sometimes predicated on forgetting previous joys as the speaker trusts that memory can lead him back to it in private thought.[4] Such thinking opens lines of inquiry that will be pursued in the discussion of the body in this chapter, and continues a throughline to discussions in previous chapters on temporality and on absence as well as returns us to my opening discussion of Cavafy's "One Night" and Shakespeare's Sonnet 129 in the Introduction of this book.

The Body as Site of Shared Desire

The speaker's thoughts of the beloved's body can be fueled by thoughts of other people who might have desired or encountered that body. The most straightforward, even crass, version of this might be Sonnet 135. The poem suggests that, at least at the level of fantasy, the speaker does not take issue with sharing his lover's body with past and present lovers. With "Will" pointing toward multiple meanings including sexual desire, male and female sexual organs, and the author's

---

[3] Responding to Leo Bersani's claim that "masturbation is the truth about sex[:] we are doing it on our own even when to all intents and purposes it seems as if we are doing it with other people," Adam Phillips remarks, "To desire someone is to be sent back into yourself." Phillips, *Side Effects*, 59–60.

[4] I owe special thanks to Paul Edmondson for a lively discussion about orgasm and memory that we had in the context of a 2022 seminar on the *Sonnets* during the Shakespeare Association of America conference.

name, the poem asks the lover if she might allow him to have sex with her, especially given how she is already having sex with others.[5] Rather than being coy, the sonnet focuses more explicitly on access to the beloved's orifice. The poem ends:

> So thou, being rich in Will, add to thy Will
> One will of mine to make thy large Will more.
> Let 'no' unkind no fair beseechers kill:
> Think all but one, and me in that one Will. (11–14)

The incessant repetition of "will" gives the poem a humorous quality while also emphasizing the number of *wills* that have had access to her vagina. For all the poem's playfulness, it does nod to the interplay between recollection and the body.[6] The final line, "Think all but one, and me in that one Will," functions as a call for integration. It asks that she accept his sexual desire into those of the roll call of lovers she has had. In doing so, it invokes her memory of past lovers and asks to be included in that ordered narrative about who she has allowed to penetrate her.

Sonnet 69 gives us a more nuanced discussion of how the interplay between interiority and desire is subtended by memory. In the poem, Shakespeare imagines how the beloved's physical appearance, "Those parts of thee that the world's eye doth view," contains beauty upon which "outward praise is crowned" (1, 5). This attention to the opinions and desires of others for the beloved, combined with the dark turn that the poem will take, dramatizes the Freudian notion that the violent side of male desire is driven by jealousy. After the opening of the sonnet that simply states that others recognize the beloved's beauty, the fantasies that others have about him subsequently sully his body. Line 5 is frequently emended in modern editions to read "Thy outward thus with outward praise is crowned." However, the quarto version reads "*Their* outward thus with outward praise is crowned" (my emphasis). The emended version suggests straightforwardly that others look upon the beloved and prize his beauty. However, the original version renders visible the interoperations of subjects and objects in the poem. When "their outward" is affected by the praise they give the beloved, the onlookers themselves are changed by whom and how they desire. And their personal fantasies inform how these desiring onlookers consider what the beloved might have done—or what might

---

[5] I follow Burrow as well as Edmondson and Wells in interpreting the "Will" to be filled here as a female addressee's vagina. However, I am intrigued by the idea that it might be a male orifice. See the description of Traub's argument in the footnote below.

[6] While I only treat this poem briefly in order to move on to more direct discussions of memory, Valerie Traub has made a fascinating argument that nicely complements my discussion here in this chapter. She teases out the complexity of this sonnet to argue that "In multiplying the number of imagined participants beyond the ménage à trois of poet, youth, and lady, the erotic sharing implied in Sonnets 31, 135, and 136 enact what would seem to be a queer fantasy. These poems, each of which lacks an unequivocally gendered addressee, describe scenarios in which the beloved's body serves as a vessel or depository for other lovers." Traub, *Thinking Sex with the Early Moderns*, 249. See 249–55 for the extended discussion.

have been done to the beloved—in order to guess at his virtue. Shakespeare writes, "They look into the beauty of thy mind, / And that, in guess, they measure by thy deeds" (9–10). This turn emphasizes another way that "their" would make sense in the original version of the poem. The parallels drawn between the outward expression and appearances of the onlookers ("their outward") *and* those of the beloved imply that guessing at his inwardness involves projecting one's own experiences upon him and his outward appearance.

But here the fantasy becomes a kind of violation at the close of Sonnet 69, as the memories of the observers intermingle with fantasized notions of the beloved's memories:

> Then, churls, their thoughts (although their eyes were kind)
> To thy fair flower add the rank smell of weeds.
> But why thy odour matcheth not thy show,
> The soil is this, that thou dost common grow. (11–14)

The "weeds" here can be read in at least two ways. They may indicate that the beloved has the outward appearance of a flower, but close inspection would reveal that he is something less innocent. The weeds might also indicate that his beauty has previously spent time with much more unsavory company. The lines here contain a crux, as "soil" appears as "solye" in the quarto edition. Catherine Belsey argues that "If 'soil' is right, it not only indicates a 'ground' for the general opinion and fits in, however loosely, with the metaphor of growing things: it also brings with it associations of dirt, and perhaps especially sexual contamination."[7] These onlookers fantasize about what the beloved may remember about past erotic bodily experiences—the onlookers' own fantasies drawing upon their own past experiences real or imagined—and subsequently these thoughts, this *soiling* by others, becomes part of what the sonnet speaker remembers about the beloved.[8]

The poet's reassurance to his addressee seems to be something like this: *others may claim to know what you have experienced, but rest assured that I know the truth of what you have experienced.* Reading the poem this way helps us see how Raphael Lyne can claim that the *Sonnets* are a particularly useful case study for exploring "the question of whether memories are truly owned or not."[9] We can

---

[7] She notes also that "This is not far, surely, from 'the wide world's common place,' or that other figurative account of the dark woman as 'the bay where all men ride' (sonnet 137)." Catherine Belsey, *Shakespeare in Theory and Practice* (Edinburgh: Edinburgh University Press, 2008), 80.

[8] The speaker does not negate the fantasies of the onlookers, or the notion that the beloved has become common. This helps us see how the binary between the male beloved's virtue and the female beloved's lack of virtue breaks down. While it may seem in some sonnets that the so-called dark lady constitutes "the material conclusion of an originally immaterial imagination, the loathsome heterosexual object of an ideally homosexual desire," we find here that the object of same-sex desire is only partially idealized in the mind of a speaker who admits his faults. Fineman, *Shakespeare's Perjured Eye*, 58.

[9] Lyne, *Memory and Intertextuality in Renaissance Literature*, 112.

better understand the implications of Lyne's claim by briefly exploring a twentieth-century poem about the trans-affective experience of desiring and being desired as it relates to memory. "Body, Remember" (1918) by Constantine Cavafy opens:

> Body, remember not only how much you were loved,
> not only the beds upon which you have lain,
> but also those desires that
> glistened for you openly in the eyes,
> and trembled in the voice—and some
> chance obstacle frustrated them. (1–6)[10]

The body here is shaped by its memory, and that memory is multiple: its memories of being loved, its memories of being desired, and by extension the memories of all of those who desired the body. Cavafy wants his addressee and his readers to consider, just as Freud once remarked that "the shadow of the object fell upon the ego," that the subject is shaped not just by its own desires but also by the desires of others that have made the subject into an object.[11] In other words, it is not simply that we project onto others when we desire them. Who one desires and what one imagines doing with that object of desire counter-reflects in order to transform the desirer, regardless of whether the love is reciprocated, never obtained, or lost. In the poem, even these unrequited desires become part of personal memory:

> Now that all this belongs to the past,
> it seems as if you gave yourself also
> to those desires—how they glistened,
> remember, in the eyes that gazed at you,
> how they trembled in the voice for you, remember, body! (7–11)

So the object is also transformed under the gaze of the desiring subject. To be desired can stimulate one to question why they are desired by a certain other and why that desirer might imagine certain interactions to be particularly desirable with oneself. The body here remembers other bodies—gazing eyes, trembling throats—to acknowledge how it has been changed by becoming someone else's object of desire and in a shared memory not entirely owned by a single subject.

In the previous chapter, we heard how imagined bodies of desire accessed through memory can compensate for absence. And Cavafy's poem illustrates not only how one's own body can be a reminder of the past but more importantly

---

[10] C. P. Cavafy, "Body, Remember," in *The Collected Poems: With Parallel Greek Text* (Oxford: Oxford University Press, 2009), 107.

[11] Sigmund Freud, "*Mourning and Melancholia* [1917]," in *The Standard Edition of the Complete Psychological Works of Sigmund Freud*, vol. 14: *On the History of the Psycho-Analytic Movement, Papers on Metapsychology, and Other Works*, trans. E. C. Mayne and James Strachey (London: Hogarth Press, 1964), 158.

how the distinction between one's own body and other bodies becomes blurred as each stimulates memories of each other. We find a startling instance of the body as a site upon which an extensive database of memories might be recorded and from which memories can be derived in Richard Saunders's *Physiognomie* (1653), which contains an illustration of the human hand as a numbered field upon which to map certain memories (Fig. 4.1). The exterior of the body is a tool because "an artificial memory is nothing but an art to assist the natural," such that the figure demonstrates "an alphabet that comprehends all that we can imagine in our hand."[12]

Another instance is Filippo Gesualdo's *Plutosofia, nella quale si spiega l'arte della memoria* (1600). Gesualdo, whose treatise on the art of forgetting and remembering draws upon Giovanni Battista della Porta's *L'arte del ricordare* (1566) discussed in the previous chapter, suggests the human body could work in the same function as an imagined theater for the art of memory (Fig. 4.2).[13] The illustration here from the title page underscores his argument that the art of memory can draw on forms of thought applied in the fields of both anatomy and architecture.[14] In the same way that the rememberer's own body can be a tablet upon which to inscribe memories, might not the body of the object of desire perform the same function?

Psychoanalytic and neuroscientific notions of the body dovetail with these ideas about bodily memory from the early modern memory arts. Physiologically, sensory perception is of course linked to the body, but sensory perception is also reliant on stimulation from both the body and the psyche. Neuroscientist Antonio Damasio's own study of the relationship between feelings and the construction of the self begins with an effort to "understand reasonably well how different emotions were induced in the brain and played out in the theater of the body."[15] Just as external sensory input can influence physiology, thoughts and feelings can occur in the mind as precursors to expressions in physical reactions and displays.

---

[12] The text and image are reproduced in *The Memory Arts in Renaissance England: A Critical Anthology*, where the editors note that the text is a "straightforward if unattributed translation from Jean Belot's *Oeuvres* (1640)." Engel, Loughnane, and Williams, eds., *The Memory Arts in Renaissance England*, 89–90; and Richard Saunders, *Physiognomie, and chiromancie ... whereunto is added the art of memory* (London: 1671), 3C2r.

[13] The body was also a mechanism to be managed as part of the memory arts, especially given the central place of Aristotle's *De Memoria et Reminiscentia* and its argument that "the capacity to remember was shaped by the given constitution of the human body." Hiscock, *Reading Memory in Early Modern Literature*, 14. On early modern memory and the body, see also 28–31.

[14] Filippo Gesualdo (Gesualdi), *Plutosofia ... Nella quale si spiega l'Arte della Memoria con altre cose notabili pertinenti, tanto alla Memoria naturale quanto all'artificiale* (Padua, 1592). We find also the notion of the body as a storehouse of knowledge in *Microcosmographia: A Description of the Body of Man* (1618), where "Man is a little world and contains in himself the seeds of all those things which are contained in the most spacious and ample bosom of this whole universe." Helkiah Crooke, *Microcosmographia: A Description of the Body of Man* (London: Jaggard, 1618), 12.

[15] Damasio's book-length study of the relationship between the body and the brain opens with an extended discussion of what an actor might experience when stepping onto a stage compared to what a playgoer might experience sitting in the theater. Damasio, *The Feeling of What Happens*, 1–8; the quoted text is taken from page 8.

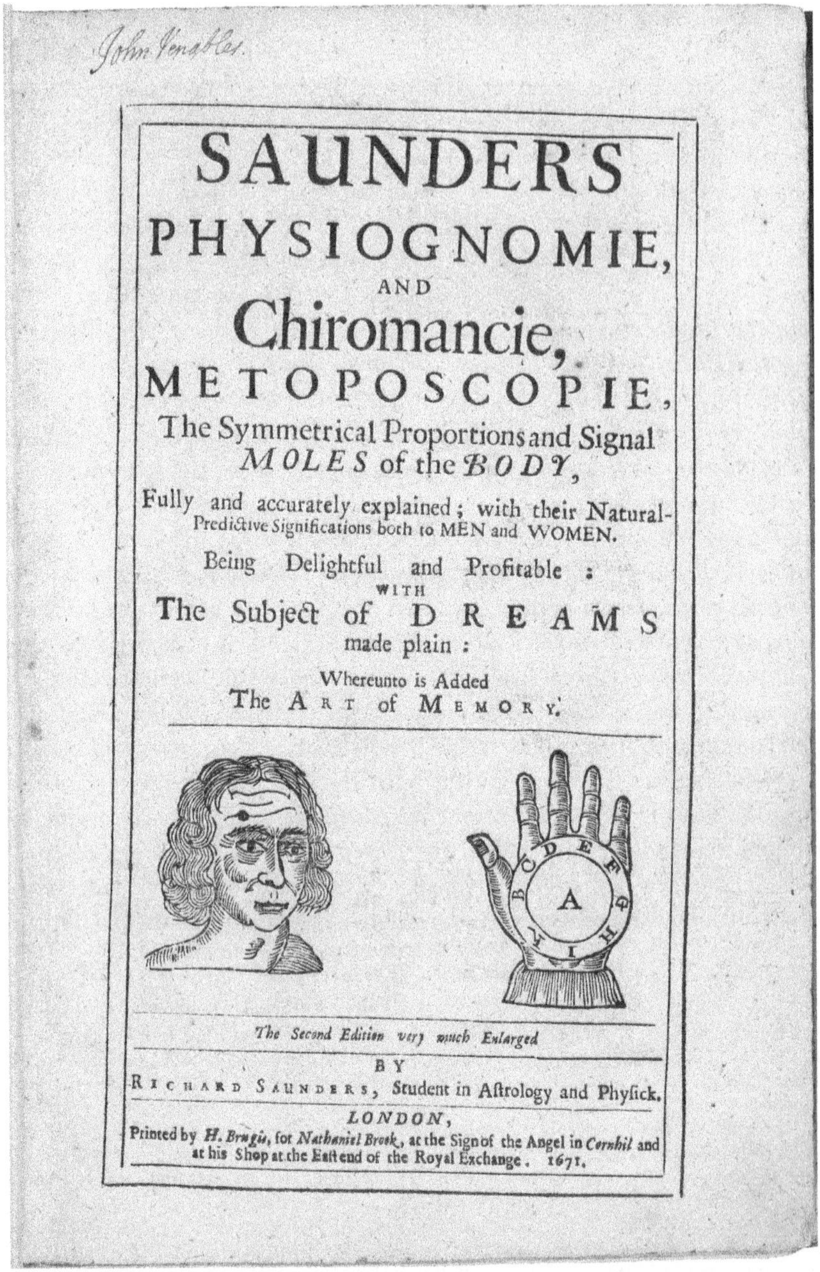

John Venables.

SAUNDERS

PHYSIOGNOMIE,

AND

Chiromancie,

METOPOSCOPIE,

The Symmetrical Proportions and Signal
MOLES of the *BODY*,

Fully and accurately explained; with their Natural-
Predictive Significations both to MEN and WOMEN.

Being Delightful and Profitable :
WITH
The Subject of D R E A M S
made plain :

Whereunto is Added
The A R T of M E M O R Y.

The Second Edition very much Enlarged

BY
RICHARD SAUNDERS, Student in Astrology and Physick.

LONDON,
Printed by *H. Brugis*, for *Nathaniel Brook*, at the Sign of the Angel in *Cornhil* and
at his Shop at the East end of the Royal Exchange. 1671.

Fig. 4.1. Richard Saunders's *Physiognomie* (1653), image 31064, used by permission of the Folger Shakespeare Library.

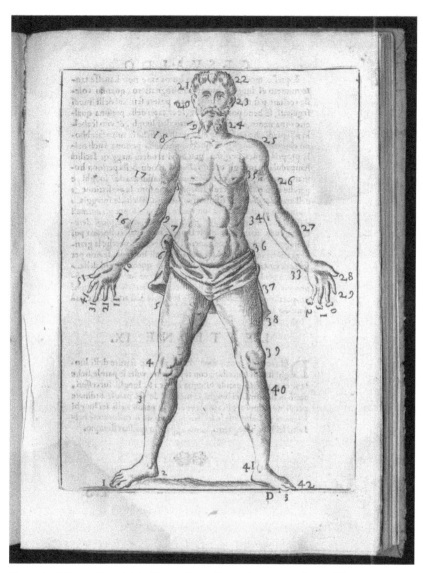

Fig. 4.2. Filippo Gesualdo's *Plutosofia, nella quale si spiega l'arte della memoria* (1600), used by permission of the Newberry Library.

A psychoanalytic approach would echo this. Freud argues that "the ego is first and foremost a bodily ego."[16] For Freud as for Damasio, the body is also that contact point with desired objects, given how "A person's own body, and above all its surface, is a place from which both external and internal perceptions may spring."[17]

Sonnet 141 explores the question of whether or not the speaker's desire stems entirely from bodily perceptions. Though he claims "In faith I do not love thee with mine eyes," he still admits the role of sight in assessing the beloved, "For they in thee a thousand errors note" (1–2). His claim, "Nor are mine ears with thy tongue's tune delighted," implies that he still hears the tune even if it is not the source of his pleasure (5). He declares that neither "my five wits nor my five senses can / Dissuade one foolish heart from serving thee," implying that part of one's desire may be driven by overcoming faults perceived through bodily sensory inputs (9–10). John Lyly's *Euphues* (1578) describes the classical paradigm of beauty, Helen of Troy, as having a scar on her chin.[18] The detail suggests that her status as the most beautiful woman in the known world relies on active work on the part of the subject who looks upon her. Lyly goes even further to posit that the friction between the flaw in her appearance and the notion of Helen as paradigmatically desirable is crucial. A perfect appearance would simply not drive the same levels of attraction as the imperfect one. Lyly explains that "in all perfect shapes, a blemish brings rather a liking every way to the eyes, than a loathing any way to the mind."[19] We find a similar idea in *The Anatomy of Melancholy*, where negative experiences constitute a whetstone against which we sharpen our pleasure, especially in the act of forgetting the hardships we have endured: "oblivion is a common medicine for all losses, injuries, griefs, and detriments whatsoever, *and when they are once past, this commodity comes of infelicity, it makes the rest of our life sweeter unto us.*"[20]

Shakespeare's poem continues as he promises fidelity to this lover who cannot promise the same. He commits,

> Thy proud heart's slave and vassal wretch to be.
> Only my plague thus far I count my gain:
> That she that makes me sin awards me pain. (12–14)

The poem offers a surprising mixture of masochism, virtue, and lovesickness. He loves this person despite her poor bodily experiences, suggesting an insight into her interiority. Yet that interiority is poorly judged, given her promiscuity. The relationship becomes highly charged then. Damasio observes how "The mapped

---

[16] Sigmund Freud, *The Ego and the Id*, trans. Joan Riviere. ed. James Strachey (New York: W. W. Norton and Company, 1960), 20.

[17] Freud, *The Ego and the Id*, 19.

[18] John Lyly, "The Descent of Euphues," in *Three Elizabethan Romance Stories*, ed. J. Winny (Cambridge: Cambridge University Press, 2015), 1.

[19] Lyly, *Euphues*, 1.

[20] Burton, *The Anatomy of Melancholy*, vol. 2, 148.

patterns constitute what we, conscious creatures, have come to know as sights, sounds, touches, smells, tastes, pains, pleasures, and the like—in brief, images. The images in our mind are the brain's momentary maps of everything and of anything, inside our body and around it, concrete as well as abstract, actual or previously recorded in memory."[21] We will return to the notion of enslavement and to disease in the following chapters. At this point, suffice to say that the ending merges psychic memory ("sin") with bodily memory ("plague") of his encounter with her. And his infection is a bodily memory of whatever partner infected her.

Yet the past partners who have encountered the beloved's body—whether real or imagined in Sonnets 135, 69, and 141—need not detract from the attraction that the sonnets' speaker might have toward his addressee. Consider how a fragment poem by our own contemporary poet Michael Ondaatje imagines the body as both inflected by its history and also as a form of history. We find the speaker expressing what might be a problem for a subject who is jealous:

> Kissing the stomach
> kissing your scarred
> skin boat. History
> is what you've traveled on
> and take with you.
> We've each had our stomachs
> kissed by strangers
> to the other. (1–8)[22]

He realizes, as perhaps many other lovers have realized, that previous people have had an intimate encounter with the body of the present beloved. This body is imagined as a vessel that is marked by its own history.

The perceived "scars" might be testimony to previous physical trauma or might be a metaphor for the appearance of wrinkles on an aging body. The stomach, with its imagined or real scars, is a particularly meaningful place upon which to project bodily memory. In his study of how emotional trauma is replayed physiologically, Bessel van der Kolk emphasizes that in order to discourage "old trauma" from seizing upon the body in the present, the traumatized individual must "integrate the memory into the overall context of their lives"; otherwise "the memory remains stuck—undigested and raw."[23] Traumatic experiences enter memory as if through the digestive system, where they sit problematically unless they are integrated into one's self-narrative. Either way, bodily memory scars represent a form of writing

---

[21] Damasio, *Self Comes to Mind*, 70.

[22] Michael Ondaatje, *The Cinnamon Peeler: Selected Poems* (New York: Vintage, 1997), 149.

[23] Bessel van der Kolk, *The Body Keeps the Score: Brain, Mind, and Body in the Healing of Trauma* (New York: Viking, 2014), 256.

that signals how the body retains and recounts its past. Early moderns were aware of the phenomenological echoes of painful memories. Robert Burton relates how,

> In Sacai, *another city, the same earthquake was so terrible unto them, that many were bereft of their senses; and others by that horrible spectacle so much amazed, that they knew not what they did. Blasius,* a Christian, the reporter of the news, was so affrighted for his part that, though it were two months after, he was scarce his own man, neither could he drive the remembrance of it out of his mind. Many times some years following they will tremble afresh at the remembrance or conceit of such a terrible object, even all their lives long, if mention be made of it.[24]

As the body receives external stimuli, the past finds its way into the present as memories are triggered. In turn, the body reacts to a degree not appropriate for the present situation but instead one appropriate for the stimuli present in the past. While this is true of trauma, it is also true of pleasure.

As we have already seen in examples from chapters thus far, the speaker's reactions to the present object of desire are informed by memories of those who have desired—or have been desired by—the speaker or the addressee. Rather than generating jealousy or devaluing the quality of the beloved, the notion of a stranger's desire might simply generate questions about the past, even titillating questions. What did the past lovers see in the beloved? What did they learn? What excitements did they derive from or incite in the beloved's body? Ondaatje's speaker finds kinship with and expresses gratitude toward his beloved's past partners:

> and as for me
> I bless everyone
> who kissed you here. (9–11)

What might be surprising about Ondaatje's poem is how the speaker is not jealous of the previous lovers of the addressee. The bodily memories symbolized by the scarred stomach become—to draw upon van der Kolk's terms—integrated rather than raw and undigested, because the pain is relegated to the past as the experience contributes to a personal narrative history that explains how this all led to present pleasures. Rather than these previous encounters rendering the body less virtuous, the previous partners are "blessed" in such a way as to suggest that they contribute to the beloved's virtue. It resembles a purification ritual here when one kisses the places on the body where the person has been kissed before. At the same time, it is an exercise in the sensual imagination. To kiss his beloved's bare stomach—and to think of others kissing it too—portrays a scene of intimacy and erotic contact.

---

[24] Burton, *The Anatomy of Melancholy*, vol. 1, 390, italics in original.

Ondaatje's positive narrative about these shared memories—his partner's memories of past loves and his own memories of having heard about them and about having known her body—stands in stark contrast to the more negative account given in Sonnet 69 above.

Elsewhere in the *Sonnets*, the speaker departs from a strict binary distinction where the judgmental speaker is counterposed to the beloved's lack of chastity. Such instances can involve an imbrication of present and past beloveds that resembles the erotics of Ondaatje's poem. For example, the speaker of Sonnet 117 admits to his own instances of psychic adultery because he:

> Forgot upon your dearest love to call,
> Whereto all bonds do tie me day by day,
> That I have frequent been with unknown minds,
> And given to time your own dear-purchased right[.] (3–6)

The poem leaves intriguingly ambiguous how the encounter with these other minds might function. Is it that he has fantasized about being with others? Or has he simply thought of others and imagined how their minds might function, in the same way that the onlookers in Sonnet 69 projected their experiences onto the beloved? We can imagine Ondaatje's poem to describe the imaginative writing process, where the poet spends his time imagining possible pasts for a body he has in mind. The same might be said here of this sonnet. The lines above could apologize for the wide-ranging imagination of such a prolific playwright and poet. As John Keats remarks in a letter to Richard Woodhouse, "A Poet is the most unpoetical of any thing in existence; because he has no identity—he is continually in form—and filling some other Body."[25] And yet another possibility for the mind-based adultery here could be the dialogic nature of the writer's relationship with multiple readers that I began to explore in Chapter Two. As Michel de Certeu has remarked, referring especially to premodern contexts when poems were much more frequently read aloud to oneself or to others, "the reader interiorized the text; he made his voice the body of the other; he was its actor."[26] Such an activity elides the stable identity of the author, rendering his mind knowable to the reader even at the level of projection. When we keep in mind Edmondson and Wells's work that has shown how the poems may address multiple beloveds beyond the paradigms of a single "Young Man" and a single "Dark Lady," the lines above could allude to poems that Shakespeare has written for others. Perhaps the most famous instance of wondering at the beloved's other lovers is in Sonnet 138, where the speaker continues to

---

[25] John Keats, "To Richard Woodhouse, 27 October 1818," in *Selected Letters*, ed. Robert Gittings (Oxford: Oxford University Press, 2009), 148.
[26] Michel de Certeu, *The Practice of Everyday Life*, trans. Steven Rendall (Berkeley: University of California Press, 1984), 176.

"lie" with his beloved though he is aware of her lying and likely adulterous lying around (13).[27]

"Her Old Loves with Me"

When the lover lies with the beloved and admires that body in Ondaatje's poem, it becomes a tablet upon which to work the imagination. That imaginative work, as we have already seen in Shakespeare's sonnets above, can involve discerning histories and generating fantasies. We encounter an evocative description of such imagination in Sonnet 138. Here, the speaker and his beloved both manipulate their own memories through active work of forgetting to co-generate a workable narrative upon which they can thrive. As an aging speaker reflects on the falsehoods that undergird the relationship with his female partner, we learn that the coupling functions because they are both false to each other:

> When my love swears that she is made of truth,
> I do believe her though I know she lies,
> That she might think me some untutored youth,
> Unlearnèd in the world's false subtleties. (1–4)

Though he knows the truth of the real situation, the speaker engages in *unknowing* as a way to exclude what he knows from the past about his partner but also to support a fantasy he has about himself. By ignoring the falseness of the beloved's claims, the two partners dwell in fantasy so that he can remain "vainly thinking that she thinks me young, / Although she knows my days are past the best" (5–6). To believe that he can be "thinking" what she "thinks," even if he admits to it being vanity, describes that process of fantasy by which the subject projects itself into other minds. Though this aging lover has the savvy to see her "subtleties," he ignores them just as a younger, more naive lover would. Thus, this unknowing contributes to the fantasy that he is of a much younger age. And the lie becomes the shared reality as the speaker asks, "But wherefore says she not she is unjust? / And wherefore say not I that I am old?" (9–10). That is, the beloved can imagine the speaker as a younger man, and so can the speaker; thus it is not just a lie. They both do know him as a younger man in their personal recollections. "Excitement and longing are preserved as memories," writes psychoanalyst

[27] Michael Schoenfeldt succinctly captures the potential imbalance inherent in the stories each partner tells themselves about each other: "The poem turns on a false comparison between the little 'white' lies that most relationships demand to some degree ('you look younger than your age') and a toxic fabrication that would erode the foundation of any relationship ('I know you are unfaithful but I will believe you are not')." Michael Schoenfeldt, *The Cambridge Introduction to Shakespeare's Poetry* (Cambridge: Cambridge University Press, 2010), 100.

Stephen Mitchell, because these memories provide "a nostalgic sense of an earlier time, at the beginning of the relationship, when it was safe to love."[28] To lie with each other now, the lovers experience not just each other as younger partners but the relationship in a younger, more exciting, less jaded form that they now long for.

There is also in this sonnet the erotic appeal of the fantasy of naiveté, something we see elsewhere in Shakespeare's work. When Portia stands before Bassanio on their wedding day in *The Merchant of Venice*, she declares:

> [...] the full sum of me
> Is sum of something which, to term in gross,
> Is an unlessoned girl, unschooled, unpractisèd,
> Happy in this, she is not yet so old[.] (3.2.157–60)

The audience knows this claim to youthful ignorance cannot be true, given Portia's savvy about the suitors' natures and about the intricacies of Venetian law. Her use of "unlessoned girl, unschooled, unpractisèd" relies on a subtle version of anaphora as it repeated "un" in such a way to suggest to Bassanio that she had not yet been exposed to the world but that suggests to the audience (and perhaps to Antonio, too) that their marriage can *undo* whatever learning or practice she may have engaged in. It is a kind of wishful thinking that she could undo what she knows about the world or what she has done in it, even if the undoing is just in Bassanio's fantasy about her. Bassanio may accept what she states as fact, or he may choose to forget the subtext here and throughout the play: that Portia is much more "schooled" than she claims to be. This is the fantasy that might underlie the arguably successful coupling and marriage described in the sonnet. Portia's lines echo those of the speaker of Sonnet 138's wish that his lover "might think me some untutored youth, / Unlearnèd in the world's false subtleties."

A friend of mine once remarked, "Some people marry believing their partner will never change. Others marry counting on the belief that the partner will change." The cleverness of Portia's pledge to her prospective husband captures both fantasies. She continues,

> But she may learn; happier than this,
> She is not bred so dull but she can learn;
> Happiest of all is that her gentle spirit
> Commits itself to yours to be directed
> As from her lord, her governor, her king. (3.2.161–5)

What she promises here is twofold. On the one hand, Portia and Bassanio will make memories together with his as the guiding mind. On the other hand, she

---

[28] Mitchell, *Can Love Last?*, 142.

will actively forget who she previously was in order to be directed by him. This "unlessoned girl, unschooled, unpractisèd" will, as she says twice in two lines, "learn." Given the rhetorical power we see her demonstrate throughout *The Merchant of Venice* and given the agency she demonstrates in the play's final scene, this speech promotes that it is a fiction that he will rule over her, no matter how much her words may reify his place in the early modern patriarchal hierarchy.

When we focus on memory as the theme of Sonnet 138, it opens the possibility that the poem meditates not just on two lovers that actively lie to each other but also on the ways in which the past selves continue to be present in a relationship over time. The addressee may truly see the speaker as the younger man that he was, and he may imagine himself clearly as he once saw himself. Sonnet 138 ends in the pessimistic mood, but this may reflect the speaker's naiveté:

> O, love's best habit is in seeming trust,
> And age in love loves not to have years told.
> Therefore I lie with her, and she with me,
> And in our faults by lies we flattered be. (11–14)

What fuels their continued sex life is "not to have years told," and they continue to "lie" with each other. After all, the "habit" in love is that which repeats itself. The fact that the poem ends with their lying together here ties erotic activity to active forgetting. That is, it may be that sustaining sexual excitement relies on forgetting his old age or her potential infidelity.[29]

It may indeed be that they both conjure the mental image of him as a younger version of himself when they are together. Writing in the sixteenth century about the operations of love, Marsilio Ficino captures nicely the thrill of such an encounter with the past-in-the-present:

> Whenever we meet that person whom we formerly loved, we are shaken, our hearts jump or quiver, or our livers melt and our eyes tremble, and our faces turn many colors (like the rainbow when the sun shines opposite the misty air). For his presence suggests to the eyes of the soul in his presence, the form lying dormant in the mind, as though rousing the fire slumbering under the ashes by blowing.[30]

Here, too, we find an instance of the body reacting—with its jumping heart, melting liver, trembling eyes, and blushing face—in a manner that is not solely a

---

[29] Frida Beckman notes that while "sexuality liberated from the predetermined and the habitual has the capacity to produce sensation that produces a becoming," it is also true that "sexuality can produce habit and cliché." In Sonnet 138, the couple appear to avoid cliché and achieve new forms of erotism through their unusual habit of lying to and with each other. Frida Beckman, *Between Desire and Pleasure: A Deleuzian Theory of Sexuality* (Edinburgh: Edinburgh University Press, 2013), 115.
[30] Marsilio Ficino, *Commentary of Marsilio Ficino on the Symposium of Plato on the Subject of Love*, trans. Sears Reynolds Jayne (New York: Columbia University Press, 1944), 201.

reaction to the presented body but also a reinvigorating of the image of the body from the past lying dormant in memory. While Ficino describes this in terms of a reunion with a former beloved, Shakespeare shows how active forgetting and remembering, working in tandem, can achieve the same effect. Both Ficino's and Shakespeare's depictions are illuminated by Deleuze's remark that "Pleasure seems to me to be the only means for a person or a subject to 'find itself again' in a process that surpasses it. It is a reterritorialization."[31] This idea that the re-encounter with the desired object can be understood in terms of mapping and laying claim to a space helps us see how the body plays a crucial role in the experiencing of past pleasure. It offers a territory upon which to impress desires and fantasies. In Sonnet 138, the territories of a lover's body function as reminders of past bodies that were younger, more beautiful, or more chaste.

Love can be self-forgetting, not of one's place in society but of one's self. It can be in the form of self-annihilation. Sonnet 138 captures the desire of the speaker to see the beloved the way she was and to imagine that she sees him as he was. In doing so, it dramatizes the appeal of projecting fantasies of the past into the present. Memory is much more knowable than the present lived experience, even if that memory is a fiction (which it may very well be in this sonnet). He says he does not know exactly how she sees him ("she says not") and that he only guesses that she lies with others. Thus, the more knowable partner is the one he and she remember from earlier in the relationship. The poem might be understood to resolve the seeming opposition between the two types of lovers in my friend's aphorism above. Sonnet 138 seems to say, *we marry people knowing they will change but can continue to relate to them as if they have not.*

Freud used the term "undoing" to capture how we wish we could rewrite our pasts in memory.[32] The German term "Ungeschehenmachen," which roughly means "making un-happened," is helpful for parsing what occurs in Sonnet 138, as the lover makes his beloved's infidelities *unhappen*, and she does the same with his years of aging.[33] Anna Freud saw forgetting as a way of undoing, one of the "modes of defense which the patient deploys against his affects" and a "form of resistance adopted by his ego."[34] Her phrasing is helpful both because it poses a

---

[31] Gilles Deleuze, "Desire and Pleasure," trans. Daniel W. Smith, in *Between Deleuze and Foucault*, ed. Nicolae Morar, Thomas Nail, and Daniel W. Smith (Edinburgh: Edinburgh University Press, 2016), 228.

[32] Sigmund Freud, "Inhibitions, Symptoms, and Anxiety," in *The Standard Edition of the Complete Psychological Works of Sigmund Freud*, vol. 20, trans. James Strachey (London: The Hogarth Press, 1961), 113.

[33] Stephen Booth notes the linkages between "beauties wear" and "minutes waste" in the figures of the "glass" and "dial" in the first two lines of Sonnet 77. That coupling offers a reminder that we can read these laments about the aging body in the context of the clock discussed in the next chapter as well as Faulkner's contemplation of what the watch might both contain and symbolize. Booth, *An Essay on Shakespeare's Sonnets*, 198.

[34] Anna Freud, *The Ego and the Mechanisms of Defence* (London and New York: Routledge, 1993 [1937]), 34.

memory as a trigger event for emotional response while also suggesting an agential element to forgetting when the subject actively represses—that is, might refuse to think about or banish a thought about—a past experience. And here is where forgetting and repetition go hand in hand. At times, erasing something from memory requires dwelling upon it, which can inadvertently only make it more indelibly written. Melanie Klein's casting of "undoing" as "a tendency to *undo harm* and put objects right magically" speaks to the role of fiction in relieving the weight of the past.[35] That is, what begins internally at the level of "feelings and phantasy" extends to "external reality [which is] drawn into this world of internal values, the compulsion to keep and put things right extends to real things."[36] We hear this in Sonnet 69 above, where the speaker's claims to the beloved's virtue seek to undo onlookers' fantasies and even the past sexual activities of the beloved.

Shakespeare's Sonnet 138 captures such dialectical efforts lyrically, even as it admits to the precarity of such management of the past within the present. The couple continue to have sex with each other, perhaps frequently with the repetition of "lie," and perhaps energized by the knowledge of others with whom the partner has slept. Even if we do not accept the speaker's suspicions that she has been unfaithful, we still find the interplay of memory as she interacts with the fantasy of his younger self and he imagines himself to be that person.

The link between Ondaatje's poem and Sonnet 138 rests in their focus on unexpected narratives about desire, aging, and the history of previous sex partners. Both dwell on the denial of some memories and the return to others in the space of romantic fantasy. Foundational psychoanalyst Wilfred Bion notes how "Desires suppress judgment by selection and suppression of material to be judged," and both poems portray the selective work done by the desiring subject of the original poem.[37] Shakespeare's Sonnet 138 depicts such "suppression" occurring as a result of the speaker dwelling on his aging and his partner's infidelity partly because, as Bion describes, "the impulse can present itself as the wish to remember something that has happened because it appears to have precipitated an emotional crisis."[38] That is, the speaker both tries to remind himself about the habituated situation that has him absent while also remembering a period that came before the reasons for the current lies. Compensating for past loves in a different way, the fragment from Ondaatje showcases a speaker who actively includes himself in the past sexual encounters where he was absent by blessing the previous partners. This assuages the presence of emotional and physical scars and, as in Sonnet 138, enables a new kind of intimacy with its own peculiar relationship to recollection.

---

[35] Joan Riviere, "On the Genesis of Psychical Conflict in Earliest Infancy," in Joan Riviere, Melanie Klein, Paula Heimann, and Susan Isaacs, *Developments in Psychoanalysis*, ed. Joan Riviere (New York: Routledge, 2018 [1952]), 61.

[36] Riviere, "On the Genesis of Psychical Conflict in Earliest Infancy," 61.

[37] Bion, "Notes on Memory and Desire," 272.

[38] Bion, "Notes on Memory and Desire," 272.

I believe this opens a series of intriguing lines of inquiry that can be applied to both poems. Does revisiting his beloved's body as she ages allow the speaker to connect with familiar nuances he has always loved? Does learning about her subtleties over time, through repetition, enhance his love for her? Or is it that her former lovers (many of whom might be old now) also lie with him just as they did with her? Just as Ondaatje helps us make (new) sense of the older poem, we might hear Shakespeare's speaker making sense of previous stages of the aging relationship. Just as the members of the couple are co-constituted with each other, previous lovers become co-constituted with the couple, especially at the level of shared memory.

The story that the Sonnet 138's speaker tells himself about his partnership is also a story about himself because, as Damasio's studies of brain science and the construction of subjectivity have found,

> the self hinges on the consistent reactivation and display of specific sets of autobiographical memories[,] reiterated display of some of our own personal memories, the *objects of our personal past*, those that can easily substantiate our identity, moment by moment, and our personhood.[39]

The speaker of Shakespeare's narrative constructs his autobiographical self by engaging in the retrospective logic-making of self-narrative that lies at the heart of recollection. He engages in pattern recognition, integrating her subtle qualities, negative or positive, into what he knows about her. As we have seen from Ondaatje's poem above, this need not be a point of concern but rather an opportunity for the celebration of the adored body and an enhancement of the erotic experience of that body.

Change and Constancy in Embodied Memory

As I have traced thus far, Shakespeare's speaker reveals concerns that his beloveds' bodies have been experienced by others, and he himself admits to his own type of psychic adultery when he discloses that he has "frequent been with unknown minds" (117.5).[40] And we can see the complexity of this problem when the *Sonnets* are read alongside Cavafy's poem "Body, Remember" and Ondaatje's "Kissing the Stomach." These poems portray how intimacy might be attenuated or intensified when the speaker knows he desires a body that has been desired by others. Such

[39] Damasio, *The Feeling of What Happens*, 196.
[40] For an excellent discussion of the ways in which literature (primarily fiction, but also drama and poetry) offers a unique site where thoughts of others can be known through the process of "psycho-narration," see Dorrit Cohn, *Transparent Minds: Narrative Modes for Presenting Consciousness in Fiction* (Princeton: Princeton University Press, 1978), 21–46 and 255–69.

knowledge threatens the balance and concordance attested to as an ideal in Sonnet 116, which celebrates "the marriage of true minds" (1). One way to interpret that sonnet is as a utopian vision of sameness between two partners with little need for compromise and sacrifice because the sailing is so smooth in the partnership:

> [...] love is not love
> Which alters when it alteration finds,
> Or bends with the remover to remove.
> O no, it is an ever-fixèd mark,
> That looks on tempests and is never shaken[.] (2–6)

Sonnet 116 seems to argue against memory in a relationship. The couple here appears to operate in a timeless present where every attribute and feeling in the *now* is the same as it was in the past. The use of polyptoton, as "alter" finds its mirror image in "alteration" and "remover" in "remove," reinforces this idea that though a word (or aging lover) might look different, the core meaning or feeling does not change. Sonnet 116 might seem the antithesis to Sonnet 138. Indeed, the former is a very popular poem to read at weddings. Perhaps it is harder to imagine someone reading Sonnet 138 at a wedding.

But maybe one should consider reading the latter poem to commemorate a friend's nuptials. Read in light of "Kissing the Stomach," we might find Sonnet 138's conception of matrimonial memory to be a particularly compelling reason that a couple might stay together. Indeed, I wonder if we might imagine any of these three poems being exemplary texts to be read if the person giving the toast truly wanted to give useful advice to a couple considering what it will mean to grow old together. When Sonnet 138 is interpreted as a poem whose message is that a couple's memory of each will allow them to re-experience earlier versions of themselves and to eroticize failed fidelity, we can see it as affirming a type of steadiness lionized in Sonnet 116. In fact, even the final lines of Sonnet 116 might be seen with new eyes:

> Love's not Time's fool, though rosy lips and cheeks
> Within his bending sickle's compass come.
> Love alters not with his brief hours and weeks,
> But bears it out even to the edge of doom.
> If this be error and upon me proved,
> I never writ, nor no man ever loved. (9–14)

With a new understanding of Sonnet 138, might this closing function just as well for either poem? When we read that "Love's not Time's fool," might we find this sonnet's speaker saying that he knows that time brings change in the form of age and "error" in the form of wandering eyes but that the emotion remains nonetheless?

Sonnet 116 and Sonnet 138, in different ways, imagine what Jessica Benjamin describes as a form of erotic freedom subtended by "the ability to share feelings and intentions without demanding control, to experience sameness without obliterating difference."[41] When the couple are of the same mind, as they are in Sonnet 116, they can know what the other might be thinking in order to face uncertainties ahead. Sonnet 138, which spotlights the common changes inherent in aging or precarious fidelity, suggests a sameness of mind that admits to fantasies about the truth of promises made in the dark. Yet the notion of shared memories within a couple, whether bound by the "one flesh" unit of husband and wife or by the "single soul across two bodies" of same-sex friends, is one with vexed implications. As I explore in the next chapter, when the *Sonnets* make claims to celebrate shared memories, they threaten to undermine the intimacy and tolerance of difference promised by the love that might be shared between the speaker and addressee.

The Body of the Friend

Friendship is lionized for the interpersonal connection it invigorates in lived experience. As Alan Bray's work has shown, the ways that it spurs one to speak and to write, as well as the way that its proofpoint is how the friend is memorialized by the living partner after death, is predicated on absence.[42] Within Bray's writing on the public expressions of male friendship common in the early modern era, the semiotics of affection have looming over them how "within only a single generation these signs had gone."[43]

To be haunted by death—of figures engraved on a tomb, of a personal friend, of an age, of oneself at an unknowable date in the future—is best known to us as

---

[41] Jessica Benjamin, *The Bonds of Love: Psychoanalysis, Feminism, and the Problem of Domination* (New York: Pantheon Books, 1988), 39.

[42] Alan Bray's scholarship has certainly been formative to my own thinking on friendship and on memory. Perhaps this is because I view him in retrospect: he is someone who has died, a figure of another era, a node of discovery from my own graduate study, someone who died before his major book *The Friend* was going to print. For this reason, it seems particularly apt that two of the essays in *GLQ*'s memorial issue focused on the work of Alan Bray are "The Work of Friendship," where Jody Greene links this title phrase to Derrida's formulation of "the work of mourning," and "Friendship's Loss," where Valerie Traub reflects on the loss of a friend as well as the loss of a scholar to the field of friendship studies. Jody Greene, "Introduction: The Work of Friendship," *GLQ* 10, no. 3 (2004): 319–37; and Valerie Traub, "Friendship's Loss: Alan Bray's Making of History, " *GLQ* 10, no. 3 (2004): 339-365.

[43] The essay from which this phrase is drawn itself constitutes a tribute to a lost friend. The co-author was a graduate student who appreciated a lecture by Bray on "the body of the friend," and the essay reflects conversations that Bray and Rey had shared before the latter's early death. Alan Bray and Michael Rey, "The Body of the Friend: Continuity and Change in Masculine Friendship in the Seventeenth Century," in *English Masculinities: 1660-1800*, ed. Tim Hitchcock and Michele Cohen (London and New York: Routledge, 1999), 66.

Shakespeare scholars in terms of the *memento mori* tradition. However, instead of picturing the familiar figure-regarding-skull visual, I would invite us to consider a different image: that of a man trapped inside a skeleton in Francis Quarles's 1635 *Emblems* with the inscription "O wretched Man that I am; who shall deliver me from the body of this Death?" (Fig. 4.3). The image offers intriguing evidence for the body as a repository for recollection. The landscape behind the skeleton is one of lifelessness. The barren tree, sunless sky, and nondescript landscape recall the "bare ruined choirs" of Sonnet 73. The skeleton's repose suggests a mode of thinking, as if death is all the living man should or can be thinking of. The man clings to the skeleton as if living his life within the overwhelming fear of deteriorating to only be that prison of bone. The image works as a *memento mori* because it throws into relief the more familiar opposite: a skeleton dwells inside each living person as if to presage their demise.

I believe, though, that this image of the person trapped inside the skeleton does different work than the person gazing at a skull. It invites us to interrupt the strict teleology of the *memento mori*. What if we read it not as a man trapped within the inevitability of his death but rather a depiction of the vibrancy of the memory of a life lived? Or, perhaps even more evocatively, what if we consider the image to depict *two* men rather than one? Such reframings allow us to ponder this image as one celebrating amity, even if we accept its macabre overlay. In turn, the depiction can help us think about the uses of friendship.[44]

Memory in the *Sonnets* is sometimes co-constituted across a network of minds. A commonplace of Shakespeare's *Sonnets* is that the speaker is older than the male addressee and thus will probably predecease this friend to whom he addresses many of the poems. Yet, as the poems tell us repeatedly, the texts will outlive them both and provide a form of immortality. In the more short term, we find the speaker lamenting his old age in contrast to the speaker's youth as well as pondering how the young man will feel about him after the speaker dies. Much of this revolves around discussions of the distance between the two men and how temporary absence foreshadows the separation of death. Sonnet 44, for example, opens with the two men apart from each other. The speaker expresses a fantasmatic wish that the body could be a form of thought and thereby reach his friend:

---

[44] Many scholars before and since Bray have covered this territory regarding male friendship incisively. To name a few excellent starting points: Tom McFaul, *Male Friendship in Shakespeare and His Contemporaries* (Cambridge: Cambridge University Press, 2007); Jeffrey Masten, *Textual Intercourse: Collaboration, Authorship, and Sexualities in Renaissance Drama* (Cambridge: Cambridge University Press, 1997); Shannon, *Sovereign Amity*; Alan Stewart, *Close Readers: Humanism and Sodomy in Early Modern England* (Princeton: Princeton University Press, 1997); and Will Tosh, *Male Friendship and Testimonies of Love in Shakespeare's England* (London: Palgrave Macmillan, 2016). For insightful studies as well as a very necessary complement to the existing body of scholarship that largely centers on male same-sex friendship, see Penelope Anderson, *Friendship's Shadows: Women's Friendship and the Politics of Betrayal in England, 1640–1705* (Edinburgh: Edinburgh University Press, 2013) and Amanda Herbert, *Female Alliances: Gender, Identity, and Friendship in Early Modern Britain* (New Haven: Yale University Press, 2014).

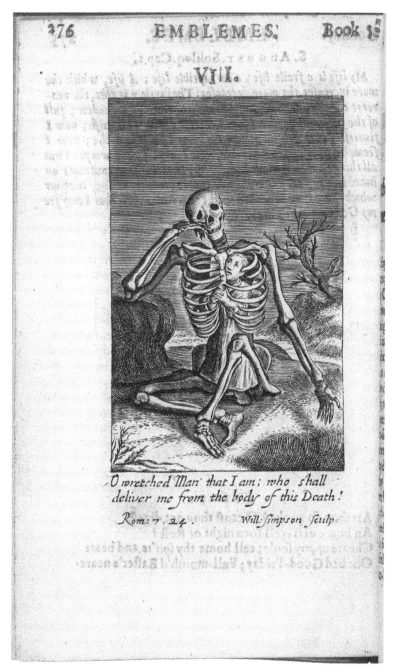

Fig. 4.3. Francis Quarles, *Emblemes* (London: Printed by G[eorge] M[iller] and sold at Iohn Marriots shope in St Dunstons Church yard fleetstreet, 1639), 272. STC 20542, page 276, image 19794, used by permission of the Folger Shakespeare Library.

> If the dull substance of my flesh were thought,
> Injurious distance should not stop my way;
> For then, despite of space, I would be brought
> From limits far remote, where thou dost stay. (1–4)

The problem at the onset of this poem is not simply that the speaker misses the beloved. It is also a problem at the heart of the idealized friendship model. Without the friend around, a man will experience longing because he needs that second body to feel complete.

In this instance where the speaker's body is "dull" and counterposed to the alacrity with which his "thought" travels to the beloved, it is tempting to see an expression of self-deprecating pleasure. That is, we might read here an instance of the psychoanalytic perspective on the masochistic components of all desire where "the investment in the delay is what lies at the basis of desire: I think about and imagine the pleasure to come."[45] But an implied lacuna in the sonnet lies in the thoughts not *about* the beloved but *of* the beloved. Does the friend think about the speaker as much as the speaker does him? Does the beloved miss him in his absence and will he miss him when he has died? The distance between them has a phenomenological capacity as it is "injurious" to the speaker, and

> No matter then although my foot did stand
> Upon the farthest earth removed from thee,
> For nimble thought can jump both sea and land
> As soon as think the place where he would be. (5–8)

Here, we see more evidence of a dialectic at the heart of the early modern friendship model. Thoughts about the beloved can "jump" from the speaker toward the beloved, but the bodily and poetic "foot" grounds the speaker in place. The use of "would" further underscores the distance that subtends their intimacy: they may share a heart and soul but one cannot be certain about the absent other's whereabouts. At the most basic level, the poet expresses a wish to instantly travel to the current location of the beloved, yet the operations of the wish introduce the counter-logics. The speaker cannot simply think of the beloved and move their bodies together.

This is not to say that the speaker cannot experience bodily pleasure in the present, and he does seem to do so by drawing on his memory of past pleasures from time spent with the beloved. He suffices to "attend time's leisure with my moan, / Receiving naught by elements so slow / But heavy tears, badges of either's woe" (12–14). These closing lines from the sonnet capture the intermingled suffering and joy of the erotic elegy. These moans in the time of leisure waiting for

---

[45] Aisenstein and Moss, "Desire and Its Discontents," 66.

the beloved echo the description of elegiac bodily pleasures in Sonnet 30 which, as we saw in the first chapter, portrays the intimate connections between bodily memory and pleasure. The body itself is a vessel for containing past pleasures—both real and imagined—and that makes it a source for present pleasure, obviating the need for reunion with the beloved. To desire someone, as Adam Phillips wonderfully puts it, "sends a depth-charge into our histories" as we consider previous successes and failures.[46] To long for the beloved here in the *Sonnets* is to imagine a future time where one of the two friends will never return. And perhaps this is the real horizon of loss against which Sonnet 44 and texts like it shore themselves up.

---

[46] Phillips, *Side Effects*, 59.

5

Scenographies of Waiting

As we saw in Chapter Three and especially in Chapter Four, the body can be a tool for memory keeping and memory making, whether or not it is actually present in the flesh. The body is at once a physical apparatus from which one can retrieve the past and also an abstract concept that can be recreated in the mind to compensate for absence. This chapter brings together the themes of the previous two chapters by focusing on the doubling that occurs when the speaker remembers the beloved or vice versa. This doubling, while initially a cause for celebration and an apt explanatory device for the operations of desirous memory, reveals the negative effects of the agential memory described in the *Sonnets*.

Sonnet 24 expresses how the body of the poet makes possible the transmutation of the beloved into memory, which then in turn can immortalize the beloved in the most complimentary way possible. At the opening, the poem describes how transcription is crucial to extending one's self into the world and into the future:

> Mine eye hath played the painter and hath stelled
> Thy beauty's form in table of my heart;
> My body is the frame wherein 'tis held,
> And perspective it is best painter's art[.] (1–4)

The poet argues that his perspective, both as an artist and as someone who deeply understands the addressee, can best render the beloved's beauty. Though the poem starts with the terms of painting, its use of "table" invokes the writing tablet and thus lets us know that it describes the transcribed poem just as well. The notion in the third line that the poet's body can hold the beloved's body invokes the intimacy of a physical tightness that goes beyond that of a physical hug, implying something more akin to the total collapse of the object of desire into the subject, a concept we saw illustrated in Chapter One with the embrace of the shirt at the end of *Brokeback Mountain*. Sonnet 24 continues to utilize the vocabulary of bodily intimacy to describe the creative process behind the poet's art. The beloved's beauty will be displayed in the poet's "bosom's shop" (7) and "breast" (11) which the addressee's "eyes" can gaze upon (8). The description suggests a close, one-to-one relationship between poet and subject, though the use of "shop" and the public nature of the printed poem emphasize that this depiction is also for broader consumption. The final couplet tells us that others may attempt to paint the beloved's beauty but "They draw but what they see, know not the heart" (14). This could imply that the

The Pleasures of Memory in Shakespeare's Sonnets. John S. Garrison, Oxford University Press. © John S. Garrison (2023). DOI: 10.1093/oso/9780198857716.003.0006

SCENOGRAPHIES OF WAITING 109

speaker knows best the beloved's heart but by leaving the possessor of this "heart" productively ambiguous, it may just as well imply that others must know the poet's heart to truly appreciate the addressee.

Sonnet 122 navigates the same conceptual terrain that Sonnet 24 does, but it brings to the surface the problems that subtend the manner in which the poet promises to memorialize the beloved:

> Thy gift, thy tables, are within my brain
> Full charactered with lasting memory,
> Which shall above that idle rank remain
> Beyond all date even to eternity:
> Or at the least so long as brain and heart
> Have faculty by nature to subsist[.] (1–6)

The terms "tables" and "charactered" once more bring to the foreground writing as a tool best suited to memorialize another's beauty and to carry that memory forward. Here, too, the body has a central role, as "brain" and "heart" are those sites which will not only inspire poetic creation but also serve as surfaces upon which memories will be transcribed. The poem functions as both a promise that the addressee will be remembered and a reminder to the speaker to do that remembering. It thus engages with what cognitive psychologists term "prospective memory." That is, the poet must recall to perform the task of remembering the poet in the future, a task for which the poem itself will serve as a cue or reminder to both him and the reader to perform this task.[1]

It becomes clear that, in order for the beloved's memory to live on, it must not only be inscribed in the "brain and heart" of the lover but also in those of future generations in order to reach "eternity." It thus seems to solve the problem of the poet's potential forgetfulness, named at the end of the poem, by enlisting readers. The sonnet continues:

> Till each to razed oblivion yield his part
> Of thee, thy record never can be missed.
> That poor retention could not so much hold,
> Nor need I tallies thy dear love to score,
> Therefore to give them from me was I bold
> To trust those tables that receive thee more.
> To keep an adjunct to remember thee
> Were to import forgetfulness in me. (7–14)

---

[1] "Prospective memory" drives a subject's desire, by reminding her of what she wants to be able to do in the future, but it also asks the subject to constantly remember that their desire is not being fulfilled in the present. For a discussion of this conundrum, see Schacter, *The Seven Sins of Memory*, 51–4.

The speaker boasts that he no longer needs his "tables" or "tallies" where he has written down his memories of the beloved. He does not need this "adjunct," or aid, to remember his object of desire whose image has been integrated into the speaker's body at the level of the brain and heart. The porous nature of their imagined bodies, where one can frame the other, allows the speaker's body to contain the beloved's body in the form of memory. Though the speaker ends the poem by placing high value on his bodily memory, he admits his potential forgetfulness and notes that the organs retaining the memory cannot subsist forever.

The use of bodily components in Sonnet 24 and Sonnet 122 suggests a way that the logic that underpins the totalizing union of idealized coupling can be deployed to describe the transmission of memory from one body to another. Indeed, this holds true regardless of the fact that we cannot say for certain the gender of the beloved here. The Book of Common Prayer stated that the married couple "shall be of one flesh," and same-sex friends were described in similar terms.[2] Montaigne's essay on friendship describes his connection with Étienne La Boétie in terms common to descriptions of idealized same-sex amity in the early modern period, as we saw in Chapter Three: "minds [...] intermix and confound themselves one in the other, with so universal a commixture, that they wear out, and can no more find the seam that has conjoined them together."[3] Yet these sonnets' use of the model of the ego-dissolving vision of the couple works against many of the promises the speaker makes.[4] On one level, it renders the beloved's presence unnecessary because he has been copied so effectively into the heart and brain of the lover.

On another level, though, it calls into question whether any real intimacy might be achieved between them. Lacan understood desire as stemming from an unacknowledged longing to recover an unobtainable, originary object of desire. In other words, individuals fail to be satisfied by their partner because they find themselves trying to find some missing piece that is, unknowingly, simply a fantasy of what (often the mother's love) was so satisfying to them in early memory. Yet more contemporary psychoanalytic thinkers, such as Stephen Mitchell, help us see a more nuanced understanding of how this might operate agentially because "desire for someone unknown and unobtainable operates as a defense against desire for someone known and obtainable, therefore capable of being lost."[5] We find a version of this in the treatise *Erotomania* (1640), where Jacques Ferrand advises that

---

[2] *Book of Common Prayer 1559*, ed. John Booty (Charlottesville: University of Virginia Press, 1976), 297.

[3] Montaigne, *Essayes*, 92.

[4] In this chapter, I focus on the breakdown of the one-flesh model of coupling as depicted in the *Sonnets*. For a broader and incisive discussion of how the early modern ideal of a couple sharing one body or one soul could result in an emotionally pernicious and physically dangerous economy of scarcity, rather than a site of abundance, see Frances E. Dolan, *Marriage and Violence: The Early Modern Legacy* (Philadelphia: University of Pennsylvania Press, 2009), esp. 26–66.

[5] Mitchell, *Can Love Last?*, 114.

"it is better to fall in love with an image" than an actual person.[6] We might understand these poems to admit the same. The poet articulates a totalizing focus on the addressee to bring them closer, all the while that the poems depict how the speaker avoids physical intimacy with the beloved himself.

What is implied in both Sonnet 24 and 122 is that the sonnet itself is a memory device that will carry forward the record of the beloved's beauty until personal and cultural oblivion. Yet this alone cannot guarantee the "eternity" promised earlier in the poem (122.4). "Because prospective memory so heavily depends on the availability of cues that trigger intended actions," Schacter notes, "the most effective way to counter absent-minded prospective memory failures is to develop and use effective external memory aids."[7] These aids will be the poem itself and the networked memories of future readers. And this creates a problem as it will ultimately attenuate control by dispersing the memories of the beloved. The speaker may position himself as a mirrored double for the addressee by relying on the model of the couple, but the multitude of readers cannot be expected to embody that role.

This flaw is embedded in Sonnet 24's more naive depiction of writing and immortality. The six instances of "eye" or "eyes" function as homonyms for "I," gesturing toward the multiple claims that different subjects might make to knowing—or possessing in memory—the addressee. In Fineman's tracing of the ways in which "I" and "eye" so frequently conflate in the *Sonnets*, he calls our attention to Sonnet 24's shifts from the past to the present tense in the final two lines and argues that "the couplet's 'eyes' persuasively express a *present* lack that, as the poem develops it, supplies the motive of the poem's desire."[8] While he interprets the poem to mean that "the poet's eyes fall short" as he longs for the beloved, I would like to stress the alternative interpretations made possible by a focus on the poem's memorializing impulse. The lack here, as discussed above, may belong to the speaker with the loss of singular subjectivity (dismantling one's own ability to say "I") with the multiplication of those who claim to know the addressee.[9] The poem, intentionally or inadvertently, stresses that the beloved's actual presence is obsolete and his memories are not his own.

---

[6] Jacques Ferrand, *Erotomania, or A Treatise Discoursing of the Essence, Causes, Symptoms, Prognostics, and Care of Love, or Erotique Melancholy*, trans. Edmund Chilmead (Oxford: L. Lichfield, 1640), 44.

[7] Schacter, *The Seven Sins of Memory*, 58.

[8] Fineman, *Shakespeare's Perjured Eye*, 138–9.

[9] As discussed in the Introduction, much of Fineman's argument relies on a strict division between Sonnets 1–124 as addressed to a Young Man and 125–54 as addressed to a Dark Lady. I suggest we resist making gendered assumptions about this poem, which may explain my different focus here and elsewhere even if Fineman and I are both interested in what insights psychoanalysis might bring to bear on the *Sonnets*. Fineman, *Shakespeare's Perjured Eye*, 139.

Imposing Memories

The notion that one can realize immortality in the memories of others is profoundly contingent, then, on those others accurately perceiving the deceased. On a more basic level, this immortality also relies on those others not becoming deceased themselves, at least without passing along the memory to a future generation. And the speaker himself confesses that he also is subject to this latter contingency. Given the poet's own aging and the frequent implication that he is older than the addressed beloved, we also find him pleading for his addressees to remember him. Sonnet 74, for example, returns to the idea that the doubling inherent in the couple form enables memorialization. It is not that the poem will retain the poet's memory but rather that the poem is an aid to remind the beloved to remember him:

> But be contented when that fell arrest
> Without all bail shall carry me away;
> My life hath in this line some interest,
> Which for memorial still with thee shall stay. (1–4)

The dynamics now reverse those of other poems discussed so far in that it is the beloved who will possess the memory of the speaker. The term "line" is multivalent, as it indicates not only the line of verse that will remind the beloved but also the line of connection between speaker and addressee. The term "interest" suggests further that the speaker needs the investment from the beloved so that his memory will be a surplus. That is, the speaker wishes that the textual body can foster memories which will exceed the limits of his own physical body and thereby extend the duration of his life in the psychic spaces of the beloved's mind. However, it is only a wish, an unconfirmable fantasy when the speaker, like Yorick, decays into dust and is left to be revived in others' imaginations. The poem utilizes the terms of doubling to explain how this recollection should naturally occur:

> When thou reviewest this, thou dost review
> The very part was consecrate to thee.
> The earth can have but earth, which is his due;
> My spirit is thine, the better part of me.
> So then thou hast but lost the dregs of life,
> The prey of worms, my body being dead,
> The coward conquest of a wretch's knife,
> Too base of thee to be rememberèd. (5–12)

The speaker's body may die but his spirit will be remembered in the beloved. The twinning of the two is signaled by the analogy that "the earth can have the earth, which is his due" in the same way that "my spirit is thine." We can understand this "spirit" to point to how one person can travel bodiless to the other in the form of his mind or his ghost. We can also go as far as to read "spirit" to mean semen in order to consider how the two individuals may have conjoined in a bodily way in the past which presaged how the mind of one will continue in the other. The absence of a corporeal connection might, then, support Daniel Juan Gil's assertion that the *Sonnets* at times "memorialize a weird, asocial experience whose felt reality is captured in depersonalized and depersonalizing emotions."[10] But another way to read this scene is as something deeply personal and deeply felt, where a form of intimacy celebrated in the *Sonnets* is one not in the present but instead in the future and reliant on prospective memory.

The poem's ending both voices self-reassurance and a request to be remembered. Its end-rhyme, "contains" and "remains," links the psychic remainder to the physical remains:

> The worth of that, is that which it contains,
> And that is this, and this with thee remains. (13–14)

The beloved will need the memory aid of the poem, and the speaker will need the beloved's remembrance. The poem ends on the note of doubling, with "that" repeated three times, "this" repeated twice, and those words tied to the final "thee" through consonance. As declarative as this ending may be, though, the moment when the addressee will fully appreciate the poet is postponed, seemingly indefinitely. In this way, the moment is surprisingly utopian in the sense of how José Esteban Muñoz defines utopia as the "not quite here yet."[11] The as-yet unrealized outcome is a reassuring ideal for the speaker to remember as he grows older. The future is the ultimate object of memory here, a notion that I will more fully explore in the final chapter.

Intimacy and the Problem of Multiple Selves

Recollection, as we have seen in various permutations thus far in the book, functions as a kind of reconstitution. It *re-collects* past experiences into new narrative arrangements or *re-members* past bodies into new or now-lost conditions. In doing so, it works against the notion of a single, homogeneous self.[12] This splitting of

---

[10] Daniel Juan Gil, *Before Intimacy: Asocial Sexuality in Early Modern England* (Minneapolis: University of Minnesota Press, 2006), 135.

[11] José Esteban Muñoz, *Cruising Utopia: The Then and There of Queer Futurity* (New York: NYU Press, 2009), 1.

[12] Memory itself offers the proofpoint for why Barthes calls photography "the impossible science of the unique being." That is, we cannot point to a photo and say, "That is me" or "That is her" because a past self is only one version of the self who preceded or followed it. Roland Barthes, *Camera Lucida: Reflections on Photography*, trans. Richard Howard (New York: Hill and Wang, 1982), 69.

Fig. 5.1. Royal Shakespeare Company: *Hamlet* (Dir. Simon Godwin and Robin Lough, Royal Shakespeare Company, 2016), screenshot from the film.

selves might be said to occur most starkly in death, and I would like to turn briefly to *Hamlet*, where we find the idea powerfully dramatized in the iconic moment when the prince contemplates a skull (Fig. 5.1). The scene at once crystallizes the *memento mori* ("remember that you will die") tradition, but more usefully teases out a variety of ways in which recollection undermines the notion of the single self. The gravedigger tells Hamlet who the skull belonged to, though there is no real evidence that this skull can be discerned from others. The prince decides to believe it embodies the face of that jovial clown, that loving jester Yorick who entertained him in the palace where he grew up. He takes the skull and recalls the beloved court entertainer of his youth:

> Let me see. Alas, poor Yorick! I knew him, Horatio—a fellow of infinite jest, of most excellent fancy. He hath borne me on his back a thousand times; and now, how abhorred in my imagination it is! My gorge rises at it. Here hung those lips that I have kissed I know not how oft. Where be your gibes now, your gambols, your songs, your flashes of merriment that were wont to set the table on a roar? Not one now to mock your own grinning? Quite chop-fallen? (5.1.179–88)

This moment is simultaneously a recreation of a child's playfulness, a dramatization of memory, an occlusion of what was likely a darker childhood, and the promise of more—"infinite"—jocularity that such memories might engender. The truth of the scene is not that Hamlet's world is in fact filled with endless future opportunities for jest. We know—and perhaps he does too—that this Prince of Denmark, like most of the characters, won't live much longer. The skull shows us

Hamlet's memory that he will die, and his knowledge that Yorick's parting fore-shadows his own parting. The truth of the scene is that the promise of Yorick's infinite jest is the promise of memory.

Yet Hamlet finds that memory cannot offer pure solace. Here retrospect shapes the present world and presages a future world. The prince's "imagination" can reju-venate the "lips" on the bone and replay the "songs" of the past for his ears now. Yet those repeated actions, where Hamlet as a child was borne on the clown's back "a thousand times," are now changed, now "abhorred." The joyful activities of the past now seem wretched. Further, the truth of the man Yorick was obscured because the prince saw it only when it was performed in the character of a clown. Hamlet "knew" him but only in his states of "jest" and his "fancy." He knew the clown that Yorick played but not the man behind the performance.

In his speech to and about Yorick, Hamlet activates his "imagination" to con-jure him. But there are now multiple Yoricks: the one in the past (whom the child did not fully know), the endlessly jovial one invoked now in present imagination, the one embodied in the skull (which might not be his), and the one created in each playgoer's imagination. We can add to these the one imagined in the afterlife. The notion that the remembered person is a different one from the actual one is captured in a variety of paintings known for their use of the phrase "et in Arcadia ego" in the title or in a visible inscription. One example is Guercino's 1618 painting which bears the title (Fig. 5.2).

Two shepherds gaze at a skull on a stone plinth with the Latin phrase, which can be translated as "I am also in Arcadia." The phrase might mean that "I," death, am also here in the pastoral paradise full of life. But it can also mean that "I," the person whose skull sits here, am also in the afterlife. That is, the deceased is both in the earthly grave and in blissful heaven. The presence of two shepherds (and such paintings usually depict a group of readers of the inscription) stages the fact that the deceased might live on differently in each of their separate sets of memories.

The prince addresses neither the Yorick of the past nor the present bodily remains but rather the spirit in the afterlife when he says:

> Now get you to my lady's chamber and tell her, let her paint an inch thick, to this favour she must come. Make her laugh at that. (5.1.188–90)

He remembers Ophelia's laughter and Yorick's gibes, gambols, and merriment. He combines them within the imagined space of heaven in a way they never inter-sected in lived experience. The arrival of a group of nobles to bury Ophelia ends the prince's contemplation of mortality and memory. The scene reminds us that memories after death are malleable, not just in the case of Yorick but also in the case of Ophelia, whose suicide is ruled an accident to justify her burial but leaving open the question of where her soul truly resides after death.

Fig. 5.2. Guercino, *Et in Arcadia Ego* (1618), courtesy of the Galleria Nazionale d'Arte Antica.

I find that the example of memorializing Yorick as a decaying skull and the graveyard setting lays bare the more subtle dynamics of the multiplying selves in the *Sonnets*. Death certainly haunts the poems, both in the form of the impending demise to which the speaker constantly returns and in the reminiscences of dead friends or previous literary figures. Moreover, death functioned for early moderns—as it does for many of our own contemporary thinkers—as an analogue for one of the more overt throughlines in the *Sonnets*: erotic connection. Both in death and in romantic coupling, the bodily ego dissolves into a state which Donne so elegantly describes when he uses the phrase "souls unbodied, bodies unclothed must be" to describe he and his mistress going to bed.[13] Early modern poetry frequently depicts *carpe diem* erotics, urging readers to seize pleasure now because we will inevitably age and die. This invokes a future memory of death in the sense that we remember our fate to die. Montaigne expresses how this sense of imminence might affect how one should live when he asserts, "you are in death, during the time

---

[13] John Donne, "Elegy XX: To His Mistress Going to Bed," in *Selected Poetry*, ed. John Carey (Oxford: Oxford University Press, 2009), 23.

you continue in life," going on to say, "you are dead after life: but during life, you are still dying: and death doth more rudely touch the dying than the dead, and more lively and essentially."[14] It is through love that one might achieve such liveliness, even if it too brings one closer to the experience of death. "There is no communication more profound," Georges Bataille claims about being in love, because "two beings are lost in a convulsion that binds them together. But they only communicate when losing a part of themselves."[15] Early modern models of friendship and marriage, as discussed below, involve finding one's double and, in that sense, involve the ego dissolution described by Bataille. And this combination of two selves represents a form of multiplicity because it generates a new self in the form of the couple. In Shakespeare's *Sonnets*, the beloveds must lose themselves in order to achieve the intimacy that ignites the speaker's immortalizing memorialization.

While the self-shattering effects of desire may be widely held concepts now among critical theorists, psychologists, and psychoanalysts, Cynthia Marshall sees a particularly early modern angle on the matter because of "the connection between the psychology of lovesickness and the rhetoric of Petrarchanism" which depicts and amplifies "the way love decenters the subject by involving emotional investment in another person and perhaps identification with the other."[16] She particularly notes "the complex resonance of masochism in Petrarchan ideology" to be at play in such dynamics.[17] The interpolation of memory into the equation yields some evocative lines of inquiry. I explore the masochistic aspect in the discussion of Sonnet 57 and Sonnet 58 below, but first I would like to consider the question of life as a process of slowly dying, as Montaigne conceives, and what complex links it may have to the pleasure that Bataille names. How might the impending loss of both the speaker's and addressee's lives bind them closer while simultaneously separating them? How might aging—typically understood in the *Sonnets* as a driver of decay, loss, and regret—be eroticized? Bodily memory, discussed in the previous chapter and further explored below, offers a consistent touchstone for the speaker exploring these polemics.

The Map of Days Outworn

Desire and death each drive the urgency of the *Sonnets*, and their charged interplay also delineates the limitations of the recuperative capacities of recollection. While the mind offers solace when the speaker or beloved forget about time, the

---

[14] Montaigne, *Essayes*, 37.
[15] Georges Bataille, "The Sacred," in *Visions of Excess: Selected Writings 1927–1939*, trans. Allan Stoekle with Carl R. Lovitt and Donald M. Leslie, Jr. (Minneapolis: University of Minnesota Press, 2004 [1985]), 250.
[16] Marshall, *The Shattering of the Self*, 57.
[17] Marshall, *The Shattering of the Self*, 57.

bodies still age in the poems. Time generates wrinkles in the skin as it "delves the parallels in beauty's brow" (60.10), etching "furrows" (22.3) and "eternal lines to time" (18.12). These multivalent phrases at times can allude to not just time's writing on the body but also lines of poetry or extended family lines that can stretch beyond death. For example, Sonnet 60's "parallels in beauty's brow" can allude to marks on a writing tablet just as much as they may refer to wrinkles from age or temporary creases on the forehead from deep thinking. Consider the depiction of "a drooping man / With anguish printed in his brow" in Abraham Holland's "A Funeral Elegy" (1626) for James I.[18] Here, where mentalization is written on the body, we find an instance of the bodily memory traced in the previous chapter. Holland's description invites us to perceive wrinkles as signs of external aging and internal feelings, and he frames these "printed" as akin to a form of writing.

These "parallels," which we see in various formulations in the *Sonnets*, are not simply signs of a past now behind the speaker and foreclosed. They are also paths or lines reaching into the past made accessible through memory. Speaking not specifically about Shakespeare's poetry but more generally about orientation and identity, Sara Ahmed ties the figure of the "line" on the body to the notion of a "lifeline":

> Lines become the external trace of an interior world, as signs of who we are on the flesh that folds and unfolds before others. What we follow, what we do, becomes "shown" through the lines that gather on our faces, as the accumulation of gestures on the skin surface over time. If we are asked to reproduce what we inherit, then the lines that gather on the skin become signs of the past, as well as orientations toward the future, a way of facing and being faced by Others.[19]

I find Ahmed's meditation on the figure of the line particularly helpful for thinking through Shakespeare's numerous references to line-like impressions in the skin and considering how they tie to memory. These lines, seen in light of Ahmed's discussion, are both signals for how the past has worn down the body and echoes of repeated gestures that the body has made. In the case of lines on the speaker's face, they are thus signs of emotion previously felt and frequently felt. The addressee, in recognizing the presence of those emotions in the speaker's bodily and psychic memory, will achieve a new closeness to the speaker. The poet offers his past as a traceable line which the addressee will eventually follow and which the two might follow together.

---

[18] Abraham Holland, *Hollandi posthuma* (London, 1626), B3r.
[19] Sara Ahmed, *Queer Phenomenology: Orientations, Objects, Others* (Durham: Duke University Press, 2006), 18.

When the speaker uses himself as a reminder to the beloved about aging, he undercuts his own appeal. Consider the complex messaging of at the center of Sonnet 73:

> That time of year thou mayst in me behold
> When yellow leaves, or none, or few, do hang
> Upon those boughs which shake against the cold,
> Bare ruined choirs, where late the sweet birds sang.
> In me thou seest the twilight of such day
> As after sunset fadeth in the west,
> Which by and by black night doth take away,
> Death's second self, that seals up all in rest.
> In me thou seest the glowing of such fire
> That on the ashes of his youth doth lie,
> As the death-bed whereon it must expire,
> Consumed with that which it was nourished by.
> This thou perceiv'st, which makes thy love more strong,
> To love that well, which thou must leave ere long. (1–14)

Line 8 has the aging speaker portray himself as "Death's second self," a phrase which Burrow notes was a conventional way of describing sleep. I would add that the phrase "second self" echoes that oft-repeated formulation of the friend as *another self* (or "alter idem" in the classical formulation) in early modern discourse. Read in this light, the phrase syncs with the pattern of thought in the poem where the speaker is a mirror in which the beloved will see himself eventually (and perhaps currently) aging. The speaker is a tether that connects the beloved to death by functioning as a double for each entity. He is his friend's second self and "Death's second self." He is both a lifeline and a deathline. The speaker, too, functions like a memory. We hear echoes of this idea in *Romeo and Juliet*, when Capulet asserts that "Life, living, all is death's" (4.4.67). The notion also links to Donne's last sermon, where he describes how "we have a winding-sheet [burial shroud] in our mother's womb which grows with us from our conception, and we come into the world wound up in that winding-sheet, for we come to seek a grave."[20] What the beloved has to learn from the speaker is that there is never truly a moment when the beloved lies outside of death's grip.[21]

The speaker's aging is both a cautionary tale for the beloved and a sign of depth of the poet's feeling. Damasio urges us to "trust Shakespeare" when it comes to understanding "that the unified and apparently singular process of affect, which

---

[20] John Donne, "Death's Duel. Preached before Charles I (25 February 1631)," in *The Major Works: Including Songs and Sonnets and Sermons* (Oxford: Oxford University Press, 2009), 410.

[21] Montaigne offers a slightly cheerier assessment of the situation, "the premeditation of death, is a forethinking of liberty. He who has learned to die, has unlearned to serve." Montaigne, *Essayes*, 34.

we often designate casually and indifferently as emotion *or* feeling, can be analyzed in parts."[22] Sonnet 73 offers an excellent example of this. The speaker's outward emotion of concern about aging is signaled by the inventory of his decaying features, described through analogies in nature. But the sonnet turns on the revelation that he meditates now on these outward signs of age because of his concern for the addressee and his desire that his beloved's love will grow. The example that Damasio gives is also from Shakespeare, the moment when Richard II asks Bolingbroke for a mirror to see how the "external manner of laments" are simply "shadows to the unseen grief" (4.1.285–6). In both Sonnet 73 and *Richard II*, the outward shows of emotion can only reveal so much, which is why we need narrative to explain the interiority of consciousness. Damasio makes the distinction that *emotion* is what we show publicly but this can be separate from *feelings*, which are private. The distinction is helpful for exploring the sonnets where the speaker may explain what is seen by the public but attempts to explain what is happening at the level of interiority. In doing so, he bolsters the line of connection between him and his addressee. After all, who better to know the thoughts of another than the friend who is his double?

Sonnet 68 reinforces the idea that the poet understands the beloved's intrinsic feelings and that this understanding comes from wisdom gained through age. Shakespeare calls upon collective memory and personal memory by stating that the beloved's face belongs to a discernible line of beautiful ones in history yet also surpasses those faces' beauty. It opens:

> Thus is his cheek the map of days outworn,
> When beauty lived and died as flowers do now,
> Before these bastard signs of fair were born,
> Or durst inhabit on a living brow[.] (1–4)

The speaker denigrates those "bastard signs" of beauty achieved with what he will call "ornament" and "false art" later in the poem. The addressee's unadorned beauty reveals his intrinsically virtuous nature as someone who avoids deception, just as the speaker's wrinkles elsewhere reveal his inner wisdom. This poem also draws upon the trope of the aging body when it suggests that the beloved's fair cheek is a map or figurative genealogical line leading to the past. The cheek is implied to be "outworn" just like those days are. There is thus a sense that everything being celebrated is something recollected, now past. That is, the presence of wrinkles underscores that there is a face without wrinkles to recall and thereby the rememberer can move along what Sonnet 18 calls "lines to time" in a way that circumvents time's seemingly unavoidable movement forward.

---

[22] Damasio, *Looking for Spinoza*, 27.

Sonnet 68 at once valorizes beauty while at the same time underscoring the inevitability of aging. The poem gives us a sense of how one's view of temporality can constrain one's relationship to time's passing. David Scott Kastan finds that, for Shakespeare, "Time cannot be deposed, but its sway need not be absolute."[23] We can couple Kastan's claim with Ahmed's thinking on the nature of the metaphor of a line, and in turn extrapolate the vexed promise of immortalization in verse. Ahmed notes that "the conventional family home [requires] a certain line, the family line that directs our gaze," and I would observe that this certainly resonates in a reading of this sonnet where the history of beautiful faces is meant to convince the young man to produce an heir to form another face like his.[24] At the same time, it promises that the verse produced by the speaker's love for the addressee might also continue this line of faces in the memories of readers. Neither solution is without peril. The sonnet ends thus:

> In him those holy antique hours are seen,
> Without all ornament, itself and true,
> Making no summer of another's green,
> Robbing no old to dress his beauty new.
> And him as for a map doth Nature store,
> To show false art what beauty was of yore. (9–14)

The notion that the young man will show others that "beauty was of yore" threatens the viability of an heir or of cultural memory to grant him immortality. It suggests that beauty standards have changed, a point which will be made again in Sonnet 127 ("In the old age, black was not counted fair"), and that the current world as well as future readers may not appreciate the beloved for how he or his heir might look.

We can begin to see that many of the sonnets do not uncategorically orientate themselves toward a positive future (e.g., beautiful heirs, timeless verse) nor do they entirely negatively portray those things that might frustrate future progress (e.g., adulterous partners, unrequited love). Narrowly reading the *Sonnets* as desiring such "straight" lines ignores how the poems' expressions are made more complex when viewed through a lens that admits the peculiar operations of desire and memory. Ahmed remarks that "certain objects are available to us because of lines that we have already taken: our 'life courses' follow a certain sequence, which is also a matter of following a direction or of 'being directed' in a certain way (birth, childhood, adolescence, marriage, reproduction, death)."[25] The speaker seems to undermine the appeal of such well-worn lines on occasion. A fall into memory

---

[23] David Scott Kastan, *Shakespeare and the Shapes of Time* (Hanover: University Press of New England, 1982), 165.
[24] Ahmed, *Queer Phenomenology*, 90.
[25] Ahmed, *Queer Phenomenology*, 21.

at times offers an alternative to focusing too much on the future or to assessing life's elements in terms of how they affect that future, suggesting a means to evade the "absolute" of Time's sway, as Kastan describes. Yet recollection, too, has its drawbacks with emphasis on recursivity, belatedness, backward-looking gazes, and stasis.

Night and Day, Day and Night

Thus far, I have traced several ways in which the promise of commemoration breaks down in the *Sonnets*. These failures include the undermining of intimacy, the admission of contingency, and the calling into question of idealized social relations. Before I turn to my closing examples in Sonnets 57 and 58, I would like to consider a bit more the cost of the constant attention needed to sustain the prospective memory upon which this commemoration relies. Prospective memory becomes a burden for the speaker as he works hard not to forget the beloved or becomes preoccupied with anticipating their reunion. Remembering the object of desire, while a testimony to love, threatens to overwhelm the speaker. Sonnet 43 has the friend shining in the night.

> When most I wink, then do mine eyes best see,
> For all the day they view things unrespected,
> But when I sleep, in dreams they look on thee,
> And, darkly bright, are bright in dark directed. (1–4)

The speaker presents a positive binary opposition. The quotidian world of the daytime is filled with base, "unrespected" elements. At night, the speaker can recollect the bright beloved in dreams. It seems to realize the wish expressed in Goldwell's treatise on perfect amity, a wish that "I would have my friend in one respect like a glow-worm: to shine most in the dark."[26] However, actually attaining such a shining object proves not altogether positive. Just as Proust likened memory to "a sort of pharmacy, a sort of chemical laboratory" within which "our groping hand may come to rest now upon a sedative drug, now on a dangerous poison," the memories here offer both. They intermingle a desired deep sleep with an obsession tinged with pernicious effects.[27]

The brightly shining vision of the beloved in the speaker's mind resembles the *phantasma*, "the image of the beloved [that] occupies the entire *via imaginativa*," whose dangerous effects include that "it feeds upon incessant recollection, and it

---

[26] Goldwell, "My Friend," M12r–v.
[27] Marcel Proust, *The Captive & The Fugitive*, Vol. 5 of *In Search of Lost Time* (New York: The Modern Library, 1993), 526.

gathers the vital spirits around it."[28] Lina Bolzoni, in her study of treatises provid-ing remedies for lovers who suffer from overactive recollection of a beloved, finds: "If memory, by nature, plays an essential role in affixing and feeding the amorous *phantasma*, the art of memory proves to be keenly interested in reversing the pro-cess, in using it for its own ends."[29] In the sonnet speaker's incessant efforts to prove his commitment to recalling his beloved, the speaker admits his failures to master the art of memory. His constant need to remind himself proves his ineffectiveness at being able to remember his love. As Bolzoni describes, "if the zones of memory are like a mass of wax on which a seal leaves its imprint, lovesickness transforms them into a hard block in which the *phantasma* of the object is fixed."[30] When we read this sonnet in the context of others that allude to the mind or heart as a wax writing tablet, the beloved's image closely resembles such a dangerous fixation.

Sonnet 43 continues to underscore the doubling of the speaker and beloved as well as the doubling of the speaker and the shadows.

> Then thou, whose shadow shadows doth make bright,
> How would thy shadow's form form happy show
> To the clear day with thy much clearer light,
> When to unseeing eyes thy shade shines so?
> How would (I say) mine eyes be blessèd made
> By looking on thee in the living day,
> When in dead night thy fair imperfect shade
> Through heavy sleep on sightless eyes doth stay?
> All days are nights to see till I see thee,
> And nights bright days when dreams do show thee me. (5–14)

On the one hand, the poem's excessive repetition (e.g., "shadow" and "shadows"; "form" and "form"; "clear" and "clearer") seems to imply parity within pairs and increased power that comes from doubling. However, the poem just as much couples opposites in close proximity to each other (e.g., "shadow" and "bright"; "shade" and "shines"; "fair" and "shade"; "nights" and "bright"). This paradox may point to the inverted memorial dynamics. In other words, memory should allow the speaker to not need to think about the beloved constantly, rather than repet-itively envisioning his image. The poem perverts discourses of friends as doubles as well as guides to each other, as Goldwell describes the true friend: "I would have him to me as I would be to him: when occasion shall make me the orb, then him be the planet [...] that we might follow one another's motion."[31] Yet such par-ity is missing from this depiction of the obsessively dreaming speaker. This is not

[28] Bolzoni, *The Gallery of Memory*, 145.
[29] Bolzoni, *The Gallery of Memory*, 146.
[30] Bolzoni, *The Gallery of Memory*, 145.
[31] Goldwell, *The True Choice of a Friend*, M13v.

friends as glowworms or orbs serving as guiding lights to each other. This is one friend occluding all other thinking and dulling other elements in the world.

Because the poem does not simply describe a metaphorical shadow but instead the actual darkness, Paul Innes observes that the terminology of Sonnet 43 "confuses the bodily subject with the shadows of the night," and this observation further emphasizes the baselessness of the nighttime image of the beloved.[32] The actual body—that material reality that suggests a single, bounded self—is absent. What is left is the imagined body, the double, the fantasy. In this sonnet and arguably across many other sonnets examined in this volume, we see little evidence of balance or equity between the speaker and addressee.

The speaker's incessant desire to write about the friend, even as he is haunted by his beloved at night, reflects the polemic nature of his desire to remember. On the one hand, the poet's alertness may seem to signal his becoming more adept in the art of memory. Garrett A. Sullivan has traced the connections between lethargy and forgetfulness in early modern treatises on bodily health, finding that memory "is intimately linked with notions of discipline and order; forgetfulness, associated as it is with practices and physiological processes antithetical to ideals of bodily comportment, connotes idleness, sloth, lethargy, and excessive sleep."[33] The speaker's persistent thinking here makes it difficult to discern how we should interpret his sleep. Here, the "heavy sleep" is described as involving effective recollection, but the state of drowsiness that induces such intense slumber indicates otherwise, and of course these are dreams, not the active work based in the memory arts.

Trapping the beloved's essence in dreams, much as it is trapped in a perfume bottle in Sonnets 5 and 6 or in a frame or shop in Sonnet 24, might work against the speaker's desire to seem appealing to the addressee. While some enclosed spaces can heighten erotic excitement, Jane Kingsley-Smith finds that "the Sonnets' claustrophilia appears less erotic and more lonely."[34] This helps us see the difficulty of navigating the positive notion of loving an image rather than a person—a less risky endeavor as characterized by contemporary psychoanalyst Stephen Mitchell and sixteenth-century physician Jacques Ferrand, as described above. Both triangulate well with Kingsley-Smith's argument that "Shakespeare's speaker yearns to enclose the beloved, but also to feel limits around himself, to reinforce a subjectivity that is constantly threatened by desire."[35] Yet the speaker must also remain vigilant of the threat of the *phantasma* described above.

---

[32] Innes, *Shakespeare and the English Renaissance Sonnet*, 165.

[33] Garrett J. Sullivan, "Lethargic Corporeality On and Off the Early Modern Stage," in *Forgetting in Early Modern English Literature and Culture: Lethe's Legacies*, ed. Christopher Ivic and Grant Williams (London and New York: Routledge, 2004), 41–58, 52.

[34] Kingsley-Smith, "Shakespeare's Sonnets and the Claustrophobic Reader," 189.

[35] Kingsley-Smith, "Shakespeare's Sonnets and the Claustrophobic Reader," 189.

In Sonnet 27, the speaker similarly encounters the object of desire shining in the night. Here, though, the speaker is even more overt about the cost of that encounter:

> Weary with toil, I haste me to bed,
> The dear repose for limbs with travail tirèd
> But then begins a journey in my head
> To work my mind, when body's work's expirèd.
> For then my thoughts (from far, where I abide)
> Intend a zealous pilgrimage to thee,
> And keep my drooping eyelids open wide,
> Looking on darkness which the blind do see;
> Save that my soul's imaginary sight
> Presents thy shadow to my sightless view,
> Which, like a jewel (hung in ghastly night)
> Makes black Night beauteous, and her old face new.
> Lo, thus, by day my limbs, by night my mind,
> For thee, and for myself, no quiet find. (1–14)

This sonnet characterizes the speaker as enjoying a closeness with the addressee by way of his "journey" and "pilgrimage," but this union is only psychic. Like Sonnet 43, this poem has the lover thinking incessantly about the beloved, remembering him and remembering how he loves him. By constructing a parallel between the daily "work" that makes him weary and the nightly "work" of his mind, the poet reveals that this form of sleep is as tiring for his mind as the daytime toil is for his limbs. José Esteban Muñoz finds the central conflict in this sonnet to be that "The lover wonders whether the beloved seen in dreams is rendered more present or more absent."[36] Muñoz does not resolve this question. I believe we can find the speaker wondering this in both Sonnet 27 and Sonnet 43. And, in light of Kingsley-Smith's commentary above, we ourselves might wonder if the speaker is more or less lonely because he has this image of the beloved to keep him company in bed. A pattern seems to emerge across the sonnets in this chapter where the speaker realizes less and less parity with the addressee, particularly in terms of who spends their energy remembering whom.

Waiting as Service, as Pleasure, and as Memory

For my final case study in this chapter, I would like to consider how Sonnet 57 and Sonnet 58 function as a diptych with their shared references to the speaker as enslaved. In examples thus far, we have seen how the speaker argues that he and

---

[36] José Esteban Muñoz, "The Sense of Watching Tony Sleep," in *After Sex? On Writing since Queer Theory*, ed. Janet E. Halley and Andrew Parker (Durham: Duke University Press, 2011), 142–50, 145.

his beloved can carry memories of each other especially because of the way they function as doubles of each other. With sometimes dubious levels of effectiveness, the speaker activates retrospective memory to combat the loneliness identified by Kingsley-Smith, or he activates prospective memory to remind himself that he will reunite with the beloved, who he commits to make unforgettable. In Sonnets 57 and 58, the operations of memory conjoin with the fantasy of bodily doubling in yet another way.

With the example of Quentin's watch from *The Sound and the Fury*, we found two relationships that an individual might have to time: watching the clock with regret or forgetting about time's passing. These two sonnets position clock watching as a form of pleasurable submission, especially when it allows the beloved to not need to watch the clock. Counter-intuitively, the speaker stresses the difference between him and his beloved, who he encourages to be absent, in order to build intimacy between them:

> Being your slave what should I do but tend
> Upon the hours, and times of your desire?
> I have no precious time at all to spend,
> Nor services to do, till you require.
> Nor dare I chide the world-without-end hour
> Whilst I (my sovereign) watch the clock for you,
> Nor think the bitterness of absence sour
> When you have bid your servant once adieu.
> Nor dare I question with my jealous thought
> Where you may be, or your affairs suppose,
> But like a sad slave stay and think of nought,
> Save where you are how happy you make those.
> So true a fool is love, that in your will,
> Though you do anything, he thinks no ill. (57.1–14)

Although the speaker elsewhere engages in the self-abnegation characteristic of the Petrarchan tradition, here he stresses even more the difference in status between him and his addressee. The beloved's time is more valuable than that of the speaker, as the latter will "tend" upon the "hours" and "times" of the beloved's "desire." As it does today, "tend" can mean "to wait upon as attendant or servant; to attend on; to escort, follow, or accompany for the purpose of rendering service or giving assistance" and this fits nicely with the metaphor of enslavement being used in the poem. "Tend" here may also carry the now-obsolete meaning of "to turn one's ear, give auditory attention, listen, hearken."[37] With this latter connotation, we find the speaker both waiting to hear if the beloved commands him while also being aware

---

[37] "Tend, v.1b." OED online.

of the beloved's "desire." That is, he pays attention to how the addressee is finding his needs met during their separation. Another meaning of "tend" is "to have the care and oversight of; to take charge of, look after."[38] When we take special note of the fact that it is the "hours" and "times" that the speaker will be tending, we find how the individuals' relationship complicates that binary distinction showcased by Faulkner: the lover will pay attention to the clock so that the speaker does not have to.

The speaker will "watch the clock for you" and will do so with pleasure as he will not "think the bitterness of absence sour" (57.6–7). The sonnet offers a type of performance of the speaker's devotion as it fantasizes a level of intimacy generated through the speaker's experience of waiting. We might think here of that famous last line of John Milton's Sonnet 16, "They also serve who only stand and wait," which pinpoints how inaction can be an active expression of servitude to a superior.[39] In the case of Shakespeare's clock-watching lover, it is an expression of how "the masochist receives pleasure from the material symbols of submission while continually producing desire for the impossible—absolute submission."[40] The speaker cannot simply state his submission to the addressee. He needs the material object of the clock to show his attentiveness, and he needs to produce the written sonnet as proofpoint that his thoughts dwell on his master figure so much as to produce this regularized, rhythmic evidence. The sonnet itself represents the mental work that the poet must do to occupy himself during the time of waiting. We might also consider this pair of sonnets within the context of the other sonnets where the speaker does imagine some form of meeting with the addressee. Consider how "someone who is in love and who is going to see the object of their desire in a week, or in a month, is able to wait because they have learnt to find pleasure in psychic work and fantasy scenarios that they create of the forthcoming encounter."[41] Yet memory short-circuits this formula as it obviates the need for the object to be present and redirects the craving not toward future fulfillment but toward the resuscitation of past fulfillment.

In both sonnets, the poet experiments with the relationship model of a master and an enslaved person to describe his devotion, yet for all the ways that the friend relation might involve such unconditional commitments, this alternative relation perverts the terms of equity that such a form celebrates and emphasizes the elements of utility that this social form is meant to reject.[42] The function of

---

[38] "Tend, v.2a." OED online.

[39] John Milton, "Sonnet 16 (When I consider how my light is spent)," in John Milton, *John Milton: The Major Works*, ed. Jonathan Goldberg and Stephen Orgel (Oxford: Oxford University Press, 2008), 81.

[40] Amber Musser, "Masochism: A Queer Subjectivity?," *Rhizomes* 11/12 (Fall 2005/Spring 2006): para 3.

[41] Aisenstein and Moss, "Desire and its Discontents," 66.

[42] Aristotle, in his *Nichomachean Ethics* upon which many early modern treatises relied, outlined three types of friendship based on their desired "ends" and framed only the third type as matching the

one friend to take the place of the other was indeed built into the early modern understanding of idealized amity. In his 1612 essay "Of Friendship," Francis Bacon articulates one of the classical period's most repeated formulations of perfect friendship, writing that "it was a sparing speech of the ancients, to say, that a friend is another himself."[43] He goes on to say:

> the manifold use of friendship [...] is to cast and see how many things there are, which a man cannot do himself; and then it will appear, that for that a friend is far more than himself. [...] So that a man hath, as it were, two lives in his desires. A man hath a body, and that body is confined to a place; but where friendship is, all offices of life are as it were granted to him, and his deputy. For he may exercise them by his friend.[44]

Bacon imagines that one's friend can function as an extension of oneself and thereby offer both some utility (as a proxy, perhaps) and (more surprisingly) as a means to double one's pleasure. To experience "two lives in his desires" suggests that a man with a friend gains access to forms of excessive pleasure unavailable to the friendless man. In that early modern calculus where a pair of friends shared a single soul across two bodies, the relation based in amity challenges our notions of the singular subject. However, Sonnet 57 takes the proxy relation that Bacon suggests is possible and extrapolates to an extreme end where one friend doubles the fulfillment of his desires because he is freed by the clock watching done by the other man.[45]

The masochistic performance of waiting uses memory to make the waiting bearable. The poet thinks only of the beloved, simultaneously encouraging him to forget about the time so that he can enjoy himself while also asking him to remember that his devotee is there waiting for him. Just as Gilles Deleuze describes the masochist who "experiences waiting in its pure form" because he "waits for pleasure as something that is bound to be late," Shakespeare's speaker seemingly awaits delayed pleasure either in news of the speaker's pleasure or in reunion with him.[46] However, neither Sonnet 57 nor Sonnet 58 gives us a vision of what will happen after the speaker's suffering. There is only promise of further clock watching as he resigns, "I am to wait," at the end of Sonnet 58. We can thus see this pair of sonnets longing for a line of connection while also troubling the notion of that line

---

ideal: those for pleasure, those for utility, and those for the joint pursuit of the good. Despite his claims of friendship with the addressee, Shakespeare's speaker seems to many times only focus on a friendship of pleasure and/or utility. Aristotle, *Nicomachean Ethics*, Book VIII, 1159 b2–3.

[43] Bacon, *Major Works*, 395.

[44] Bacon, *Major Works*, 395.

[45] Even Bacon reiterates the idea in his *Essays*, saying "It is friendship, when a man can say to himself, I love this man without respect for utility." Bacon, *Major Works*, 301.

[46] Gilles Deleuze, "Coldness and Cruelty," trans. Jean McNeil, in *Masochism: Coldness and Cruelty & Venus in Furs* (New York: Zone Books, 1991), 71.

charting a straight course. Karmen MacKendrick argues that masochistic pleasure is characterized by "delay," which "opposes both the productive and the teleological."[47] Seen through the lens of Deleuze's and MacKendrick's shared concepts of masochistic delay, the sonnets depict the speaker's intentional waiting to interrupt the possibility of *straight* time. This interruption occurs not because the relationship depicted necessarily lies outside heterosexual experience but because it postpones, possibly indefinitely, a desirable end of coupling. Quite to the contrary, the speaker's clock watching enables the liberated partner's infidelity, denying the possibility of "jealous thought" (57.9) over his "affairs" (57.10).[48] The speaker encourages the addressee to enjoy his "liberty" (58.6) to pursue "what you will" (58.11), with all the sexual connotations of that term "will" as sexual desire or sexual organ. The opposition he sets up between "what you will" and "I am to wait, though waiting so be hell," an opposition accentuated by the consonance in the repeated initial "w-" sound and terminating "-ll," underscores that the beloved's liberal pleasure is made possible by the speaker's self-imposed bondage.

These two sonnets, especially with their masochistic underpinnings, leave open the question of how much pleasure and how much suffering is entailed in the speaker's experience. Bruce Smith observes that "Shakespeare's sonnets, taken as a whole, are rather longer on the pains than the pleasures."[49] Yet the terms of masochism listed above help us see that these two categories are difficult to disaggregate. The speaker welcomes the humiliation of the denial of his own liberty. Wayne Koestenbaum nicely encapsulates a pattern that we have seen in many of Shakespeare's poems highlighted in this book:

> In a sonnet, the ratio of humiliation to uplift is 8:6. Eight lines of humiliation (*I'm a social outcast*); then the sonnet undergoes a turn, and the last six lines are uplift, change of heart (*I'm no longer depressed; I see tomorrow's potential glory*).[50]

Sonnets 57 and 58 break from this pattern in interesting ways. They portray the speaker constantly thinking of the beloved, rather than such thought serving to alleviate pain toward the end of the poem. "Tomorrow's potential glory," as Koestenbaum puts it, is endlessly postponed in both sonnets. The speaker thinks only of the present and, in fact, posits such constant thinking about time as what he can offer his beloved. Koestenbaum helps us see the pleasure inherent in this, even if the speaker denies the possibility of future reunion. He suggests

---

[47] Karmen MacKendrick, *Counterpleasures* (New York: State University of New York Press, 1999), 111.

[48] Burrow notes that "affairs" was "more likely to have suggested 'business matters' than 'love affairs' to a contemporary reader, but the context pushes it towards amours." Burrow, *The Complete Sonnets and Poems*, 494.

[49] Smith, "Shakespeare's Sonnets and the History of Sexuality," 7.

[50] He cites Sonnet 29 as paradigmatic of such a formula. Wayne Koestenbaum, *Humiliation* (New York: Picador, 2011), 43.

that "humiliation involves a triangle: (1) the victim, (2) the abuser, and (3) the witness." This is because "the humiliated person may also behold her own degradation or may imagine someone else, in the future, watching it or hearing about it. The scene's horror—its energy, its electricity—invokes the presence of three."[51] The poet memorializes his suffering for the beloved and for the reader, both of whom he may only encounter through the transmission of the textual depiction.

These sonnets show us how there is a pleasure in waiting, in watching the time, and in allowing oneself to be subject to time's mastery. This waiting links to the self-abnegation that characterizes the genre of the sonnet. It combines both identitarian concerns—the speaker's low self-worth in the face of the beloved—and action—the performance of waiting as testimony to the speaker's love. The pleasure for the masochist is often characterized as embedded in the delay of pleasure, and this might be true of all desire. As Aisenstein puts it, "the structure of desire is masochistic in essence, for it is inconceivable without the renunciation of immediate satisfaction and the cathexis of waiting."[52] Yet here the speaker receives pleasure from the knowledge of the beloved's pleasure and in his hopes that the suffering, framed within the terms of human slavery, will remind the beloved of his enduring love.

It might not seem surprising that Shakespeare draws upon the terms of slavery, given the prevalence of human enslavement within the larger economic and cultural discourses of the early modern period.[53] As Melissa Sanchez observes, "Shakespeare's Sonnets 57 and 58 cannot be separated from a long history of bondage whose racial referent was rapidly constricting in his time."[54] She goes on to trace how the racialized valences in the poems' central analogy of slavery are problematic in terms of the relational ideal the poems seek to achieve. Sanchez finds that, by taking enslavement as their central analogy, these sonnets "rigorously contest an ideal of homonormative friendship as a uniquely virtuous and respectable relation between a male pair 'by nature free' of irrational and self-destructive appetite."[55] The speaker's constant remembering of the addressee, who

[51] Koestenbaum, *Humiliation*, 43.

[52] Marilia Aisenstein, "Thinking as an Act of the Flesh," in *An Analytic Journey: From the Art of Archery to the Art of Psychoanalysis* (London: Routledge, 2017), 189.

[53] On the resonances of metaphors of enslavement for early modern audiences, see Patricia Akhimie, *Shakespeare and the Cultivation of Difference: Race and Conduct in the Early Modern World* (New York: Routledge, 2018), especially 83–116 where such discourses enable a new reading of Shakespeare's *The Comedy of Errors*. An excellent resource that traces the expansive interests in enslavement in the early modern imagination and economic reality is Feisal G. Mohamed, "On Race and Historicism: A Polemic in Three Turns," *English Literary History* 89, no. 2 (Summer 2022): 377–405. The essay models how attention to such historical contexts helps us see the charged nature of John Milton's *Samson Agonistes*. See also Fred Moten, "The Dark Lady and the Sexual Cut: Sonnet Record Frame / Shakespeare Jones Eisenstein," *Women and Performance: A Journal of Feminist Theory* 9, no. 2 (1997): 143–61.

[54] Melissa E. Sanchez, *Queer Faith: Reading Promiscuity and Race in the Secular Love Tradition* (New York: New York University Press, 2019), 84.

[55] Sanchez, *Queer Faith*, 85.

is encouraged to forget him and to forget the passing of time, undergirds the dynamics that Sanchez nicely pinpoints here.

When we pay attention to the role of delay and waiting in the speaker's portrayal, we can identify even further tension in these poems as they ignore differences of privilege.[56] On the one hand, we might argue that an awareness of privilege is crucial to the poems' argument. The poet relies on the formula that his beloved can be free to enjoy his "pleasure" (58.2) and "leisure" (58.4), and he knowingly depicts this as a performance of romantic devotion in the poem. Barthes writes, "There is a scenography of waiting: I organize it, manipulate it, cut out a portion of time in which I shall mime the loss of the loved object and provoke all the effects of minor mourning. This is then acted out as a play."[57] In light of this characterization, we could choose to see Sonnets 57 and 58 as dramatizations of the speaker's love as he casts himself as someone waiting and watching the clock. However, the performative elements of the role-play in Shakespeare's scene overlook the lived experience of suffering by reducing enslavement to metaphor. Commenting on our own contemporary cultural dynamics, Sandra Ruiz recognizes these same performative dynamics of waiting but renders visible the racialized charge of that experience. She writes, "Brownness is accessed through a shared sense of endurance experienced within various scenographies of waiting. Brownness-as-waiting transpires within the senses, informed by moments that feel longer than the actual time elapsed."[58] Shakespeare stages this "scenography of waiting," a phrase Ruiz adopts from Barthes, but it is only the poet scripting the scene and imagining that it is at the command of a master.

Shakespeare seemingly ignores not only the ways in which the relationship between a master and enslaved person calls into question the virtue and parity of his relationship to his friend. He also ignores the power differential when the enslaved person, whether literally enslaved as property or enslaved by a racist system, is forced to watch the clock. Ruiz argues that we need to understand that "waiting" is "not a neutral act: it is a political existence for a Brown subject whose intersubjective encounters are framed by states of perceived incompletion."[59] By co-opting the terms of how the enslaved person is forced to wait, Shakespeare nonetheless signals his own liberty because his imagined scenario is divorced from the actual terms by which a human can be sold to another.

---

[56] Aisenstein and Moss remark, "The work of desire demands that the object, before being found, be kept in mind. Such work insists on delay." Aisenstein and Moss, "Desire and its Discontents," 71.

[57] Barthes locates waiting at the center of erotic experience: "Am I in love?—yes, since I am waiting. The other one never waits." He is victim to his own desire: "The lover's fatal identity is precisely this: I am the one who waits." Sanchez also makes the connection to this section from *A Lover's Discourse* in the context of her discussion of Sonnets 57 and 58. She finds that, although we find Barthes and Shakespeare in states of suspension as they await their beloved, "waiting may threaten the very love it should demonstrate." Barthes, *A Lover's Discourse: Fragments*, 40; and Sanchez, *Queer Faith*, 88.

[58] Sandra Ruiz, "Waiting in the Seat of Sensation: The Brown Existentialism of Ryan Rivera," *Women & Performance: A Journal of Feminist Theory* 25, no. 3 (2015): 336.

[59] Ruiz, "Waiting in the Seat of Sensation," 336.

Sonnet 58 opens by reiterating that the speaker is enslaved to the beloved before introducing a wider vocabulary to describe their uneven relationship:

> That god forbid, that made me first your slave,
> I should in thought control your times of pleasure,
> Or at your hand th' account of hours to crave,
> Being your vassal bound to stay your leisure.
> O let me suffer (being at your beck)
> Th' imprisoned absence of your liberty,
> And, patience-tame to sufferance, bide each check
> Without accusing you of injury. (1–8)

Shakespeare invokes terms both racially and economically charged in this sonnet. He shifts from declaring himself "slave" to becoming a "vassal," as he will "suffer" states associated with tropes of being "bound" and "imprisoned." Despite his passionate claims otherwise, his status as not actually being legally bound by such terms call into question his devotion. The poem ends thus:

> Be where you list, your charter is so strong
> That you yourself may privilege your time
> To what you will: to you it doth belong
> Yourself to pardon of self-doing crime.
> I am to wait, though waiting so be hell,
> Not blame your pleasure be it ill or well. (9–14)

This second poem pivots away from the poet's suffering, though it does emphasize his status as the one who waits. This focus instead is on giving the addressee permission to forgive himself despite his vices, reiterating a dynamic one can find in Sonnet 35. Late in his exploration of masochism, Freud began to see a difference between "erotogenic masochism," a sexualized "pleasure in pain," and "moral masochism," characterized by "having loosened its connection with what we recognize as sexuality" and instead focusing on unconscious guilt.[60] In light of the way the depiction of enslaved clock watching ultimately results in the beloved being pardoned, we might interpret the suffering in Sonnets 57 and 58 to depict the speaker accepting torment in the place of the addressee's suffering. The speaker not only urges the beloved to engage in self-forgiveness but also expresses his willingness to accept punishment by proxy.[61]

---

[60] Sigmund Freud, "The Economic Problem of Masochism," in Sigmund Freud, *The Standard Edition of the Complete Psychological Works of Sigmund Freud*, Vol. 19, trans. James Strachey (London: The Hogarth Press, [1924] 1961), 159–70, 162 and 165.

[61] Elizabeth Freeman asserts that "the body in sadomasochistic ritual becomes a means of invoking history—personal pasts, collective suffering, and quotidian forms of injustice—in an idiom of pleasure." Shakespeare's speaker embraces the role as part of his performance of his dedication. Freeman, *Time Binds*, 137.

Taken together, Sonnets 57 and 58 show us the suffering which can be intrinsic to obsessive attention to another person's pleasure. Within these poems, the speaker's subjugation to the desires and identity of the beloved takes on much more ego-dissolving qualities than are implied in the idealized couple forms to which he claims to aspire. His offer to "watch the clock for you" (57.6) recalls the positive quality of the father's wish for his son in Faulkner's novel to "forget [time] now and then for a moment and not spend all your breath trying to conquer it." However, it grants the beloved liberty to pursue other partners and denies the speaker even his right to jealousy. The speaker's time and identity, in essence, is overwhelmed by the beloved's time and identity. While Hamlet may claim that "There is nothing either good or bad, but thinking makes it so," it would begin to seem that no amount of positive thinking about the speaker's self-narrative about this formulation—or about others surveyed in this chapter—can lead him to remember these as the best of times (2.2.252).

6

Remembering, Repeating, and Writing Through

Inevitably, when I teach a cluster of the poems from Shakespeare's *Sonnets*, a student remarks that they are repetitive. The comment is not necessarily a negative one, but it does point to a peculiarity about the poems when we consider them as a collection. Even just in the selection I have surveyed thus far in the previous chapters, the poet seems to repeat the same message or to use the same figurations again and again. If we imagine groupings of the *Sonnets* as pleas to a particular addressee (and we don't need to think of them this way), they begin to feel like unacknowledged communication. The so-called procreation sonnets, for example, often strike my students as the most repetitive and the students are quick to interpret Sonnets 1–17 as a reflection of obsessive fantasizing on the part of the speaker. Then if we look at poems which are internally reiterative (perhaps most famously Sonnet 135 in which "will" appears thirteen times), there might be a tendency here also to see evidence of a compulsion to repeat.

To say that something is *repetitive* often carries negative connotations, but it does not need to. One might think of repeated phrases and sentiments as often losing their power in successive iterations and subsequently becoming dull in their capacity to excite. In the case of one sonnet that very strongly echoes another, a reader might be compelled to compare them, to ask which is the better version. Repetition has practical implications, of course, especially in the early modern period. In the context of the schoolroom, it was useful for an individual attempting to memorize a text as well as for learning how to translate a text. For example, Roger Ascham, who served as Elizabeth I's tutor in Greek and Latin, devised a model method for language learning which involved "the double translation of a model book." In his treatise on education entitled *The Scholemaster* (1570), Ascham described his own successful experience using the method:

> I had once a proof hereof, tried by good experience, by a dear friend of mine[.] A young gentleman was my bedfellow who, willing by good nature and provoked by my advice, began to learn the Latin tongue, after the order declared in this book. We began after Christmas: I read unto him [...] *de Amicitia*, which he did

The Pleasures of Memory in Shakespeare's Sonnets. John S. Garrison, Oxford University Press. © John S. Garrison (2023). DOI: 10.1093/oso/9780198857716.003.0007

every day twice translate out of Latin into English, and out of English into Latin again.[1]

This scene of two men in bed together, repeating phrases back and forth to learn the "Latin tongue," emphasizes that repetition can be a means to building intimacy. Indeed, it is not a coincidence, I think, that they repeat back to each other snippets from Cicero's treatise on perfect friendship.

In the *Sonnets*, reading and writing cannot not be disaggregated from the intimacies they describe or generated between speakers, addressees, and readers. We find a flashpoint for this in the final couplet of Sonnet 15:

> And, all in war with Time for love of you,
> As he takes from you, I engraft you new. (13–14)

The speaker fights on behalf of his beloved, taking his place on the battlefield against Time, and compensating for casualties by replicating in his writing whatever is lost. The caesura in the last line evenly divides the syllables, reassuring the reader that whatever is lost can be found here again. The ongoing resuscitation of Shakespeare's poetry across generations, too, can be linked to pleasurable repetition. It is not just that the successive printing of the *Sonnets* for willing readers led to the canonization of a national poet. Brian Boyd has argued that the popularity of Shakespeare's poems lies, in part, to the ways that their lyrical language and layers of meaning set off pleasure centers in the brain in a way that other poems do not.[2]

Early modern discussions of rhetoric stress the propensity of repetition to produce pleasure. Henry Peacham's *The Garden of Eloquence* (1577), for example, describes how "this figure is very pleasant, for that it doth as it were, strike a double stroke."[3] Ben Jonson advises to "repeat often what we have formerly written; which [...] quickens the heat of imagination, that often cools in the time of setting down, and gives it new strength, as if it grew lustier by the going back."[4] And we find another variation in John Hoskins's *Directions for Speech and Style* (1600), which underscores repetition's ability to stimulate toward a desired end: "Climax

---

[1] Roger Ascham, *The Scholemaster* (London: John Daye, 1570), Kiiij r–v. For a wonderful contemporary depiction of how memorizing one of Shakespeare's sonnets can build familial intimacy, see Barbara Johnson, "Speech Therapy," in *Shakesqueer: A Queer Companion to Shakespeare's Works*, ed. Madhavi Menon (Durham: Duke University Press, 2001), 328–32.

[2] Boyd argues that the human brain's chemical reaction to repetition and difference in Shakespeare's *Sonnets* is key to their popularity. See Brian Boyd, *Why Lyrics Last: Evolution, Cognition, and Shakespeare's Sonnets*, esp. 1–23.

[3] Henry Peacham, *The Garden of Eloquence (1593)*, ed. William Crane (Gainesville: Scholars' Facsimiles and Reprints, 1954), 47.

[4] Ben Jonson, "*De stilo et optimo scribendi genere*," in *The Cambridge Edition of the Works of Ben Jonson*, vol. 7, ed. David Bevington, Martin Butler, and Ian Donaldson (Cambridge: Cambridge University Press, 2012), 556, 556–8.

is a kind of anadiplosis [repetition] leading by degrees."[5] It is not hard, as it were, to see the erotic resonances of this pleasurable stroking that grows ever lustier until it leads to climax.[6] Although the *Oxford English Dictionary* states that "climax" did not have the connotations of sexual orgasm until the nineteenth century, the early modern understanding of the word does thrive on the same operations through which erotic activity makes use of repetition. As early as 1572, "climax" referred to "a rhetorical device consisting of a series of related ideas or statements arranged in order of increasing force, intensity, or effectiveness."[7] Such a description may well describe rhetorical strategy but it surely describes the ways in which stimulation of increasing force and intensity (in the context of either solitary fantasy or interpersonal encounter) can effectively help a person reach peak levels of satisfaction.

Repetition, as this chapter argues, has a variety of ties to memory in the *Sonnets*. And repetition also has an erotic quality. Outside the experience of obsession, the operations of pleasurable memory rely on repeated behavior, ritual, or attention, all of which have a complex relation to whom and how a subject desires. We might think of repetition as one of the operations by which memory becomes eroticized or romanticized. Indeed, one might argue that memory operates as repetition and perhaps so too does love. Leo Bersani remarks, "Love is perhaps always [...] a phenomenon of memory."[8] Shakespeare follows these rhetoricians in activating repetition's capacity to heighten excitement about what is to come, even if he ultimately describes his experiences of love and desire as aftereffects of recollection.

Returning to the Freudian Body

Consider, for a moment, what Freud terms the "repetition compulsion." When he first introduces the phrase, he does so in order to explain repetition as a dramatization of repression: "the patient does not *remember* anything of what he has forgotten and repressed, he *acts* it out, without, of course, knowing that he is repeating it."[9] In this early formulation, repetition constitutes a barrier to pleasure

---

[5] John Hoskins, *Directions for Speech and Style*, ed. Hoyt Hudson (Princeton: Princeton University Press, 1935), 12.

[6] Though he does not address the sexual connotations of the pairing, William Walker has convincingly traced how classical and early modern rhetoricians linked *anadiplosis* (repetition) closely with *gradatio* (climax). William Walker, "Anadiplosis in Shakespearean Drama," *Rhetorica: A Journal of the History of Rhetoric* 35, no. 4 (Autumn 2017): 399–424.

[7] "climax n.1a," OED online.

[8] Leo Bersani, "Conclusion," in Leo Bersani and Adam Phillips, *Intimacies* (Chicago and London: University of Chicago Press, 2010), 125.

[9] Sigmund Freud, "Remembering, Repeating and Working-Through" (1914a), in *The Standard Edition of the Complete Psychological Works of Sigmund Freud*, vol. 12, edited by James Strachey (London: Hogarth Press, 1950), 150.

because the subject continually returns to an approach that has led to unpleasant failure in the past.[10] The notion that repetition could lead to pleasure emerges when Freud extrapolates on his earlier thinking six years later in *Beyond the Pleasure Principle* (1920). He observes the juvenile thrill of Fort-Da, a game where a very young boy cries "fort" ["gone"] as he throws a toy out of sight, and then reels it back and cries "da" ["there"]. Freud finds of the child, "At the outset he was in a *passive* situation [...] but by repeating it, unpleasurable though it was, as a game, he took on an *active* part."[11] Freud saw this game as a way for the child to build skills in the ability to manage the experience of loss, especially of the mother who has left the room. Lacan, however, suggests that Freud reads too much into the game, arguing that the child takes pleasure simply from the repetition of the terms themselves.[12] I would argue that we see Shakespeare engaging in retention toward both ends in his poems.

We might ask the same question about the speaker composing the *Sonnets* that Freud does of the child inventing Fort-Da: "How then does his repetition of this distressing experience as a game fit in with the pleasure principle?"[13] If my students wonder why Shakespeare repeats himself in his poems—why he seemingly forgets that he already used the same formulations—we might answer that he has turned loss into a pleasurable game through which he can guarantee the return of his desired object—even just in memory or at the level of writing.[14] That line quoted above, "As he takes from you, I engraft you new," mirrors the dynamics of Fort-Da both in its promise to recover lost objects and in the playful, singsong quality of its internal rhyme linking its two halves. Freud's thinking leads Bersani to assert that "repetition may be inherent in the logic of sexuality itself."[15] Such a claim finds evidence in the *Sonnets*. Shakespeare can be seen to be *working through* the conflict between the promise of reciprocated love and the threat of unfulfilled desire by *writing through* repeated permutations for how he might resolve that conflict.

---

[10] Freud writes that the subject "is obliged to *repeat* the repressed material as a contemporary experience instead of [...] *remembering* it as something belonging to the past [...] the compulsion to repeat the events of his childhood in the transference evidently disregards the pleasure principle in *every* way." Freud, "Remembering, Repeating and Working-Through," 153.

[11] Sigmund Freud, *Beyond the Pleasure Principle*, in *On Metapsychology* (Middlesex: Penguin Books, 1987), 285.

[12] For an incisive discussion of how Freud and Lacan differentially interpret the game, and the broader connections between preposition and pleasure, see Gertrudis Van de Vijver, Ariane Bazan, and Sandrine Detandt, "The Mark, the Thing, and the Object: On What Commands Repetition in Freud and Lacan," *Frontiers in Psychology* 8 (December 2017): 1–10.

[13] Freud, *Beyond the Pleasure Principle*, 285.

[14] For an intriguing discussion of how Freud's observation of the Fort-Da game helps us see the connection between repetition and pleasure, see Bruce Reis, *Creative Repetition and Intersubjectivity: Contemporary Freudian Explorations of Trauma, Memory, and Clinical Process* (New York: Routledge, 2020), 101–16.

[15] Leo Bersani, "The Pleasures of Repetition," in *The Freudian Body: Psychoanalysis and Art* (New York: Columbia University Press, 1986), 61.

Repetition is central to how Shakespeare constructs the erotic objects in the poems. Christopher Bollas remarks that "character is pattern," meaning that subjects make the Other desirable by making legible those repeated patterns of behavior that define them.[16] This is by no means unpolemical. One might say that over-familiarity can kill desire, and one even more evocatively might say that the more time one spends with someone, the less they feel that they actually know them.[17] As we have already seen, the pleasure-seeking speaker can attain agency in the patterns he delineates, especially when he brings fantasy productively into play. An individual can choose to accept the fantasy about the other person. After all, there is "pleasure at finding a pattern," as Bollas adds, even if that pattern involves aligning observed characteristics to fit a fantasy about the beloved.[18] The *Sonnets*, then, can be interpreted as a set of hypotheses about what the beloved might mean to the speaker, and what the speaker might mean to the beloved. This is especially true when we view "introspection" in the way that many cognitive scientists do, as a form of narrative where our exploration of ourselves functions "like literary criticism where we ourselves are the text to be understood."[19] As readers see the many versions of the lover and beloved reflected in the *Sonnets*, it serves as a reminder that "just as there is no single truth that lies within a literary text, but many truths, so are there many truths about a person that can be constructed."[20] One way to read the *Sonnets* is as a series of repeated interpretations of the lover and his beloveds in an attempt to find which versions ring most true for the speaker and for the addressee.

One can find repetition depicted as a sort of game, as pattern recognition, as self-work, and as erotic pleasure in Sonnet 76. The speaker overtly points to the repetition found across his poems when he opens:

> Why is my verse so barren of new pride,
> So far from variation or quick change?
> Why with the time do I not glance aside
> To new-found methods, and to compounds strange? (1–4)

One could read this as self-deprecation where "barren" implies that there is something inherently unproductive about repetition and "far from [...] quick" implies a lack of youthful liveliness. However, I would challenge us to see the poet as Freud sees the child playing Fort-Da. Shakespeare asks here how his patternistic method might prove an alternative form of pleasure outside the terms of heterosexual reproduction and the renewal offered by youthfulness that seem so celebrated

[16] Christopher Bollas, *The Freudian Moment* (London: Karnac, 2008), 58.
[17] A wonderful resource for discussions of this is Mitchell, *Can Love Last? The Fate of Romance over Time*, esp. 93–118 and 173–201.
[18] Bollas, *The Freudian Moment*, 59.
[19] Wilson, *Strangers to Ourselves: Discovering the Adaptive Unconscious*, 162.
[20] Wilson, *Strangers to Ourselves: Discovering the Adaptive Unconscious*, 162.

elsewhere in the *Sonnets*. One might even find him lionizing a lack of desire when he wonders why he does not glance in new directions. The thinking in the subsequent stanza evolves into a line that finds him introspective, reading the repetition in his literary text as a reason to question his motives as well as a means to look inward at himself: "Why write I still all one, ever the same" (5).[21]

Yet his reiterative verse, seemingly treated with derision at the opening of the poem, is redeemed as we reach the volta: "O know, sweet love, I always write of you" (9). Rather than leave ambiguous whether "love" means the beloved or the abstract emotion, the next line underscores that he speaks of both: "And you and love are still my argument" (10). The "O" of line 9 imbues the poem with resonances of apostrophe. However, it also reminds us that *wanting*—that word that means both desire and lack—can itself be a pleasure-delivering experience. That is, his writing about the recollected beloved brings about the feeling. "Memory for me is always fresh," Toni Morrison has remarked, "in spite of the fact that the object being remembered is done and past."[22] For Morrison, it seems to be memory itself, the phenomenon of something already experienced returning in ephemeral form, that is so pleasingly and paradoxically "fresh." Like Morrison, Burton names the pleasure of memory plainly in *The Anatomy of Melancholy*, writing, "Atque haec olim meminisse juvabit [recollection of the past is pleasant]," and he makes even plainer that the pleasure derives from repetition: "*the privation and want of a thing many times makes it more pleasant and delightsome than before it was.*"[23] Perhaps this is because the remembered experience happens in a new context, with a more mature version of the self as witness. The resurgence of memory when Shakespeare ponders his beloved can have both positive and negative valences as it keeps the past in the present.

Sonnet 76's final couplet collapses erotic desire into the act of writing in a familiar formulation that, I think, is still quite moving: "For as the sun is daily new and old, / So is my love, still telling what is told" (13–14). We return here to the conflation of the loved one and the love itself that the speaker feels for him in the single word "love." There is also a productive ambiguity in the phrase "still telling what is told." It recalls the use of the verb "tell" that the speaker seized upon in Sonnet 12 to acknowledge that his experience of the present and his recollection of the past are based in self-narrative. Note the two verb forms in the final line of Sonnet 76: "told" occurs in the past but continues into "telling," which occurs in the present and will extend in the future. This emphasizes that repetition carries the positive connotation of constancy in romantic relations. If we read the comma here to signal an appositive, then the "telling" is equivalent to both the beloved and the emotion felt toward him. In light of that apposition, we find the speaker

---

[21] The theme continues across the *Sonnets*. In Sonnet 108, the speaker must "must each day say o'er the very same" to express his love (108.6).

[22] Toni Morrison, "Memory, Creation, and Fiction," in *The Source of Self Regard*, 327.

[23] Burton, *The Anatomy of Melancholy*, vol. 2, 148, italics in original.

asserting that his very description of his romantic desire is what produces love and is that which satisfies him.

Let's Go Again

Recognizing that pleasure can derive from patterns and from repetition, the speaker seeks them out in order to make sense of his romantic and erotic life. In Sonnet 35, the beloved repeatedly disappoints the speaker but also is simply a repetition of tedium in the broader world. The poem evokes memory in its first line, as it urges the addressee to let go of regret especially in light of the presence of flaws in all things. In fact, Stephen Guy-Bray notes two forms of memory occurring here in the first quatrain, where "It is not merely that the lover remembers his appalling behavior, but also that the speaker presents the lover's memory of how the natural world operates as something that should comfort him."[24] The poem opens:

> No more be grieved at that which thou hast done:
> Roses have thorns, and silver fountains mud,
> Clouds and eclipses stain both moon and sun,
> And loathsome canker lives in sweetest bud. (1–4)

The parallels drawn here point to the tension between outside and inside, between appearance and interiority. The rose appears beautiful but stings when one touches the stem to draw it closer. The fountain appears refreshing until one steps into it or deeply penetrates it with the hand. The third line reverses the dynamic, where the outer "stain" might hide beauty that one remembers seeing previously.[25] Burrow observes that the "loathsome canker" suggests a caterpillar or worm destroying the bud of the plant.[26] I would also note what the *Oxford English Dictionary* describes as a now-archaic meaning of "a chronic, non-healing sore or ulcer, esp. one that extends into surrounding tissue."[27] This is related to our own

---

[24] Guy-Bray, "Remembering to Forget," 46.

[25] The use of "stain" here may also have racialized valences. The clouds threaten to pollute the beloved's fairness for which he is so praised in other sonnets, where typically "foulness is the opposite of cleanliness and beauty, but it is also the opposite of whiteness." Melissa E. Sanchez, "Was Sexuality Racialized for Shakespeare?," in *The Cambridge Companion to Shakespeare and Race*, ed. Ayanna Thompson (Cambridge: Cambridge University Press, 2021), 129. On the use of "stain" as a marker that conflated non-whiteness, moral failing, and sexual impurity, see for example Joyce Greene MacDonald, *Women and Race in Early Modern Texts* (Cambridge: Cambridge University Press, 2002); and Ian Smith, *Black Shakespeare: Reading and Misreading Race* (Cambridge: Cambridge University Press, 2022), 90–101.

[26] Burrow, *The Complete Sonnets and Poems*, 450.

[27] "canker, n.1a," OED online. For more on the multiple meanings and uses of this word in the early modern period, see Sujata Iyengar, *Shakespeare's Medical Language: A Dictionary* (New York: Bloomsbury Arden Shakespeare), 51–4. For discussion of the term specifically in Shakespeare's *Sonnets*, see Alanna Skuse, "The Worm and the Flesh: Cankered Bodies in Shakespeare's Sonnets," in *Disability,*

contemporary "canker sore" in the mouth, but the early moderns understood the canker as a sore that will spread into the healthy, unirritated tissue near the sore. With this meaning in mind, we can see how the speaker suggests that the world with which the addressee might come in contact could infect him, but it also suggests how the points of contact between the speaker, the poem, and the addressee make transmission of memories containing "what thou hast done" possible.

The poet points to how the beloved's sin becomes his own sin when he finds "myself corrupting salving thy amiss" (7). By excusing the other man's sins, he doubles them in his own mind by revisiting them, justifying them, and making it possible to live with the memory of them.[28] This creates a repetition of those sins as he recollects them to defend them, and this reels into excess as he ends up "excusing thy sins more than thy sins are" (8). As Burrow notes, "the poet is corrupting himself, and by extension his art, in his excessive efforts to exculpate his friend."[29] The reiteration of the word "sin" in this line emphasizes Burrow's point because there are now two sets of sins where there was once one: those in the speaker's mind and those in the addressee's mind. The poem concludes:

> For to thy sensual fault I bring in sense—
> Thy adverse party is thy advocate—
> And 'gainst myself a lawful plea commence:
> Such civil war is in my love and hate
> That I an accessary needs must be
> To that sweet thief which sourly robs from me. (9–14)

The speaker, in defending the addressee, sins. And while this stains the speaker, it also generates an intimacy with him as the poet proves himself not only to be on the beloved's side but also to be drawn deeper into him as they look inward at their shared recollections of sin. The intimacy for which the poet argues is emphasized by his asserted status as an "accessary." In combining "sweet" and "sour" and by making the "adverse party" into an "advocate," Sonnet 35 reminds us that negative experiences can also be pleasurable. The text offers an instance of what Raphael Lyne has traced across Shakespeare's poems, where they "bring poetic expression and intense, troubled thought into conjunction" to exemplify "the friction between the tools of rhetorical inquiry and the predicaments encountered in passionate

---

Health, and Happiness in the Shakespearean Body, ed. Sujata Iyengar (New York: Routledge, 2014), 240–59.

[28] While the poet urges the addressee to forgive himself, he does not go as far as to tell him he can forget his sins. Instead, he suggests that his faults might be hidden from the public world in order to reduce his shame because their two minds can hold the memories in private. Such sins might be impossible to truly expunge from memory, especially if one fears that they are publicly known because "occasions of humiliation are so difficult to forget; it is often easier to forget physical pain than to forget humiliation." Paul Connerton, "Seven Types of Forgetting," *Memory Studies* 1, no. 1 (2008): 67.

[29] Burrow, *The Complete Sonnets and Poems*, 450.

situations."[30] The poem uses repetition in various forms to render thinking about sin beautiful. And, keeping in mind those descriptions of the rhetorical device with which I opened this chapter, this repetition heightens Sonnet 35's erotic stakes.

In the tension between "sweet" and "sour," we find this same complement that we have seen elsewhere: the beloved can make desirable even that which initially repels. Like the two men sharing a bed in Ascham's model of learning, the poet and addressee grow closer as Shakespeare translates the sins into poetry and into his own mind, only to be reflected back. The accessory, then, is both a confidant who uniquely understands the accused and also an individual who should be pitied for the burden of carrying the other's memories which he has assumed. The final line thus links to the first, and in turn links the lover to the beloved, by way of recollection. The grief that the beloved feels at looking back on his past actions is coupled with the grief that the speaker suggests he himself feels now that he has been robbed by this thief. Although these memories are implied to resurface involuntarily, that does not mean that the mourning that accompanies them needs to be interpreted as negative. Schacter observes that, with involuntary memories, "persistence serves a healthy function: events that we need to confront come to mind with a force that is hard to ignore."[31] The speaker not only urges the beloved to confront his memories in order to integrate them into a story he knows about the world but also to recognize the other man's love for him.

Cedar Sigo's adaptation of the poem, "XXXV," helps illuminate the pleasure inherent in the original poem. It opens more crassly than Sonnet 35 does, "Fuck off with your crippling guilt," before pointing to the flaws of the world. Rather than stating that "all men make faults," as the original poem does, Sigo states, "no one is beyond reproach except the indians."[32] He points to his own indigenous identity as a member of the Suquamish Tribe, as well as to his status as a queer person, throughout the poem. Thus, he deploys a double action of noting that he belongs to groups typically marginalized but that this also allows him a claim to virtue and to unique insight. The closing of the poem takes up the themes of repetition, excess, memory, and erotism in ways only implied by Shakespeare's original. As he considers the beloved's dual state as alluring for his pure desirability yet also abject for his sinful state, Sigo's speaker cannot help but "suffer this reversal right beside you" (9). Desire in the present is informed by memories of previous behavior, so much so that the poem is characterized by the sense of sexuality and excess—the speaker's desire is described as filling a "whore bath beyond the brim" (8)—as well as the intimacy of shared, toxic experience of the "zombie dust" (14) that fills the beloved's lungs and draws them into mutual breathing.

---

[30] Lyne, *Shakespeare, Rhetoric, Cognition*, 214.
[31] Schacter, *The Seven Sins of Memory*, 183.
[32] The text of this poem is drawn from Cedar Sigo, *Language Arts* (Seattle: Wave Books: 2014), 21.

The encounter with the beloved, both in Shakespeare's original and in Sigo's version, is a surrender to a desired object that offers contact and interaction with alluring elements beyond the subject's control. As Lauren Berlant remarks, "The object [of love] is the encounter between negativity and nonsovereignty, the problems of radical incoherence and relational out-of-synchness that threateningly traverse the subject and the world."[33] Sigo's poem shows us the truth of Shakespeare's poem. Both texts posit shared sin, for all its negativity, to be exciting and, more importantly, suggest that transgression within the private thoughts and interactions of the couple allow a way to confront the world's inherent instability in a confined context. Both poems, then, exemplify the sometimes traumatic component to what Freud describes as the height of love, that point at which "the boundary between ego and object threatens to melt away. Against all evidence of his senses, a man who is in love declares that 'I' and 'you' are one."[34]

This ego dissolution, though it asks the speakers of both poems to give up control and confront the more unsavory elements of coupling, nonetheless frames the encounter as one begging to be repeated. Sigo demands this so eloquently in the final three words, such that Guy-Bray suggests that the poem "ends with an invitation to sex that is also an appeal to memory."[35] When the speaker says, "lets go again" (15) in the final words of the poem, he elides the apostrophe that should be placed in "let's" and the period that should end the poem. There is no need to hesitate to repeat the memorable encounter with this partner. In fact, Sigo's speaker seems to already be re-engaging with him as he adds a fifteenth line to his adaptation of this sonnet.[36] Perhaps what Sigo is doing to Shakespeare's poem is the same thing his speaker is doing with the beloved. The contemporary poet is taking what is, arguably, one of the less memorable of Shakespeare's *Sonnets* and one whose erotic charge is minimal and making it more memorable by remembering it in a much more intoxicating form. He gives it a flashbulb-like quality, acknowledging that "we remember more high and low moments in our lives than mundane ones, though psychologists have long-debated whether positive experiences are better remembered than negative ones."[37] Shakespeare and Sigo both seem to be saying that either will do.

Genealogies of Past Desire

Repetition in Shakespeare's Sonnet 35 works at cross-purposes. At first, it increases the weight of guilt by implying that the speaker and beloved share obsessive thoughts about sin. Then it goes on to lighten that weight by stating that inner

---

[33] Lauren Berlant and Lee Edelman, *Sex, or the Unbearable* (Durham and London: Duke University Press, 2014), 65.

[34] Sigmund Freud, *Civilization and its Discontents*, trans. James Strachey, ed. Peter Gay (New York: W. W. Norton and Co., 1989), 13.

[35] Guy-Bray, "Remembering to Forget," 49.

[36] Schacter, *The Seven Sins of Memory*, 164.

[37] Schacter, *The Seven Sins of Memory*, 164.

faults are replicated in the nature of elements in the external world. Sonnet 35 thus connects to Sonnet 76 and to other sonnets discussed in this book, where the speaker offers his own mind and the poem as a glass in which the addressee can see his own reflection. And that reflection works both ways: the addressee might learn more about the poet and the abnegated speaker might become more like the addressee who he, at times, admires and at other times abhors.

These sonnets promise to contribute to the project of self-knowledge and self-cultivation in which memory plays an integral role. Montaigne writes:

> We are all framed of flaps and patches, and of so shapeless and diverse a composition, that every piece plays his part. And there is as much difference found between us and ourselves as between ourselves and others.[38]

The self is constantly changing with new experiences that must be integrated into the story of how one's life makes sense as a narrative. Damasio observes, "autobiographical memory is architecturally connected, neutrally and cognitively speaking, to the nonconscious protoself and to the emergent and conscious core self of each lived instant."[39] Montaigne crystallizes the way that the subject is constantly changing with his image of the individual as "flaps and patches," where the present self is stitched to connect with previous versions of oneself. All go by the same name but each has its own set of memories that are updated and re-narrativized by the later version.

As we have seen in previous chapters, this notion that one self is composed of multiple selves finds expression across Shakespeare's work. The more one looks for it, the more one sees it repeated, even as it may find its most paradigmatic expression in the "seven ages" of Jaques's speech from *As You Like It*. I would now like to return to this trope, linking it to earlier discussions of the narrative self and tying it to the curiously reproductive work of repetition. Richard II believes that he can overcome the isolation of prison through mental work that first bifurcates him into male and female before generating new children based in thought:

> My brain I'll prove the female to my soul,
> My soul the father, and these two beget
> A generation of still-breeding thoughts;
> And these same thoughts people this little world[.] (5.1.6–9)

The king believes that he can place multiple parts of himself in dialogue with each other, and he frames those parts at first as a parental couple, suggesting a type of romantic fulfillment even in isolation. He sees himself as a patchwork, much in

---

[38] Montaigne, *Essayes*, 196–7.
[39] Damasio, *The Feeling of What Happens*, 173.

the same way that Montaigne describes personal identity. By reflecting on how he might compare the private world of the prison to the larger world, he engages in that same work that the speaker of Sonnet 35 does: he draws parallels between the physical outside and the psychic inside. That Richard does so in the confines of his cell, where he imagines his "vain weak nails / May tear a passage through the flinty ribs / Of this hard world, my ragged prison walls" (5.1.19–21), is all the more telling in terms of his own looking into his mind or soul to make sense of how his life has led him to this fallen state.

Richard II's monologue, where he descends into his thoughts and fantasies of digging out, dramatizes the terms with which cognitive psychology describes the autobiographical self, where "one version of the narrative viewpoint is perfectly compatible with the archaeology metaphor: people can excavate many things about themselves through introspection, which they then weave into a story."[40] We have our own evolving story about ourselves, and that story is intertwined with our stories about others and about those lives we did not lead. Richard contemplates:

> Thus play I in one person many people,
> And none contented. Sometimes am I king;
> Then treasons make me wish myself a beggar,
> And so I am. Then crushing penury
> Persuades me I was better when a king.
> Then am I kinged again, and by and by
> Think that I am unkinged by Bolingbroke[.] (5.1.31–7)

These different individuals are not imagined characters but rather versions of himself throughout his adult life. Like those paradigmatic roles listed in the "seven ages" speech, where each man is at one point a schoolboy then a soldier then a justice and so on, Richard II's imagined selves are both stock characters from literature and his own identities at different times. And that ability to be multiple people simultaneously is fueled by memory, as he revisits his self who was king, his self who is now a beggar, his self who wishes to be king again, and the implied fourth self who does not wish to be king again because this would only lead to treason against him anew. This cell, in its own way, is its own "mausoleum of all hope and desire" for it contains all of Richard's memories and possible pasts.

And just as Quentin in *The Sound and the Fury* inherits a device to contain his own regrets and hopes, so too is Richard trapped in a genealogy of others who have worn the crown. Earlier in the play, he will give one of Shakespeare's most famous speeches as he mourns what he has lost upon being overthrown by Bolingbroke:

[40] Timothy D. Wilson, *Strangers to Ourselves: Discovering the Adaptive Unconscious* (Cambridge, MA: Harvard University Press, 2002), 162.

> For God's sake, let us sit upon the ground,
> And tell sad stories of the death of kings—
> How some have been deposed, some slain in war,
> Some haunted by the ghosts they have deposed,
> Some poisoned by their wives, some sleeping killed,
> All murdered. (3.2.151–6)

The speech places his own personal memory of being king and being betrayed within the larger collective memory of kings who have been portrayed. History already tells the audience that he, too, will be killed. He is linked to these past kings because of his elevated status and because all of these figures share "the hollow crown / That rounds the mortal temples of a king" (3.2.156–7). We see in this speech and in the one delivered from his prison cell that, as Jonathan Baldo puts it, "the past has usurped [Richard's] present" such that "[a]ll that remains is the traumatized compulsion to repeat."[41] All of these figures prefigure him, both elevating him for leading such an elite life and diminishing his uniqueness as his life has been lived before. The speaker of the *Sonnets* engages in a similar rhetorical strategy in his appeals to the beloved. However, he attempts to offer a more nuanced consideration of such genealogies of previous paradigms, one that both relies on the power of retention but also promises to break from pattern.

The Erotics of Literary History

Sonnet 53 wrestles with the uniqueness of the beloved, struggling as Sonnet 18 does with the question of how to celebrate his superlative qualities without likening him to other similarly elevated figures. The poet asks, "What is your substance, whereof are you made, / That millions of strange shadows on you tend?" (1–2). The beloved draws comparison to others, though none of them can compare to him as they are but as dim reflections, followers, or "shadows." The speaker can only make sense of the beloved's exemplary qualities by drawing upon the past and by naming a genealogy to which the beloved belongs yet also does not belong. Whereas Richard II placed himself in a long line of (doomed) nobles who have worn crowns, the beloved is placed among (doomed) beauties from collective, literary history:

> Describe Adonis, and the counterfeit
> Is poorly imitated after you.
> On Helen's cheek all art of beauty set,
> And you in Grecian tires are painted new. (5–8)

---

[41] Baldo, *Memory in Shakespeare's Histories*, 15.

The speaker does not simply say that the beloved is more desirable than Adonis and Helen. He further suggests that these figures were patterned after him.[42] Thus the beloved is placed outside time while also placed in a long genealogy of those who have been celebrated similarly, just as King Richard imagines himself connected to all those who have worn the hollow crown. Elizabeth Freeman has observed that "contact with historical materials can be precipitated by particularly bodily dispositions, and that these connections may elicit bodily responses, even pleasurable ones, that are themselves a form of understanding."[43] It may be titillating for the speaker to invoke these paradigmatically attractive individuals, and he hopes it will titillate the beloved or reader as well.

Both Adonis and Helen are highly desirable figures, but they are also figures who are associated with destruction because of their desirability. Madhavi Menon, in her analysis of *Venus and Adonis*, argues that Shakespeare understood Adonis as an entity who resists teleology. She keenly observes, "In Ovid, Adonis both has sex and lives on after his death to remind Venus of the pleasures of fulfilled desire; in Shakespeare, he both spurns her and fails to leave behind a recurrent image of himself."[44] Helen, too, seemed to be for Shakespeare a force associated with termination. In *Troilus and Cressida*, Paris states that any man should be spurred to draw a sword for her, and her own choice of song is "This love will undo us all" (2.2.155–9; 3.1.106).[45] It remains unclear why Shakespeare invokes these doomed lovers as the paragons of excellence within whose genealogy the beloved should be placed. However, the anti-teleological impulse to frame ancient figures as patterned after the beloved may suggest that their inferiority as copies resulted in the tragic ends with which they are associated.

The way the poem presents a genealogy that links two doomed lovers from literary history to a present couple echoes a scene in *The Merchant of Venice* which

---

[42] Other instances in the collection speak to a line of thought in the poems where the beloved's beauty ties not just to the external world but to collective and personal memory of previous beloveds. For example, in Sonnet 98, flowers are "figures of delight / Drawn after you, you pattern of all those" (11–12) and, in Sonnet 106, descriptions of beauties in previous ages are "all you prefiguring" (10). While such claims might seem nonsensical, I would aver that desire itself often seeks to reconcile paradoxes. In his discussion of the "noticeable paradox in the equation of Adonis and Helen" in this sonnet, Stephen Booth goes as far as to argue that "the substance of the sonnets is paradox, so the style is paradoxical." Booth, *An Essay on Shakespeare's Sonnets*, 104.

[43] Freeman, *Time Binds*, 95–6.

[44] Edmondson and Wells suggest that this sonnet was written within the 1595–7 period, shortly after the 1593 publication of *Venus and Adonis*. Edmonson and Wells, *All the Sonnets of Shakespeare*, 179; and Madhavi Menon, "Spurning Teleology in *Venus and Adonis*," *GLQ: A Journal of Lesbian and Gay Studies* 11, no. 4 (2005): 499.

[45] For an exploration of Helen as a time-defying figure, see Dustin W. Dixon and John S. Garrison, "The Spectacle of Helen in Euripides' *Helen* and Marlowe's *Doctor Faustus*," *Classical Receptions Journal* 13, no. 2 (April 2021): 159–77.

remains difficult to interpret. Toward the end of the play, Jessica and Lorenzo compare their mutual love to that of famous lovers with tragic ends:

LORENZO: The moon shines bright. In such a night as this,
  When the sweet wind did gently kiss the trees
  And they did make no noise, in such a night
  Troilus, methinks, mounted the Trojan walls
  And sighed his soul toward the Grecian tents
  Where Cressid lay that night.
JESSICA: In such a night
  Did Thisbe fearfully o'ertrip the dew
  And saw the lion's shadow ere himself
  And ran dismayed away.
LORENZO: In such a night
  Stood Dido with a willow in her hand
  Upon the wild sea-banks, and waft her love
  To come again to Carthage.
JESSICA: In such a night
  Medea gathered the enchanted herbs
  That did renew old Aeson.
LORENZO: In such a night
  Did Jessica steal from the wealthy Jew,
  And with an unthrift love did run from Venice
  As far as Belmont.
JESSICA: In such a night
  Did young Lorenzo swear he loved her well,
  Stealing her soul with many vows of faith,
  And ne'er a true one.
LORENZO: In such a night
  Did pretty Jessica, like a little shrew,
  Slander her love, and he forgave it her.
JESSICA: I would out-night you did nobody come,
  But hark, I hear the footing of a man. (5.1.1–30)

I quote the full interchange here to tease out the questions it helps raise about the strategy being used in the *Sonnets*. The two characters invoke lovers from literary history: Aeneas and Dido; Cressida and Troilus; Pyramus and Thisbe; and Jason and Medea. On some level, these are paragons of what love should be: they pine for each other, risk death for each other, remain faithful after saying goodbye to each other, and care for each other's family. But each of these loving couples will ultimately end up betrayed, mournful, or at least direfully unhappy. When Jessica and Lorenzo place themselves in this inventory of great loves, it is also unclear whether

Shakespeare means the present lovers think they can break from the pattern of the figures they name or if they believe that, even knowing these past instances, they will inevitably repeat that pattern. Or it could be that these lovers think it is enough to experience joy in the moment, remembering but then forgetting the pattern to which they have adhered. It might be tempting to imagine Shakespeare wishing to assert his poetic authority in *The Merchant of Venice* and in the *Sonnets*. That is, we could see him as treating loss as a game, where that which is lost can be found (to paraphrase the Oracle from *The Winter's Tale*), because one can outsmart the rules of the game if one knows them. However, we might also argue that reviewing literary history functions like the game of Fort-Da, where loss is inevitable and all one can control is how one reacts to it.[46]

Sonnet 53 engages some of the same logic as Sonnet 35. Here, the external world does not justify the beloved's faults. Instead, nature's beauty reflects the beloved's beauty, even if it is just a pale reflection of it:

> Speak of the spring and foison of the year,
> The one doth shadow of your beauty show,
> The other as your bounty doth appear,
> And you in every blessèd shape we know.
> In all external grace you have some part,
> But you like none, none you, for constant heart. (9–14)

Like Sonnet 35, this poem states that the speaker knows the beloved's thoughts. The beloved's constancy is what makes him stand out from other lovely elements of his beauty in the world, and the formulation suggests his beauty derives from repetition. He is part of "every blessèd shape we know," and that infinite series of reflections indicates his worthiness.

It is thus the speaker's intimate knowledge of the beloved and his knowledge of literary history that justifies the truth of his true praise and forms their shared intimacy. We find this same trope in Sonnet 59, which locates an image of the beloved "in some antique book" (7) showing the "composèd wonder of your frame" (10). The "image in some antique book" now seems different to the speaker because the present beloved casts the past in a new light. Kristine Johanson argues that, in Sonnet 59, the "desire for memory and history to recuperate the past performs a temporal move that brings the reader and speaker towards that past just as it

---

[46] We can think of this exchange between Jessica and Lorenzo, as well as the exchanges between the poet and addressee, as invoking the public history of famous lovers from the past as an analogue for invoking one's own personal history of past romantic relations. And the fact that past relationships may have ended poorly, or simply just ended, may heighten the need to enjoy the present relationship while in its exhilarating phase. What Deleuze finds in Proust, we might also find in Shakespeare: "It is quite true that we repeat our past loves; but it is also true that our present love, in all its vivacity, 'repeats' the moment of the dissolution or anticipates its own end." Gilles Deleuze, *Proust and Signs: The Complete Text*, trans. Richard Howard (London: Continuum, 2008), 13.

affirms its distance."[47] Sonnet 59 thus links to Sonnet 53, where former figures are invoked as a shared cultural memory but then are dismissed as only particle like-nesses. Bollas's notion described above, where "character is pattern," incorporates the idea that in "very intimate relations there is deep mutual character perception taking place."[48] This is yet another way in which desire links to narrative. The sub-ject creates the Other to whom he is attracted by determining a pattern about them. One determines who someone else is by recognizing patterns within their behav-ior and language but also—as these poems' paeans to literary history attest—by recognizing patterns in previous acquaintances or archetypes.

The closing couplet of Sonnet 59 admits the ways that memory functions on the basis of projection. The speaker remarks, "O, sure I am the wits of former days / To subjects worse have given admiring praise" (13–14). We hear the deep impres-sion of the character—of the written text, of the individual being portrayed—in the largely unnecessary adjective "admiring," a term which implies looking but surely functions as a synonym for praise. Johanson argues that, "In Sonnet 59, Shake-speare offers a poetics of temporal instability as his speaker attempts to chart the tension between the security of constancy through repetition and the knowledge that everything must change, that *tempus edax rerum*."[49] But, if the speaker simply repeats praise delivered to previous beauties in history, he runs the risk of being seen, in retrospect, as one of those short-sighted wits he criticizes at the end of the poem.

It is difficult not to read some self-doubt, or at least some self-awareness regard-ing the use of hyperbole, in Shakespeare's attempts to place his addressees within the genealogies of cultural memory. For example, consider how Sonnet 106, which I touched upon briefly in the first chapter, opens:

> When in the chronicle of wasted time
> I see descriptions of the fairest wights,
> And beauty making beautiful old rhyme
> In praise of ladies dead, and lovely knights[.] (1–4)

Here, the beauty of the figures being praised enhances the quality of the verse from a previous age. Because these older poems engage in "the blazon of sweet beauty's best," we know that they are selective (5). Margreta de Grazia helps us understand the poet's strategy in engaging this canon of previous praise. De Grazia sees that "the only option is repetition" when Shakespeare confronts the writing of the past, because "immortality, whether for himself or for the friend, can be

[47] Kristine Johanson, "Ecclesiastes and Sonnet 59," in *The Sonnets: The State of Play*, ed. Han-nah Crawforth, Elizabeth Scott-Baumann, and Clare Whitehead (New York: Bloomsbury Arden Shakespeare, 2017), 66.

[48] Bollas, *The Freudian Moment*, 58.

[49] Johanson, "Ecclesiastes and Sonnet 59," 57.

attained only through such poetic reiteration."[50] This functions as well at the level of Shakespeare's choice of genre. Vasiliauskas argues that "Outmodedness creates the conditions for a private love to develop in the first place in the sonnets, and the absence of progress makes it possible for that love to be recovered by the young man, even after the death of the speaker."[51] We can synthesize these two insights as we trace the function of the literary past to which the *Sonnets* turn in their loving praise. The immortality promised by the poems may not be realized in the beloved being remembered in the present by future readers. Instead, it may be that the beloved will be seen as counting among those forgotten or failed relationships of the past and that the poems will testify to the power of the love felt in the wake of the awareness of inevitable failure. Such a reading would place the poems in line with at least one reading of the curious exchange between Jessica and Lorenzo. That is, it is the speaker's love for the beloved which will be immortalized rather than the beloveds themselves.

When the speaker of the *Sonnets* states that the beloveds portrayed in previous literature are inferior copies of the addressee, he may point less to the singularity of his object of desire and more to his own literary influences. Sonnet 106 states that the ancient writers' depictions are unknowingly anticipatory because "all their praises are but prophecies / Of this our time, all you prefiguring" (9–10). The lines link the beloved to those praised in the past, but note the ambiguity of the phrase "our time." It may suggest the present which the speaker and addressee occupy, but the use of the plural pronoun "our" emphasizes that the poem celebrates their time together and their love, or more specifically the poet's experience and writing about that love. The lines also underscore that the poet's reading of these previous praises enables his writing now. In that way, we might hear Sonnet 106 as echoing the first sonnet of Sidney's *Astrophil and Stella* (1591), where:

> I sought fit words to paint the blackest face of woe,
> Studying inventions fine, her wits to entertain;
> Oft turning others' leaves, to see if thence would flow
> Some fresh and fruitful showers upon my sunburnt brain.
> But words came halting forth, wanting invention's stay;
> Invention, Nature's child, fled step-dame Study's blows;
> And others' feet still seem'd but strangers in my way.
> Thus great with child to speak and helpless in my throes,
> Biting my truant pen, beating myself for spite,
> "Fool," said my Muse to me, "look in thy heart, and write." (5–14)[52]

---

[50] Margreta de Grazia, "Revolution in *Shake-speare's Sonnets*," in *A Companion to Shakespeare's Sonnets*, ed. Michael Schoenfeldt (New York: John Wiley & Sons, 2006), 64, 66.

[51] Vasiliauskas, "The Outmodedness of Shakespeare's Sonnets," 781.

[52] The text of this poem is drawn from Sir Philip Sidney, "Astrophil and Stella," in *Sir Philip Sidney: The Major Works*, ed. Katherine Duncan-Jones (Oxford: Oxford University Press, 2008), 153.

Sidney echoes some of the concerns we have seen in the sonnets discussed above. He describes his anxieties about his writing in sexually reproductive terms, and he grapples with the writers of the past as he attempts to articulate the uniqueness of his own object of desire. Despite their similarities, though, a striking difference between Shakespeare's and Sidney's formulations helps us see a strand of thought in the *Sonnets* I have been exploring. Sidney needs to break from the past in order to find his voice and to appeal to his beloved. Shakespeare, on the other hand, seems much more comfortable with placing himself and his love in a repeated pattern he sees in literary history.[53]

Sidney himself makes the claim in his *Defense of Poetry* that the poet can "bring forth, quite anew, forms such as never were in nature."[54] It is intriguing to consider that Shakespeare does the reverse with his genealogies of love. He brings forth a form that is present in nature (an actual beloved in the external world of the present) and adulates that form by separating it from forms within the imaginative work of previous writers. Shakespeare's *Sonnets*, like other media intended for a public audience, generate "worlds that a memory community would not know without them."[55] Contemporary readers of Shakespeare's poetry might locate irony in the fact that the *Sonnets* promise immortality to the beloved, but the identity of any addressee is far from knowable. It could be argued, however, that the poems are not so much mnemonic devices for public commemoration of the beloved but rather memoriams to the sincerity and strength of the speaker's experience of love.

Moving Away from Monumental Memory

A typical way to think about the *Sonnets* is to imagine them as working against cultural forgetting. That is, the poems act as monuments to an addressee or to the author, such that they will never be forgotten. A frequent touchstone for such an interpretation is Sonnet 55. The poem lionizes the power of the text as a memory device superior to physical objects, and seemingly reassures the addressee that they will not be recollected:

> Not marble, nor the gilded monuments
> Of princes shall outlive this pow'rful rhyme,

---

[53] Shakespeare's expressed need to place himself and his beloved in a long history of repeated adoration attests to how the desiring subject does need to have a prior achievement of pleasure—whether in their personal past or in their knowledge of others' past pleasures—in order to expect a similar experience to generate similar pleasure. As Deleuze observes, "habit, in the form of a binding synthesis, precedes the pleasure principle and renders it possible." Gilles Deleuze, *Difference and Repetition*, trans. Paul Patton (London and New York: Bloomsbury, 2004), 121.

[54] Sir Philip Sidney, "The Defence of Poetry," in *Sir Philip Sidney: The Major Works*, ed. Katherine Duncan-Jones (Oxford: Oxford University Press, 2008), 230.

[55] Astrid Erll, *Memory in Culture*, trans. Sara B. Young (Hampshire: Palgrave Macmillan, 2011), 116.

> But you shall shine more bright in these contents
> Than unswept stone besmeared with sluttish time. (55.1–4)

The claim feels not particularly evocative and indeed familiar: the texts will outlive physical memorials. Amanda Watson links Sonnet 55's "pow'rful rhyme" to Sonnet 16's "barren rhyme" (4), tracing a larger pattern across the collection where "the procreation sonnets set up an implicit competition between visual commemoration and poetic commemoration, with the latter eventually prevailing."[56] She incisively pinpoints a throughline in the poems that praises the reproductive quality of verse more often than—and as superior to—human terms of reproduction. I am interested, though, in putting pressure on the question of what the poems commemorate and how they call into question their own ability to generate collective memory. As we saw in the previous chapter, attempts to transmit accurate recollections about the beloved are attenuated by the unreliability of the future minds that will receive those memories. Even in the poet's present, when he watches the clock such that the beloved can forget time and even forget him, the reliability of any form of commemoration outside the poet's mind is anything but certain. The "sluttish time" in the fourth line of this poem would just as aptly describe the vicissitudes of public interest as it would the beloved's own tendency to invest his or her energies in others.

Sonnet 55 assures the beloved of the sanctity of "The living record of your memory / 'Gainst death and all-oblivious enmity" (8–9). The poem thus imbues itself with a long life, if verse is the "living record" to which Shakespeare counterposes physical monuments. However, the phrase "living" directs the reader's attention to the living person who holds the memory being discussed: the poet. The poem provides no real physical detail about the beloved, in contrast to how a stone monument might replicate a person's body or face. All we have recorded here in this lyric is the fact that the poet loves him and will remember him. Sonnet 55 ends:

> Shall you pace forth, your praise shall still find room,
> Even in the eyes of all posterity
> That wear this world out to the ending doom.
> So, till the judgement that yourself arise,
> You live in this, and dwell in lovers' eyes. (10–14)

In the broadest sense, "the eyes of all posterity" could belong to any reader of the poem or even any person (any "I") who hears about the beloved. Yet the poem narrows the scope of these "eyes" to be only "lovers' eyes" where the beloved will continue. What is repeated until the "ending doom," or the world on judgment day, is not the beloved himself but rather the experience of looking at another person

---

[56] Watson, "'Full character'd," 348.

with the feeling of love. Future readers will attach not to Shakespeare's beloved but instead to the feeling Shakespeare remembers feeling when he experienced a love for the ages.

We can counterpose two forms of love in the poem, and each is tied to different forms of memory. Sonnet 55 uses the idea of the monument in order to separate a pure form of desire from a more lascivious form. The "sluttish time" is promiscuous in the sense that, over time, people may turn their attention to other objects of interest and discard old ones. The attention to a single, physical monument is also "sluttish" in the sense of how it occupies a large group's attention in terms of what early twentieth-century scholar Maurice Halbwachs has famously described as "collective memory," or more specifically the "social frameworks of memory."[57] The monument, in essence, has many onlookers or lovers in a given time period and that attention will prove unfaithful as time goes by. This form of memorial desire is quite different from the personal love that the speaker describes. That love is monogamous, at least on the speaker's side, as he takes his beloved as his singular object of affection. Others may express love for this beloved, but the speaker has special knowledge of his worth based on his knowledge of the function of private and public memory. What achieves immortality at the end of the poem is not the specific beloved but the love the speaker feels, endlessly repeated in "lovers' eyes" for their own objects of desire. The role of verse, then, is to place Shakespeare and his anonymous beloved in this long genealogy of famous and unknown lovers, as well as to perhaps help those future lovers find language to express how they feel.

The Art of Forgetting

In the *Sonnets*, the art of forgetting is as integral as the art of memory in achieving pleasure. For all his work to not forget and store memories effectively, Shakespeare acknowledges what contemporary psychology has documented: forgetting and fading memory are part of a housekeeping that allows us to store and recall memories efficiently.[58] He shares the sentiment expressed by Etienne Pasquier in *Monophylo*, his 1572 philosophical treatise on love, where:

> I hold opinion with an ancient captain of Athens, who being asked if he took not pleasure to learn the art of memory: "no, rather," said he, "I delight in the art of forgetfulness."[59]

---

[57] Maurice Halbwachs, *On Collective Memory*, trans. Lewis A. Coser (Chicago: University of Chicago Press, 1992), 37–192.

[58] Much of our understanding of the science of forgetting comes from studies of those with amnesia or other conditions affecting the ability to recollect the past. A useful starting point for understanding the sciences is Angelica Staniloiu and Hans J. Markowitsch, "Towards Solving the Riddle of Forgetting in Functional Amnesia: Recent Advances and Current Opinions," *Frontiers in Psychology* 3 (November 2012): esp. 403.

[59] Etienne Pasquier, *Monophylo*, trans. Sir Geoffrey Fenton (1572), Q3v–Q4r.

Knowing when to remember and when to forget can help a lover engage in a type of housekeeping not just for effective storage of memory but also for effective management of desire. On the one hand, the speaker continually reminds the beloved of the love he feels. Such expressions can communicate what is invisible to the external onlooker. Consider, for example, how the early modern memory artist and playwright Della Porta characterizes his repetitive thoughts in a way that echoes Shakespeare's depiction of thinking of his shining beloved in the nighttime in his *La Sorella* (1604):

> I'm sorry that I cannot open and show her my heart, where she would see shining forth her resplendent and beautiful image, as if in a bright and polished mirror; it is so taken up and filled with this image that there is no longer space for others and the way is closed to all.[60]

The constant return to the beloved in the heart can be offered as a testimony to the lover's devotion and to his singular interest. For the poet, the best way to transmit these internal feelings is through writing on the page, which we have seen Shakespeare liken to the heart-as-writing-tablet during the discussion of Sonnet 24 in the previous chapter. Composition of sonnets, even with their repeated elements, may also be a way for him to work through, or write through, his own compulsion to repeat desirous thoughts in his mind.[61]

Forgetting, though, can also be key to not overfilling one's heart and mind to a detrimental degree. However, it can also involve a kind of forgetting the beloved as this obsessive repetition can lead to an imagined figure rather than an accurate recollection of the beloved. There are dangers in the repeated, patternistic thinking that stems from love. Robert Burton underscores the connection between repetition and lovesickness this way, "as he that is bitten with a mad dog, thinks all he sees dogs, dogs in his meat, dogs in his dish, dogs in his drink; his Mistress is in his eyes, ears, heart, in all his senses."[62] The *Sonnets* suggest that the speaker largely avoids such a trap, except in the cases we have seen where he sees the beloved distributed into elements of the natural world around him. For the most part, however, it seems as if the poems express a habit the poet encourages in himself, where he expresses new permutations of his love less for a beloved who might have forgotten him and more for his own pleasure.[63]

---

[60] Qtd. in Lina Bolzoni, "The Art of Memory and the Erotic Image in Sixteenth- and Seventeenth-Century Europe: The Example of Giovanni Battista Della Porta," in *Eros and Anteros*, ed. Donald A. Beecher and Massimo Ciavolella (Ottawa: Dovehouse, 1992), 115.

[61] Remembering the beloved and forgetting the beloved must work in tandem to fuel the writing of new poems. As Garrett Sullivan has argued, "Forgetting entails not merely the loss of memory traces, it also clears a space for and initiates a fresh act of judgment; it is the precondition of something new being done." Sullivan, *Memory and Forgetting in English Renaissance Drama*, 47.

[62] Burton, *The Anatomy of Melancholy*, vol. 3, 170.

[63] Such reveries, where the speaker reinvents the beloved in new ways rather than relentlessly trying to recreate him with pinpoint accuracy, may evince his mastery of the arts both of forgetting and of

There is also the danger of too much forgetting, a concern which seems largely centered on the addressees' ineffective management of memory in the *Sonnets*. In the case of the procreation sonnets, Garrett A. Sullivan, Jr. finds that the speaker urges the young man to remember his social position and what he owes to society in terms of a failure of memory. In the young man's case, "self-forgetting is a violence done to identity (as well as to others) through the influence of overmastering sexual desire."[64] The speaker also predicts that he will be forgotten by his beloved. Sonnet 71 opens by asking that the beloved "No longer mourn for me when I am dead." The poet frames this permission to forget in a way that rejects the need for the beloved's memory but also elevates his own love as selfless:

> Nay, if you read this line, remember not
> The hand that writ it, for I love you so
> That I in your sweet thoughts would be forgot,
> If thinking on me then should make you woe. (5–8)

Sonnet 72 similarly gives the beloved permission to forget him in an effort not to be a burden to him:

> O, lest the world should task you to recite
> What merit lived in me that you should love
> After my death (dear love) forget me quite[.] (1–3)

In this light, we might imagine the discussion of Sonnets 57 and 58 in the previous chapter being a case of encouraged forgetting. In those sonnets, the beloved is encouraged to forget time while the speaker suffers for his love. In Sonnets 71 and 72, he is encouraged to forget him entirely. Such a strategy might be interpreted as a ploy not to be forgotten, just as Montaigne observes that "nothing so deeply imprints anything in our remembrance, as the desire to forget the same."[65] However, as Sullivan notes, the beloved is described as someone with a strong propensity to forget.

In the cases of these four sonnets, it seems just as likely the case that we, the readers, are encouraged to remember not the beloved but the speaker's love for the

memory. Psychologist Charles Fernyhough notes that cognitive science dismisses "the idea that memory is a static, indivisible entity, an heirloom from the past," but instead "a memory is more like a habit, a process of constructing something from its parts, but subtly changing ways each time, whenever the occasion arises." Charles Fernyhough, *Pieces of Light: The New Science of Memory Illuminates the Stories We Tell about Our Past* (New York: Harper, 2013), 6.

[64] Sullivan also notes the threat where "the dark lady is explicitly figured as the cause of the *poet's* forgetting himself." Sullivan, "Voicing the Young Man," 337 and 339, respectively.

[65] Montaigne, *The Essayes*, 286.

beloved.[66] This claim might be extended to many of the other sonnets which read as excessively repetitive internally or as repetitive of other ones in the collection. The poems themselves are a form of work that depict how the speaker sustains his experience of love, reflected back and processed through *not* interactions with the beloved in lived experience *but instead* ones depicted in literature. In fact, this may also help us understand the negative experiences depicted in many of the poems as the written page offers a safe space within which to work through traumatic memories through such techniques as analogue, metaphor, and simile. Seen this way, those sonnets that name literary characters as evidence for what the speaker loves about the beloved make sense as evidence for the experience of love he attests to being true. Shakespeare's writing is a culmination of experiences imagined by previous writers and experiences imagined by him in each poem, repeated so the poet can reach a climax in each short poem.

---

[66] The reader might look negatively upon a beloved who would forget so devoted a lover and thereby hold the speaker's moral qualities in higher esteem. The proofpoint for the lover's virtue is that he will continue to think of his beloved regularly. Such an assessment fits with Aristotelian tradition where repetition led to habituation, relying on "the crucial role memory was thought to have in the shaping of moral judgment and excellence of character." For a description of this tradition, see Carruthers, *The Book of Memory*, 85.

7

Contagious Memory

When someone talks about the future or even when one is just thinking about the future—sometimes *too much* when someone might be, as a friend of mine calls it, "future tripping"—what a person really has on their mind is the past. In the mind and at the level of fantasy, the past and the future are so closely intermingled that they share a kind of intimacy. This is something that early moderns knew. In his 1562 treatise *The Castle of Memory*, William Fulwood asserts that "neither is invention or imagination of that one part of the soul or brain, and memory of the other, but they are [the] functions of the same part of the soul."[1] This notion finds its neuroscientific proof-point in recent research that shows that the prediction of the future and the recollection of the past utilize the same area of the brain.[2] Or, in psychoanalytic terms, "The future is not some place we're going to, but an idea in our mind now. It is something we're creating, that in turn creates us. The future is a fantasy that shapes our present."[3] Every new experience, every new memory, it seems, shapes someone's vision of what is to come.

Throughout this book, I have explored the relationship between memory and pleasure by placing the *Sonnets* in dialogue with texts from their own contemporaneous present as well as texts from our own present. In this final chapter, I will engage even more directly and expansively with contemporary texts that evince a pattern of thought that connects our era to that of Shakespeare. It seems inescapable to discuss our current moment without taking into account the deep uncertainty about the eventual toll of COVID-19 as well as how the pandemic has opened up awareness about the instability inherent to imagined outcomes of any present moment. Right now, everyone is generating the raw material of what will become their own memories of this period. For me, as a gay man who came of age in the 1980s and is now navigating this new pandemic, I find myself irresistibly

---

[1] Fulwood translates Gratarolo's *De memoria reparanda, augenda confirmandaque ac de reminiscentia*. Fulwood, *The Castel of Memorie*, A1v.

[2] See, for example, Daniel L. Schacter, Donna Rose Addis, Demis Hassabis, et al., "The Future of Memory: Remembering, Imagining, and the Brain," *Neuron* 76 (November 21, 2012): 677–94 and Sinéad L. Mullally and Eleanor A. Maguire, "Memory, Imagination, and Predicting the Future: A Common Brain Mechanism?," *Neuroscientist* 20, no. 3 (June 2014): 220–34. A simpler introduction to the subject is Julie Beck, "Imagining the Future Is Just Another Form of Memory," *The Atlantic* (October 17, 2017).

[3] Stephen Grosz, *The Examined Life: How We Lose and Find Ourselves* (London: Random House, 2013), 157.

The Pleasures of Memory in Shakespeare's Sonnets. John S. Garrison, Oxford University Press. © John S. Garrison (2023). DOI: 10.1093/oso/9780198857716.003.0008

returning to the narrative of an earlier one. Not the plague of Shakespeare's time, though many writers have made that connection.[4]

Instead, recent times have vividly recalled for me the HIV/AIDS pandemic.

Disease as Persistent Recollection

As a contagious illness with uncertain origins and outcomes, the plague surely haunted the minds of early moderns but was also not the only disease that coursed through the cultural imagination. Without effective treatments available, sexually transmitted infections made the outcome of intimate encounters and the predictability of a healthy life uncertain. Just as they are today, new erotic encounters would be haunted by the threat of transmitting the embodied memory of previous ones in the form of disease. I can think of no more stunning example of the relationship between disease, memory, and futurity than Sonnet 147. In it, Shakespeare likens the memory of erotic desire to infection and in turn evinces memory's propensity to be transmitted from person to person as well as from the past into the future. The poem famously opens,

> My love is as a fever, longing still
> For that which longer nurseth the disease[.] (1–2)

Desire here is a hunger, a sickness. The speaker leaves ambiguous whether he simply likens his love to a fever or if he actually suffers from a fever after an encounter with the beloved. When one reads the poem with the possibility that the speaker has contracted venereal disease that induces bodily fever, he appears gripped not only by "longing" for further encounters but also by extended bodily memory of the beloved.[5] The use of "still" and "nurseth" places the time of the poem in something resembling the perfect-continuous mood: he knows he has been infected, he is currently infected, and the infection will continue in the time to come.[6]

---

[4] Of course, readers of the present book may have in mind our own current pandemic, and its connections to Shakespeare have already been explored in interesting ways. See, for example, Anoushka Sinha, "King Lear under COVID-19 Lockdown," *Journal of the American Medical Association* 323, no. 18 (April 10, 2020): 1758–9; Emma Smith, "What Shakespeare Teaches Us about Living with Pandemics," *The New York Times* (March 28, 2020). For a humorous take on these pontifications, see Daniel Pollack-Pelzner, "What Shakespeare Actually Did during the Plague," *The New Yorker* (April 1, 2020).

[5] I am not the first scholar to posit that Sonnet 147 suggests the transmission of a sexually transmitted infection. See, for example, Graham Holderness, *Nine Lives of William Shakespeare* (New York: Continuum, 2011), 142, and Olga L. Valbuena, "The Dyer's Hand: The Reproduction of Coercion and Blot in Shakespeare's Sonnets," in *Shakespeare's Sonnets: Critical Essays*, ed. James Schiffer (London: Taylor and Francis, 2013), 344n22. For a discussion of the speaker of Sonnet 147 as suffering from lovesickness as a medical disease, see Ian Frederick Moulton, "Catching the Plague: Happiness, Health, and Disease in Shakespeare," in *Disability, Health, and Happiness in the Shakespearean Body*, ed. Sujata Iyengar (New York: Routledge, 2014), 212–22.

[6] While certainly the poem resonates with longing, the speaker's experience counters a conception of desire-as-lack here because his experience of the beloved has left him with more than he wanted.

For the speaker, as for anyone who realizes that a disease now inhabits their body, knowledge of infection in the present is an awareness of continued infection for an unknown period of time. The disease refuses to leave the patient just as he refuses treatment prescribed by the physician:

> Feeding on that which doth preserve the ill,
> Th' uncertain sickly appetite to please.
> My reason, the physician to my love,
> Angry that his prescriptions are not kept,
> Hath left me, and I desperate now approve
> Desire is death, which physic did except. (3–8)

The grasp of the virus on his psyche leads the speaker to proclaim that "desire is death" (8). The pronouncement crystalizes how self-obliteration has come to be associated with sexual satisfaction, yet it also once more points to the role of futurity in the poem.[7] Given that desire is marked by a need in the present for something that may or may not come in the future, one might interpret the speaker as decrying an emotionally charged present moment with no real foreseeable closure. Viral infection and romantic infatuation both promise a kind of undying death. Desire here is, on one level, a *lack* of something the speaker hopes he will yet receive from the beloved. After all, "desire," as Lauren Berlant tells us, "describes a state of attachment to something or someone, and the cloud of possibility that is generated by the gap between an object's specificity and the needs and promises projected onto it."[8] As Berlant so incisively demonstrated with her notion of "cruel optimism," even obtaining the object of desire obviates the subject from obtaining the fantasy of what the object promised to provide. Berlant has coined the phrase "cruel optimism" to describe situations "when something you desire is actually an obstacle to your flourishing."[9] The phrase aptly describes the situation of Sonnet 147's speaker, who has an *over-abundance* of the beloved in the sense that he now carries a virus, something he did not intend to take away from the encounter.

Composing this chapter now and meditating on the intertwined characteristics of desire and disease, I am reminded of David Wojnarowicz's memoir *Close to the Knives*. In it, he shares how living with HIV made him feel "in a clearer than clear way that at this point in history the virus' activity is forever."[10] He means both that

---

[7] For two excellent discussions of how the link between sexual desire and dissolution of the subject manifests in early modern literature, see Jeffrey Masten, "Is the Fundament a Grave?," in *The Body in Parts: Fantasies of Corporeality in Early Modern Europe*, ed. David Hillman and Carla Mazzio (New York: Routledge, 1997), 128–45, and Marshall, *The Shattering of the Self*, especially the discussion of the genre of the sonnet from 56–84.

[8] Berlant, *Desire/Love*, 6.

[9] Berlant, *Cruel Optimism*, 1.

[10] David Wojnarowicz, *Close to the Knives: A Memoir of Disintegration* (New York: Vintage Books, 1991), 118.

he, as an HIV-positive person living in the early 1990s, shares the sonnet speaker's status of feeling "past cure" (9) *and* that he can now only imagine the world as if it will always be plagued by the new virus. The memoir and the sonnet showcase the relentless hold of memory which, as Montaigne puts it, "memory represents unto us, not what we choose, but what pleases her."[11] To know that one is infected with a virus, or to know that one might become infected, is a state of precarity predicated on what may or may not come to pass. And once more we have an early modern writer articulating what neuroscience has only recently discovered: that memory is future-oriented. Its nature is to linger in the mind only to be revivified later. In Shakespeare's poem, the speaker's intertwined knowledge of being infected and being infatuated underscores the challenge of letting go of the past.

Sonnet 147 portrays a speaker unable to control either his compulsion to think about and to talk about both his lover and his acquired infection:

> Past cure I am, now Reason is past care,
> And, frantic-mad with evermore unrest,
> My thoughts and my discourse as madmen's are,
> At random from the truth vainly expressed. (9–12)

He is plagued by thoughts of the beloved, which only drive him mad and which exhibit activity that will be forever causing "evermore unrest." The sonnet vividly and viscerally captures the connection between the speaker and his lover as the message he is transmitting now while he reels from disease. At the same time, it admits how mad he will sound to future readers.

The speaker's experiences of the present moment surge with emotional charge because they are points where unresolved feelings about the past collide with concern about the future. Martin Conway remarks that erotic memory evokes "feelings of surprise, recognition, perplexity, even wonderment, and triggers an intense sense of the self in the past."[12] The claim helps us see that the speaker's reaction is less "random" than he suggests: he may not realize that he is simply at the midpoint where his "sense of the self in the past" straitjackets him to a certainty that his future self will be unchanged. Eric Langley argues that we should see Sonnet 147 as part of "a sonnet *cycle* or *course*" where the speaker and reader "are bound to follow the purgative course of an excessively sweet yet ultimately astringent cure in the form of one-hundred and fifty-four sweet doses of bitter sonnet-medicine."[13] While I agree that poems such as this one can be read as something akin to an

---

[11] Montaigne, *The Essayes*, 286.
[12] Conway is the clinical psychologist who coined the term "flashbulb memory" to denote how intense emotion at the time of experience informs the likelihood that we will recall that experience. Conway, "Memory and Desire," 550.
[13] Eric Langley, *Shakespeare's Contagious Sympathies: Ill Communications* (Oxford: Oxford University Press, 2018), 116–17.

immune response to lovesickness, I favor reading the poems as resisting such a teleology toward cure or purging of disease. Instead, Sonnet 147 and others like it show the negative aspects of the close linkages between desire and recollection as the speaker's tenacious attraction makes the bitter memory of the encounter all the more unforgettable. Infection, like recollection, keeps us from forgetting. In the context of sexually transmitted disease, symptoms constitute the lingering, gnawing, and burning sense that something acquired in the past will resurface in the future.[14]

Textually Transmitted Infection

The speaker turns from internal lament to direct address of the beloved in the final couplet, where Helen Vendler finds that "anger finally erupts as the self-enclosure of the sickroom is broken for one final *j'accuse*."[15] The poem ends,

> For I have sworn thee fair, and thought thee bright,
> Who art as black as hell, as dark as night. (13–14)

Especially in light of the praise of the male beloved's fairness elsewhere in the *Sonnets*, we might interpret this poem turn as turning on a familiar theme in the collection that intertwines misogyny and racist tropes in order "to conclude that only *female* fairness is flawed."[16] However, the poem offers no definitive indication of the gender. The similitude between the beloved now perceived as "dark" and the space of "hell" nonetheless may locate this sonnet's final couplet within the long genealogy of racist thought to which Shakespeare contributes, as Ruben Espinosa has compellingly traced, wherein "the perception that Blackness is indicative of

---

[14] Tracing the vexed erotics of the disease/memory nexus in Sonnet 147 allows us to set aside the predominant discussion of futurity in the *Sonnets* as represented by the potentiality of the young man's heir and the immortality of the poet's verse. By choosing such an approach, the present essay seeks to respond to Melissa Sanchez's call for early modern scholars to join queer theory's collective effort to trace "forms of intimacy and community in which perverse, shameful, and irrational feelings and desires have a place." Melissa E. Sanchez, "'Use Me but as Your Spaniel': Feminism, Queer Theory, and Early Modern Sexualities," *PMLA* 127, no. 3 (May 2012): 496.

[15] Vendler, *The Art of Shakespeare's Sonnets*, 619.

[16] Sujata Iyengar, *Shades of Difference: Mythologies of Skin Color in Early Modern England* (Philadelphia: University of Pennsylvania Press, 2005), 140–1. The use of the term "hell," which functioned as slang for female sexual anatomy in the early modern period, opens the possibility that this poem is addressed to a female beloved even though no pronoun is used here to make certain such a claim. If this poem does address a woman, then its final condemnation could reflect what Moya Bailey has termed "misogynoir" because the speaker renders judgment upon the female addressee for the blackness he has newly discovered about her. The term was coined to describe discourses that intermingle anti-Black and anti-woman sentiments, and the neologism aptly fits this scenario as well. Moya Bailey, "New Terms of Resistance: A Response to Zenzele Isoke," *Souls: A Critical Journal of Black Politics, Culture, and Society* 15, no. 14 (2013): 341–3.

moral, aesthetic, and/or intellectual inferiority."[17] The use of "hell" in the demo-nization of the beloved underlines another operation of futurity in the poem: the addressee will experience the repercussions of their actions into the afterlife. Yet so will the speaker, whose own sin promises that the suffering from viral infection now will only be translated into a space of non-bodily punishment after death.

Despite his efforts to spotlight the origins of his infection, he cannot absolve himself of his own faults. The speaker's own infection breaks down any binary distinction between him and his blamed beloved. The movement of his speech from largely Latinate elegance to a blunter lashing out in the vernacular under-scores that his own desires are polluted with the baseness that he projects onto his object of desire.[18] Such a reading of the poem contributes to the project that Ambereen Dadabhoy has recently urged, wherein Shakespeare scholars (especially white scholars such as myself) should seek to render visible and undermine the textual sites where "the normative gaze is always already rooted in the logics and epistemologies of whiteness."[19] Dilating on the interstice between the "I" and "thee" who encounter each other in the couplet underscores the way that sexual transmis-sion functions as a metaphor for textual transmission. However, it is vital to note that diverse readers might differentially imagine themselves interpolated into the textual space of the poem as well as the temporal space between the moment when the speaker utters this invective and the later moment when the beloved might receive the message.

As one reads this and other poems in the 1609 collection, one might feel that the speaker's deeply intimate utterances about his isolation and longing represent a wish for connection not just with the beloved to which a poem is addressed but to a larger world. Michael Warner remarks that erotic partners relish "the public world of their privacy" because "it is the pleasure of belonging to a sexual world, in which one's sexuality finds an answering resonance not just in one another, but in a world of others."[20] This poem seems to aspire toward a similar dynamic where, even if the speaker's specific dilemma sounds alien, a reader still might feel what he claims to feel or empathetically connect different experiences to his. In reading this poem, one need not ask the question of whether the sexually transmitted disease actually occurred; instead, one can pursue the question of how sexuality operates

---

[17] Ruben Espinosa, *Shakespeare on the Shades of Racism* (New York and London: Routledge, 2021), 15.

[18] I thank Carla Mazzio for this insight and for excellent feedback on my reading of the poem. Some portions of this chapter appear in an earlier form in her edited collection *Histories of the Future: On Shakespeare and Thinking Ahead* (forthcoming from University of Pennsylvania Press).

[19] Ambereen Dadabhoy, "The Unbearable Whiteness of Being (in) Shakespeare," *postmedieval: a journal of medieval cultural studies* 11, 2–3 (2020): 230.

[20] Michael Warner, *The Trouble with Normal: Sex, Politics, and the Ethics of Queer Life* (Cambridge, MA: Harvard University Press, 1999), 179.

as a category for understanding the trans-subjective and trans-temporal operations of feeling.

Instead of hiding his feelings of dejection and his embarrassment of being infected, Shakespeare's speaker fully embraces the affective capabilities of this short body of text to connect with its reader. Indeed, Francis Meres's *Palladis Tamia* gives us an intriguing glimpse into how early moderns might have considered such a textually active experience of a text to be inherent in the act of reading.[21] As discussed in Chapter Two, Meres suggests that "as we see ourselves in other men's eyes, so in other men's writings we may see what becomes us."[22] In the case of the speaker's beloved, Shakespeare seems to want the addressee to remember the pain they have caused him and to know that his infatuation continues to burn. In the case of a larger readership, the poet may want future readers of the poem to recall similar pains they have experienced as well. As Meres suggests, reading is integral to a self-fashioning not just through the advancement of learning but through a process by which one looks for reflections of one's own self or representations of who one might aspire to be. In the case of Sonnet 147, the interaction might be a mix of identifying with a previous sense of the same remorse and committing to avoid situations that might engender such a sense of remorse. We thus find a new implication of Meres's suggestion that "what thou read is to be transposed to thine own use."[23] In Shakespeare's case, the poem seems dually purposed to be transposed upon both his present beloved and his future readers for an array of uses: shame, empathy, avoidance, or inspiration.

Writing as Reversal

What must it be like to suffer from a fever as one longs for a beloved? How does the beloved perceive the lover's suffering? How do readers see themselves in a text? How does undesirable desire and irrepressible memory have us looking backward and looking forward at once? We find a startling display of answers to these questions in Maureen Owen's twenty-first-century adaptation of Sonnet 147.[24] The poem appears this way on the page:

---

[21] While Meres is well known for his commentary on Shakespeare's early career, Catherine Nicholson has recently observed that "few have ventured beyond his comments on Shakespeare." Nicholson, "Algorithm and Analogy," 643.

[22] Meres, *Wits Treasury*, 268v.

[23] This quotation is also discussed in Chapter Two. Meres, *Wit's Treasury*, 268v.

[24] Maureen Owen, "Sonnet 147," in *The Sonnets: Translating and Rewriting Shakespeare*, ed. Sharmila Cohen and Paul Legault (Brooklyn: Nightboat / Telephone Books, 2012), 225.

night as dark as hell as black as art   who

bright thee thought and fair thee sworn have I   for

express'd vainly truth the from random   at

are madmen's as discourse my and thoughts   my

unrest evermore with mad-frantic   and

care past is reason now am I cure   past

except did physic which death is   desire

approve now desperate I and me left   hath

kept not are prescriptions his that   angry

love my to physician the reason my

please to appetite sickly uncertain   the

ill the preserve doth which that on   feeding

disease the nurseth longer which that   for

still longing fever a as is love my

The poem might first seem like the madmen's discourse that Shakespeare's speaker describes afflicting him. Yet setting aside impulses to find the sequential logics of subject/predicate, before/after, and if/then, a reader can begin to make some sense of the writing. Having discussed this poem at length with my students, I can tell you that this seemingly jumbled transcription of words does make sense in many parts even before one realizes that it is Shakespeare's poem written backwards (with some alterations to typography, grammatical marks, and spacing). One certainly can read this lyric as a feverish utterance: the very madman's thoughts and discourse that the speaker tells us are his symptoms. As the adaptation throws into relief the jumbled nature of the original speaker's thoughts and speech, it underscores the strained quality of the speaker's attempt to claim the superiority of his own fairness. Shakespeare's original poem instantiates that pattern which Kim F. Hall has identified within the *Sonnets*, where readers encounter "fairness as an emergent ideology of white supremacy."[25] The original Sonnet 147 and its adaptation underscore how we might extend Hall's claim that "the young man sonnets" reveal the "difficult task [of] maintaining fairness as a stable and pure linguistic and social quality."[26] Afflicted with disease and filled with regret, the speaker finds his own fairness polluted by desire and further finds that desire has corrupted his ability to discern fairness from blackness in his shifting evaluation of the beloved.

[25] Kim F. Hall, "'These Bastard Signs of Fair': Literary Whiteness in Shakespeare's Sonnets," in *Post-Colonial Shakespeares*, ed. Ania Loomba and Martin Orkin (London: Taylor and Francis, 1998), 67.
[26] Hall, "Literary Whiteness in Shakespeare's Sonnets," 67.

Owen invites the reader to make sense of Shakespeare's poem by seeing it in reverse, to imagine her poem as the earlier one now transposed onto the contemporary page. Its surface unintelligibility speaks to both its representation of feverish discourse and its status as a reflection of the inherent queerness of seeking to render legible early modern sexuality within our own contemporary contexts. Might one say that this poem answers Valerie Traub's call for scholars to "render adequately the complexity and alterity of early modern sexuality"?[27] The ravings of Shakespeare's desiring speaker are simultaneously recognizable and unintelligible in this adaptation. All the while, the poem seems to call our attention to work of similitude. The top line showcases the work of "as" in both the original and the adapted poem, as the reader is asked to crosswalk a range of concepts—venereal disease and desire, lover and beloved, past and present. Owen's spacing of the poem, which places "my" in a particularly noticeable position, emphasizes the speaker's ownership of the disease and the desire for which he blames the addressee. She thus underscores what Melissa Sanchez has identified within the *Sonnets*: a pattern where the racial and gendered valences of distinctions between the "fair" young man and the "black" mistress in Shakespeare's *Sonnets* serve to undermine the opposition between these figures in terms of their connection to purity, agency, and fidelity.[28]

Owen's "Sonnet 147" is thus both a mirror image of the original and, in its reverse transposition of the text, the opposite of the original poem. By reversing the order of the words, the poem becomes a search for origins not just in the sense of the textual origin of the adaptation but also the origin of the speaker's madness. In this new version, we find that the inciting element is not love but a hateful attitude toward the Other. Owen's "Sonnet 147" commences with the speaker in a state of despising his beloved for the quality of blackness and hating himself for his own inability to discern fair from black. By opening the poem with a series of instances of "as" rather than "is" in the original, Owen's reverse version depicts the speaker actively seeking similes and creating narratives to justify his hate by tracing it to love-as-disease. This, in turn, concretizes Owen's own poetic authority as someone who has not simply transcribed the poem backwards. As an adapter and memorializer of Shakespeare's sonnet, she has given readers a new way to close read the poem. We can look anew at the poem's "who," now startlingly showcased through the poet's use of white space, and render visible the active work of the speaker—as well as the reader, addressee, and future adapter—who might be obscured by the performance of mad discourse.

We might claim, then, that Owen sees herself—as poet and as speaker—in the original poem but looks at it through a visualized retrospect on the

[27] Valerie Traub, "The Sonnets: Sequence, Sexuality, and Shakespeare's Two Loves," in *A Companion to Shakespeare's Works*, vol. 4: *The Poems, Problem Comedies, Late Plays*, ed. Richard Dutton and Jean E. Howard (Oxford: Blackwell, 2003), 285.

[28] Sanchez, *Queer Faith*, 131–42.

page, an example of moving backwards or reverse transcription. She mirrors the original poem but queers it too. Margaret Owen's poem engages in that same project as queer research into the past by "suspending determinate sexual and chronological differences while expanding the possibilities of the nonhetero, with all its connotations of sameness, similarity, proximity, and anachronism."[29] This adaptation looks back on the past from the vantage point of the future, seeing it clearly and not seeing it clearly by stunningly not changing a word of the poem.

Early Modern Memories of AIDS

Shakespeare's *Sonnets* have done much to catalyze contemporary efforts to discern who and how Shakespeare desired, especially given how he seems tantalizingly public about his passion yet leaves its objects anonymous. It is not hard to see how this poem and sonnets such as 153 and 154, which depict Cupid quenching his love torch in a bath in a futile attempt to quench its flame, inform the BBC biopic *A Waste of Shame: The Mystery of Shakespeare and His Sonnets*.[30] The film has the playwright abandoning his family, frequenting brothels, and pining after both the "fair youth" and the "dark lady" of the *Sonnets*.[31] In one of its more memorable scenes, he takes a mercury-infused bath in an effort to cure himself of syphilis. While speculations such as these certainly might be matters of personal curiosity or even of identity politics, they instantiate an enduring longing on behalf of readers to relate to the much earlier writers they read. It only urges us to want to understand how Shakespeare might have felt and to wonder if those feelings are anything like ours. I have always loved The Smiths' song "Cemetry Gates," where the melancholic speaker spends a sunny day visiting the graves of Keats, Yeats, and Wilde. He pines that the dead have *loves and passions just like his*. And he seems to speak simultaneously to a friend who has joined him on the cemetery visit and to his audience when he concludes the song stating that Keats and Yeats may be on his friend's side but Wilde is on his.[32] While it is a mistake to imagine that Shakespeare desired in the same way a modern subject does, it is nevertheless tantalizing to imagine such a possibility and that this, in turn, might explain one's connection to him.

[29] Jonathan Goldberg and Madhavi Menon, "Queering History," *PMLA* 120, no. 5 (October 2005): 1609.
[30] The title quotes the first line of Sonnet 129, which begins "Th'expense of spirit in a waste of shame." *A Waste of Shame: The Mystery of Shakespeare and His Sonnets*, directed by John McKay (BBC Four, 2005).
[31] In the film, Shakespeare has sex with a commercial sex worker and thus the venereal disease is traceable to her. This fits with the misogynistic pattern in the *Sonnets* where the female reproductive body is "associated with inconstancy, disease and death and with the absence of temporal progression." Callahan, *Shakespeare's Sonnets*, 99.
[32] The Smiths, "Cemetry Gates," by Morrissey and Johnny Marr, recorded 1986, track 5 on *The Queen Is Dead*, Rough Trade Records.

An intriguing meditation on Shakespeare's passion, on memory's curious relationship to the future, and on epidemic can be found in Timothy Findley's 2000 play *Elizabeth Rex*. The play opens during late evening on Shrove Tuesday 1601. Three characters are among a group of people staying in a barn not too far from the Tower of London. They are there for the night because a curfew has been set. William Shakespeare is there, with a group of actors who have just performed *Much Ado about Nothing* nearby, and he is feverishly working on *Antony and Cleopatra*. I say "feverishly," a term adapted from rhetorics of disease to describe work, especially writing. Elizabeth I is also there. She saw the production of *Much Ado* and finds herself stuck here under curfew with a group of waiting women. The playwright and the monarch share something. Imprisoned nearby in the Tower are a group of conspirators who attempted to stage a coup. Among them is Robert Devereux, Earl of Essex, who had been Elizabeth's advisor and favorite at one time. He is sentenced to die the next day for leading the rebellion. He is joined by Henry Wriothesly, the Earl of Southampton, who had been Shakespeare's patron and is often assumed to be the dedicatee of the *Sonnets*.[33] The audience never sees these two alleged conspirators on stage, but the two will be recalled in memory within the dialogue amongst the characters.

Oh, and there is a third figure of importance. The audience meets Edward Lowenscroft, or "Ned" as he is referred to throughout the play.[34] He is a member of Shakespeare's acting troupe, and he has just played the role of Beatrice in the play that evening. He is an actor famous for playing female roles. The most famous cross-dressing actor in England, in fact. He also has "the pox," or syphilis.[35] The stage directions describe him as having "open sores," and when I saw a production of the play several years ago at the Chicago Shakespeare Theater, these lesions immediately struck me as Kaposi's sarcoma.

My experience of temporal disorientation that night in Chicago was more layered than the usual heterochronic experience of theater where one finds themselves in the presence of events taking place centuries earlier. The AIDS-related Karposi's sarcoma of my present did not exist in seventeenth-century England, and such pock marks are rarely if ever seen now. Yet they were ever-present as telltale signs of later-stage HIV disease in the widespread images and in social interactions with my friends in the 1980s and 1990s. I found myself thereby interpolated into an ambiguous time poised between the 1601 of the play and the 2010s of viewing the play. Reviewers of different productions over the years have similarly seen Ned as dying of HIV infection, and his pox to be a thinly veiled signifier

---

[33] Wriothesly was in fact deeply involved in Essex's rebellion. His life was spared, but Devereux was executed in the Tower on February 25, 1601.

[34] Timothy Findley, *Elizabeth Rex* (Winnipeg and Niagara Falls: Blizzard Publishing, 2002).

[35] Findley, *Elizabeth Rex*, 16.

for Kaposi's sarcoma.[36] Tim Dean has observed that to become aware that one is infected with HIV is to "serve as a host for not only a virus but also another time, one that viscerally connects a body in the present to a period—and, indeed, a set of socio-sexual relations—in the historical elsewhere."[37] Dean, like Wojnarowicz, captures the strange relationship of infection to futurity. For some, infection means wondering when it will end, whether through a disease abating or in death. (HIV was not yet a manageable chronic condition when Wojnarowicz composed his memoir or when Findley wrote the play.) Infection brings the future into a state of unknowability but also makes us acutely aware that there will be a future after us. To become sick is to join a long historical genealogy of others who have been sick, and this is acutely visible in *Elizabeth Rex* because early modern syphilis functions as a natural analogue for HIV disease. As Susan Sontag remarks in *AIDS and Its Metaphors*,

> syphilis [...] in the earliest descriptions by doctors at the end of the fifteenth century, generated a version of the metaphors that flourish around AIDS: of a disease that was not only repulsive and retributive but collectively invasive.[38]

Sontag goes on to note that both syphilis and AIDS carry with them reactions of victim-blaming and connotations of promiscuity. We can thus link the figure of Ned to the speaker of Sonnet 147, and in turn to the twinned eroticism and guilt over possessing multiple sexual partners that I have explored in Chapter Four.

But what are the origins of Ned's AIDS-like illness? He has contracted the pox from his former lover, a soldier who has died in war. In an interview around the time the play premiered, Findley revealed that he based Ned on a young actor he knew who was dying of AIDS.[39] The actor's partner was someone who had been Findley's lover in the 1950s and with whom he remained very close. So Ned is a memory of a dying friend of the playwright and—in that moment of playgoing—also a memory of dying friends of mine. He is a mirror image in the past now transposed onto figures in the present. But he also is very much a figure *of the present*. Unlike other characters in the play, he speaks in modern slang and behaves much more like a stage diva or drag queen figure that one might encounter in the documentary *Paris Is Burning* or the television series *Pose*. The anachronism is not entirely effective, especially in a scene that feels dated now where Ned explains to

---

[36] A reviewer who saw the same production I did describes Ned this way: "dying from syphilis—which Findley clearly intends us to see as a metaphor for AIDS—contracted from a man he loves." Chris Jones, "On a Rough Night, Queen Elizabeth I Hangs out with Actors," *Chicago Tribune* (December 9, 2011).

[37] Tim Dean, "Bareback Time," in *Queer Times, Queer Becomings*, ed. E. L. McCallum and Mikko Tuhkanen (Albany: State University of New York Press, 2011), 93.

[38] Susan Sontag, *Illness as Metaphor and AIDS and Its Metaphors* (New York: Picador, 2001), 134.

[39] Sandra Martin, "Prize Play Hits Close to Home," *The Globe and Mail* (November 17, 2000). Accessed October 1, 2020. https://www.theglobeandmail.com/arts/prize-play-hits-close-to-home/article18427663/.

Elizabeth how to be a woman while she explains to him how to be a man. At other times, though, Findley does seem productively involved in contemplating how the rhetorics of disease and desire intertwine to render visible how the echoes of the past cannot be disaggregated from contemplations of futurity.

Clever but often mournful banter —about acting, about aging, about gender roles—fills the play. The three characters—Shakespeare, Elizabeth, Ned—speak into the wee hours. Late night Shrove Tuesday becomes early morning Ash Wednesday in the final act. Toward the end of the play, the tension on stage increases as the story comes closer to the time when it will be too late for the queen to pardon Devereux or Wriothesly. As tragedy looms, Ned demands that Elizabeth and Shakespeare admit that they loved the two imprisoned men, respectively. They refuse to admit it, but Ned persists. Had not Devereux and Elizabeth flirted openly in court and then slept together furtively when they could? Was not Wriothesly the beloved, "the fair youth," to whom Sonnets 18 and 20 are addressed? Had not Shakespeare and the young man had sex in secret?

Whether Devereux and Elizabeth, or Shakespeare and Wriothesly, had ever been romantically involved is something that scholars can never know. Yet Findley seizes upon the dying actor's desire to hear these famous figures' memories to drive the high drama at the closing of the play. Ned needs to know that they, too, are haunted by memories of a lost beloved. He is like the queen of England and the country's best-known playwright, he insists, because they have had insatiable passions just like his. And he has known what it is like to lose someone. But Ned is not in the historical record. He is just an actor, a friend, someone with a disease. Ned wants these famous historical figures to *feel like he does*. And in the climax of the play, he addresses his deceased lover and cries:

> How does one do this? I've done it a hundred times on stage. But you ... you had to suffer it. And did. On that day you rose from your bed thinking there was still *forever*. Yet in the afternoon—in the evening—in the twilight—you sank into the earth. Out of all sight forever. How does one do this? How? To be alive—no more. [...] No more connections, no more responses.[40]

As Ned imagines his lover's final hours, he captures the profound purchase that disease has upon futurity. The day begins just like any other day with infection surely on the mind but the lover without a sense that this state of being infected is about to end along with his life. Then this twinned finality arrives for Ned's infected lover, though his death commences a new state of suffering for the man who will grieve for him. Judith Butler observes that mourning entails that a person "accepts that by the loss that one undergoes, one will be changed, possibly for

---

[40] Findley, *Elizabeth Rex*, 77.

ever."[41] The audience hears a powerful expression of this as Ned likens his lover's state of being dead to that of his own state of mourning. Grieving, he tells us, is not a temporary state that ends with closure but rather is "still *forever*." It is a future-perfect state of undying doubt expressed in the phrase "How does one do this?"

The open question has Ned turn to the two other characters in an attempt to evoke a response:

(*He looks at WILL.*) No more wonder. No more words. [...] No more warmth of breath—or the touch of fingertips on skin. Of all these joys—no more. All the way over. You're gone. You're safe. Safe. (*He goes to ELIZABETH.*)[42]

Derrida's notion that "the work of mourning" is a "confused and terrible expression" is acutely dramatized here by Ned's speech.[43] He swirls in the fever pitch of memory. He remembers all the times he practiced losing a loved one. He remembers how his lover must have felt the day he died. He remembers the gentleness of their union. The speech powerfully deploys the rhetorical device of apostrophe as it is used to lament loss and to address the beloved who cannot return. And how haunted the scene is by AIDS as one witnesses the pox-covered speaker lament the loss of the dead, same-sex lover and as one hears him long for the unavailable status of being—choosing that familiar keyword for disease prevention, particularly HIV prevention—"safe."

After this speech, Elizabeth and Shakespeare are rendered frozen by the sound of distant canon fire that signals the death of the chief conspirator. Moved by Ned, Queen Elizabeth had even given the order to stop the execution of Devereux, but it was too late. Shakespeare has admitted that he loves Wriothesly but says they have never had sex (just as the stage directions tell us he is "possibly lying").[44] So the two historical figures share Ned's status as fellow lovers and mourners. Ned achieves what he wants: that Shakespeare and Elizabeth should understand his suffering and know what it is like to lose a lover. And this might be someone's experience, too, as they watch the play or even when they read Shakespeare's or Owen's Sonnet 147. One might become afflicted with what Derrida characterizes as "archive fever," that feeling to "burn with a passion [...] an irrepressible desire to return to the origin, a homesickness, a nostalgia for the return to the most archaic place of absolute commencement."[45] Yet, in the play's overt heterochrony that places a flamboyant queen with AIDS in the early modern period, *Elizabeth Rex* exposes that such connections to the past are subtended by fantasy. That is, one need not

[41] Butler, *Precarious Life*, 21.
[42] Findley, *Elizabeth Rex*, 77.
[43] Derrida, *The Work of Mourning*, 200.
[44] Findley, *Elizabeth Rex*, 55.
[45] Jacques Derrida, *Archive Fever: A Freudian Impression*, trans. Eric Prenowitz (Chicago and London: University of Chicago Press, 1995), 91.

read the play as if Findley insists that Shakespeare and Queen Elizabeth had passions just like ours. Rather, Ned's insistence that they must have had such passions dramatizes how "the projects of knowing sex, thinking sex, and making sexual knowledge are situated within the space of an irresolvable contradiction."[46] Just as one's visions of the future are so often really just extrapolated memories of the past, so too is the past its own kind of wish-fulfillment when viewed from the present.

In the minute before the stage goes dark, the audience hears "BOYS: (*Calling from the past.*) Will! Will! Over here—over here!" One way to interpret this ending is that Shakespeare reaches back into memory to avoid thinking about the unfolding present heartache. Another way to interpret this is as a final nod to the theme of disease in the play. Langley suggests that the young man of the *Sonnets* "avoids infection by attending only to himself."[47] And perhaps Shakespeare's dive back into himself here, this outstretching of his mind into the past, is an attempt to remember a time when the promise of the love of other willing bodies was not coupled with the threat of infection.

The Persistence of Viral Memory

In the literary case studies that I have discussed in this chapter and in our broader, contemporary tropic discourse, one finds that recollection, writing, and disease are not easily disaggregated. And now it seems that memories carry forward into the future in a means that truly is viral. Neuroscience has come to understand that recollection occurs by one brain cell transcribing what it knows onto another cell, in a way that "structurally and functionally resembles a retrovirus such as HIV."[48] Through *reverse transcriptase*, one cell writes or imprints its contained memory onto another cell, creating a copy that can create more copies. The *Sonnets* make clear that such a dynamic would be familiar to Shakespeare. The way that the memory-formation process is described in Sonnet 147 and in the scientific literature underscores the strong grip that narratives and figures of viral epidemics have on our imaginations. Writing is a form of viral transmission just as it is a way to reconcile oneself with the presence of a virus.

Elizabeth Rex connects collective memory to personal memory: there is always a previous pandemic, there are always others who have loved and grieved. Sara Ahmed has posited that "hope in the future rests with the objects that are behind us," and perhaps that is true in the sense that one can be reassured that others

---

[46] Traub, *Thinking Sex with the Early Moderns*, 34.

[47] Langley, *Shakespeare's Contagious Sympathies*, 21.

[48] Elissa Pastuzyn, "Are Our Memories Formed by an Ancient Virus?" *The Biologist* 65, no. 3 (2018): 14–17; see also Elissa D. Pastuzyn et al., "The Neuronal Gene *Arc* Encodes a Repurposed Retrotransposon Gag Protein that Mediates Intercellular RNA Transfer," *Cell* 172, nos. 1–2 (January 2018): 275–88.e18.

have overcome times like the ones we are diversely experiencing now.[49] Earlier pandemics and experiences of loss may haunt one in the present at the level of collective and personal memory, but they are also part of the positivistic fantasy of connection between individuals living in the past and those who will live into the future. All three case studies that I have discussed this far are concerned with the process of *transposing*, to borrow the term Meres chooses to describe reading, or with *writing in reverse*, to conjure both Owen's creative process and the cellular replication of memory described above. One finds characters, readers, and writers transmitting emotions to each other and transposing their experiences onto each other. In doing so, these figures shore up one's fantasy that connection to the past is possible, if only as material from which one can conjure fantasies of the future.

Sonnet 147 and *Elizabeth Rex* are just two data points in a pattern of thought that links memory and contagious disease. Another flashpoint for this inter-mingling is the 1953 novel *Funeral Rites*, where Jean Genet's narrator recounts how—after his lover had died—he realized that he had caught from him a case of pubic lice. He decides not to treat the problem. Indeed, for him, the parasites are far from a problem:

> I saw to it that they stayed there and in the vicinity. It pleased me to think that they retained a dim memory of that same place on Jean's body, whose blood they had sucked. They were tiny, secret hermits whose duty it was to keep alive in those forests the memory of a young victim. They were truly the living remains of my friend.[50]

Surely this depiction offers one of those "obscene postures," as Kadji Amin describes Genet's flashes of literary spectacle meant to eroticize the abject through "performances [...] designed to solicit the reader's hatred, pity, and disgust."[51] Without idolizing Genet, as Amin notes that many previous queer scholars have done, I do believe there is room for "being willing to pursue his wily and some-times contradictory affective motivations" and to note the productive erotics of disease-inflected mourning here.[52]

The deceased beloved (named Jean) never dies because his living memory con-tinues upon the body of his lover (also named Jean) as this first-person narrator blends into the voice of the author (yet a third, and perhaps all the same, Jean). In this depiction, we can trace the intertwined discourses of memory and of roman-tic affairs—"secret" invokes the private world engendered and occupied by lovers, "sucked" invokes an erotic connection between bodies and the transfer of fluid between them. Then we have the tripling of names, the twinned site of infection

[49] Sara Ahmed, *The Promise of Happiness* (Durham: Duke University Press, 2010), 198.
[50] Jean Genet, *Funeral Rites*, trans. Bernard Frechtman (New York: Grove Press, 1994 [1953]), 41.
[51] Kadji Amin, *Disturbing Attachments: Genet, Modern Pederasty, and Queer History* (Durham: Duke University Press, 2017), 2.
[52] Amin, *Disturbing Attachments*, 176.

on the body (that particular site itself an erotic zone), and the mild itching from the presence of parasites. All of these speak to the nagging function of recall. The "dim memory" that the lice are imagined to possess is the protagonist Jean's recollection of the now-deceased Jean. And now perhaps this infection—I mean the notion of this infection—is embedded in our memory. The description is at once unusual, abject, heartbreaking. Infection is something that keeps us from forgetting.

When I first began to contemplate how to conclude this book and decided to think through this particularly evocative triptych—Shakespeare, contagion, memory—my thoughts turned to this moment in Genet's novel. It is, in fact, a textual instance I have not thought of in many years and—as I think of it now—I realize that the experience Genet describes struck me as utterly alien when I read it as an undergraduate. I encountered it in a French literature course I had taken, on a lark more or less, in my last semester in college. Upon reading this in the first instance, I wondered: Did all French literature speak so frankly about sex? And, if so, why would Genet depict something typically avoided in discussion and why describe it in such moving prose? Certainly, at age twenty-one, I was not a prude. I knew about same-sex desire, about sex, about naked bodies, and I had been educated about sexually transmitted infections.

But I was only beginning to know that one might speak so frankly about sexuality. And I did not yet fathom how utterly catastrophic loss could feel, especially when that loss simultaneously vacated romantic love and the beloved from one's life in a single moment. To the twenty-one-year-old me, Genet's scenario seemed nearly as distant to me as the early modern world. Now—even just in light of my own research and thinking that I have synthesized in the present book—the novel's description (and all of its attendant emotions) don't seem so strange to me as they once did.

Coda: Every Time We Say Goodbye

I would like to close by considering a final example, albeit a non-Shakespearean one, where the early modern period proves apt for contemplating how viral transmission offers a powerful metaphor for the purchase of memory. Derek Jarman's 1991 film *Edward II* adapts Christopher Marlowe's 1594 play for the screen. It highlights the relationship between the king and his favorite Piers Gaveston, just as the original play does, but with a crucial shift. In Marlowe's version, the royal court objects strongly to the relationship because of the class differences between the two men. In Jarman's film, it is very much the same-sex nature of the relationship that so raises the ire of the court. And it was not the director's first engagement with early modern literature. In *The Angelic Conversation* (1985), he juxtaposed dream-like homoerotic imagery with Judi Dench's voice-over reading the *Sonnets*. In *Edward II*, the filmmaker retains the original language of the play but maps the narrative conflict onto the struggle for gay rights and efforts to raise awareness of the HIV/AIDS epidemic.[53]

While Jarman's *Edward II* intermingles contemporary elements in its backdrop—an anti-government protest, a rugby game, modern clothing—with non-modernized language from Marlowe's play, the most startling intrusion of the present comes when Edward must say farewell to Gaveston as he is banished. While the two speak, music comes over the scene. We hear Annie Lennox, sometime lead singer of the Eurythmics, sing Cole Porter's "Every Time We Say Goodbye." At first, it seems that the song is non-diegetic as the music simply seems to cue the audience to the mood and meaning of the interaction. Lennox does appear on screen but seems to be elsewhere, unconnected to the action of the play, the visual presence of the singer just another one of Jarman's unusual cinematic choices. And it's such an apt song for the moment between these two characters. After all, the song's speaker claims, "I die a little," upon every separation from the beloved. It's an old idea. Recall Arthur Schopenhauer's remark that "every parting gives a foretaste of death."[54] And maybe it is even more true in the context of romantic desire. Think of Juliet telling Romeo that "parting is such sweet sorrow" or even more explicitly watching him depart and saying, "Methinks I see thee, now thou art so low, / As one dead in the bottom of a tomb" (2.1.229; 3.5.55–6). We say farewell, and we're only left with the memory of the departed. We say farewell, and it is a recollection of previous farewells, an addition to the mounting calculus of loss every time we say goodbye.

Then the lovers are dancing to the song. The music is thus diegetic, linking the audience and the characters across time. The inclusion of a song from the 1940s contributes to the mixing of slices of time that characterizes the film: there is the time of the play (the early fourteenth century), the time of its writing (the late sixteenth century), the time of the song (the middle of the twentieth century), and the time of the audience's viewing (the early 1990s, the height of the HIV epidemic). The camera then pans out, giving us the whole scene in deep focus.[55] It turns out that Lennox has been there all along. She has been singing for the parting lovers the entire time, and they pause from their dancing briefly to watch her sing. And then we have that refrain one final time: "Every time we say goodbye."

---

[53] Jarman himself was deeply interested in the Renaissance. As Lee Benjamin Huttner observes, "Jarman regularly places pressure on the relevance of the historical subject to the present, inventing an anachronistic imaginary through which to envision how figures of the past continue to haunt the present." Lee Benjamin Huttner, "Body Positive: The Vibrant Present of Derek Jarman's *Edward II* (1991)," *Shakespeare Bulletin* 32, no. 3 (2014): 398.

[54] Schopenhauer, *Studies in Pessimism*, 65.

[55] While these anachronisms violate the boundaries between the past and present, they also remind us that we make sense of the past through the lens of present circumstance. It is a method that both makes the past knowable and also emphasizes its unknowability, which Jarman articulates nicely when reflecting on his decision to make the film a mixture of past and present elements: "The past is the past, as you try to make material out of it, things slip even further away." Derek Jarman, *Queer Edward II* (London: British Film Institute, 1991), 86.

It's such a simple song but a really elegant one too. That's the stuff we expect from a Cole Porter song.[56] And it works so well for this scene. Longing, separation, disapproval of loving a particular way in a cultural context. Well, that must be the stuff of Cole Porter, too, I suppose. Being gay in the 1940s could not have been easy. I can only imagine.

Lennox's own music video for the song doesn't relate to the film, at least not directly. Instead, we see her watching splices of old home video of a family with young children (Fig. 7.1). She's watching them on one of those old film projectors, sometimes sitting in a chair and other times standing with the images projected partly on her face and partly on the screen behind her. A young boy and his sister chase after a ball on the lawn, swim in the ocean, laugh with their parents. The music video doesn't reveal this, but these snippets are from home movies of the Jarman family when Derek was growing up in England in the 1940s. These celluloid memories call back to the child who Jarman was before he knew about romantic love, about heartache, about infection, about how many times he would have to say goodbye. Like those boyhood voices that call out to William Shakespeare at the end of *Elizabeth Rex*, these images tantalize us with the notion that one can go backwards in time, that memory is a way to undo the past, or at least that reverie allows us to forget about the passage of time now and then.

The music resuscitates Cole Porter's jazz standard in a way that makes the song speak so directly to the emotional weight of the HIV epidemic, even if it was written in a different time. And, in turn, both the video and the song become haunted by the shadow of the epidemic. The young child we see could not have known about AIDS nor could he have known he would contract the disease. Forty years later, Jarman was supposed to direct Lennox's music video but ended up being too sick to do so. The film of *Edward II*, too, was impacted by the director's health. He had contracted AIDS-related pneumonia and worked on the film during his homebound recovery. In his diaries, he wrote, "I'm up, and off the oxygen, though still breathless. I spend the morning working on the script for *Edward II*."[57] He would die only a few years after making the film. In its new contexts, "Every Time We Say Goodbye" takes on new meanings as it invites listeners to think about the past in a new way, to connect more closely to the urgency of the present, and to

---

[56] This Annie Lennox version is featured on the 1990 compilation album *Red Hot + Blue*, which was produced by the HIV/AIDS education and advocacy organization Red Hot Organization. It included pop performers adapting some of the best-known songs by Porter, and the title of the album comes from Cole Porter's musical *Red, Hot and Blue*. The album producers must have seen something in that musical that spoke to themes circulating in discourses about the epidemic at the time—*Red, Hot and Blue*—anger, sex-positivity, sadness. Not all the themes of the songs on the album speak to issues in the HIV/AIDS epidemic. But the one included in Jarman's *Edward II* certainly does. It is a song about two people saying farewell. That is one way to read the "we" in the title and the refrains of the song. But another way to read it is that the "we" is us, all of us, we, the living.

[57] Derek Jarman, *Modern Nature* (Minneapolis: University of Minnesota Press, 2009), 293.

Fig. 7.1. Annie Lennox, "Every Time We Say Goodbye (Red Hot + Blue)" (Dir. Ed Lachman, Chrysalis Records, 1990), screenshot from the music video.

think about what the future may bring. Lennox's music video opens with a statement by the artist. She looks directly at the camera and says, "The more cases of HIV infection we can prevent now, the fewer cases of AIDS will be seen in the future." It is a reminder that what we are about to see—the homage to Cole Porter, to Derek Jarman, and to saying goodbye—asks us to remember the past in order to shape the future.

And, in turn, the song offers a way to think about the sometimes bittersweet pleasures of memory, whether realized, sought, proposed, or just a dream.

Bibliography

Acker, Faith. "John Benson's *Poems* and Its Literary Precedents." In *Canonising Shakespeare: Stationers and the Book Trade, 1640–1740*, edited by Emma Depledge and Peter Kirwan, 85–106. Cambridge: Cambridge University Press, 2017.

Acker, Faith. *First Readers of Shakespeare's Sonnets 1590–1790*. London: Routledge, 2020.

Aguayo, Joseph. "Bion's Notes on Memory and Desire: Its Initial Clinical Reception in the United States, a Note on Archival Material." *International Journal of Psychoanalysis* 95, no. 5 (2014): 889–910.

Ahmed, Sara. *Queer Phenomenology: Orientations, Objects Others*. Durham: Duke University Press, 2006.

Ahmed, Sara. *The Promise of Happiness*. Durham: Duke University Press, 2010.

Aisenstein, Marilia. "Thinking as an Act of the Flesh." In *An Analytic Journey: From the Art of Archery to the Art of Psychoanalysis*, 185–200. London: Routledge, 2017.

Aisenstein, Marilia and Donald Moss. "Desire and its Discontents." In *Sexualities: Contemporary Psychoanalytic Perspectives*, edited by Alessandra Lemma and Paul Lynch, 63–80. London: Routledge, 1989.

Akhimie, Patricia. *Shakespeare and the Cultivation of Difference: Race and Conduct in the Early Modern World*. New York: Routledge, 2018.

Alpers, Paul. "Apostrophe and the Rhetoric of Renaissance Lyric." *Representations* 122, no. 1 (Spring 2013): 1–22.

Amin, Kadji. *Disturbing Attachments: Genet, Modern Pederasty, and Queer History*. Durham: Duke University Press, 2017.

Anderson, Penelope. *Friendship's Shadows: Women's Friendship and the Politics of Betrayal in England, 1640–1705*. Edinburgh: Edinburgh University Press, 2013.

Anonymous. *Rhetorica ad Herennium*. Translated by Harry Kaplan. Cambridge, MA: Harvard University Press, 1954.

Anonymous. *Book of Common Prayer 1559*. Edited by John Booty. Charlottesville: University of Virginia Press, 1976.

Archer, John Michael. *Technically Alive: Shakespeare's Sonnets*. London: Palgrave Macmillan, 2012.

Aristotle. *Nicomachean Ethics,* edited by Lesley Brown and translated by David Ross (Oxford: Oxford University Press, 2009).

Ascham, Roger. *The Scholemaster*. London: John Daye, 1570.

Atkins, Carl D. "The Context of the Sonnets." In William Shakespeare, *Shakespeare's Sonnets: With Three Hundred Years of Commentary*, edited by Carl D. Atkins, 1–28. Madison and Teaneck: Farleigh Dickinson University Press, 2007.

Bacon, Francis. *Francis Bacon: The Major Works*. Edited by Brian Vickers. Oxford: Oxford University Press, 2008.

Bailey, Amanda. "Hamlet without Sex: The Politics of Regenerate Loss." In *Sexuality and Memory in Shakespeare's England: Literature and the Erotics of Recollection*, edited by John S. Garrison and Kyle Pivetti, 220–36. London and New York: Routledge, 2016.

Bailey, Moya. "New Terms of Resistance: A Response to Zenzele Isoke." *Souls: A Critical Journal of Black Politics, Culture, and Society* 15, no. 14 (2013): 341–3.

Baldo, Jonathan. *Memory in Shakespeare's Histories: Stages of Forgetting in Early Modern England*. New York: Routledge, 2012.

Barber, C. L. "Shakespeare in His Sonnets." *The Massachusetts Review* 1, no. 4 (Summer 1960): 648–72.

Barnfield, Richard. *The Complete Poems*. Edited by George Klawitter. Selinsgrove: Susquehanna University Press, 1990.

Barret, J. K. "Enduring 'Injurious Time': Alternatives to Immortality and Proleptic Loss in Shakespeare's Sonnets." In *The Sonnets: The State of Play*, edited by Hannah Crawforth, Elizabeth Scott-Baumann, and Clare Whitehead, 137–56. London and New York: Bloomsbury Arden Shakespeare, 2017.

Barthes, Roland. *The Pleasure of the Text*. Translated by Richard Miller. New York: Hill and Wang, 1975.

Barthes, Roland. "The Death of the Author." In Roland Barthes, *Image—Music—Text*, translated by Stephen Heath, 142–8. New York: Hill and Wang, 1978.

Barthes, Roland. *Camera Lucida: Reflections on Photography*. Translated by Richard Howard. New York: Hill and Wang, 1982.

Barthes, Roland. *A Lover's Discourse: Fragments*. Translated by Richard Howard. New York: Hill and Wang, 2010.

Barthes, Roland. "Letter to Robert David, December 8, 1944." In *Album: Unpublished Correspondence and Texts*, translated by Jody Gladding, 51–63. New York: Columbia University Press, 2018.

Bataille, Georges. *Erotism: Death and Sensuality*. Translated by Mary Dalwood. San Francisco: City Lights Publishers, 1986.

Bataille, Georges. "The Sacred." In *Visions of Excess: Selected Writings 1927–1939*, translated by Allan Stoekle, with Carl R. Lovitt and Donald M. Leslie Jr., 178–82. Minneapolis: University of Minnesota Press, 2004.

Bate, Jonathan. "Ovid and the Sonnets; or, Did Shakespeare Feel the Anxiety of Influence?" *Shakespeare Survey* 42 (1990): 65–76.

Beck, Julie. "Imagining the Future Is Just Another Form of Memory." *The Atlantic*, October 17, 2017.

Beckman, Frida. *Between Desire and Pleasure: A Deleuzian Theory of Sexuality*. Edinburgh: Edinburgh University Press, 2013.

Beecher, Donald. "Recollection, Cognition, and Culture: An Overview on Renaissance Memory." In *Ars Reminiscendi: Mind and Memory in Renaissance Culture*, edited by Donald Beecher and Grant Williams, 367–426. Toronto: Centre for Renaissance and Reformation Studies, 2009.

Belsey, Catherine. *Shakespeare in Theory and Practice*. Edinburgh: Edinburgh University Press, 2008.

Benjamin, Jessica. *The Bonds of Love: Psychoanalysis, Feminism, and the Problem of Domination*. New York: Pantheon Books, 1988.

Berlant, Lauren. "The Female Complaint." *Social Text* 19/20 (Autumn 1988): 237–59.

Berlant, Lauren. *Cruel Optimism*. Durham: Duke University Press, 2011.

Berlant, Lauren. "A Properly Political Concept of Love: Three Approaches in Ten Pages." *Cultural Anthropology* 26, no. 4 (November 2011): 683–91.

Berlant, Lauren. *Desire/Love*. Brooklyn, NY: Punctum Books, 2012.

Berlant, Lauren and Lee Edelman. *Sex, or the Unbearable*. Durham and London: Duke University Press, 2014.

Bersani, Leo. "The Pleasures of Repetition." In *The Freudian Body: Psychoanalysis and Art*, 51–80. New York: Columbia University Press, 1986.

Bersani, Leo. "Sociality and Sexuality." *Critical Inquiry* 26, no. 4 (Summer 2000): 261–85.

Bersani, Leo. "Conclusion." In *Intimacies*, Leo Bersani and Adam Phillips, 119-126. Chicago and London: University of Chicago Press, 2010.

Bion, Wilfred R. "Notes on Memory and Desire." *The Psychoanalytic Forum* 2 (1967): 272–3.

Boellstorff, Tom. "When Marriage Falls: Queer Coincidences in Straight Time." *GLQ: A Journal of Gay and Lesbian Studies* 13, nos. 2–3 (2007): 227–48.

Bollas, Christopher. *The Freudian Moment*. London: Karnac, 2008.

Bolzoni, Lina. "The Art of Memory and the Erotic Image in Sixteenth- and Seventeenth-Century Europe: The Example of Giovanni Battista Della Porta." In *Eros and Anteros*, edited by Donald A. Beecher and Massimo Ciavolella, 103–22. Ottawa: Dovehouse, 1992.

Bolzoni, Lina. *The Gallery of Memory: Literary and Iconographic Models in the Age of the Printing Press*. Translated by Jeremy Parzen. Toronto: University of Toronto Press, 2001.

Booth, Stephen. *An Essay on Shakespeare's Sonnets*. New Haven and London: Yale University Press, 1969.

Booth, Stephen. *Shakespeare's Sonnets*. New Haven: Yale University Press, 1977.

Borges, Jorge Luis. *Obras Completas, Tomo 3*. Buenos Aires: Emece Editores, 2005.

Boyd, Brian. *Evolution, Cognition, and Shakespeare's Sonnets*. Cambridge, MA: Harvard University Press, 2012.

Boyd, Brian. *Why Lyrics Last: Evolution, Cognition, and Shakespeare's Sonnets*. Cambridge, MA: Harvard University Press, 2012.

Boyd, William. "Two Loves Have I." *The Guardian*, November 18, 2005.

Bray, Alan and Michael Rey. "The Body of the Friend: Continuity and Change in Masculine Friendship in the Seventeenth Century." In *English Masculinities: 1660–1800*, edited by Tim Hitchcock and Michele Cohen, 65–84. London and New York: Routledge, 1999.

Burrow, Colin. "Introduction." In William Shakespeare, *The Complete Sonnets and Poems*, edited by Colin Burrow, 1–158. Oxford: Oxford University Press, 2003.

Burrow, Colin. "Shakespeare's Sonnets as Event." In *The Sonnets: The State of Play*, edited by Hannah Crawforth, Elizabeth Scott-Baumann, and Clare Whitehead, 97–116. New York: Bloomsbury Arden Shakespeare, 2017.

Burton, Robert. *The Anatomy of Melancholy*, 3 volumes. Edited by A. R. Shilleto. London: G. Bell and Sons, 1912.

Butler, Judith. *Undoing Gender*. New York and London: Routledge, 2004.

Butler, Judith. *Precarious Life: The Powers of Mourning and Violence*. London: Verso, 2006.

Butler, Judith. *Bodies That Matter: On the Discursive Limits of Sex*. New York: Routledge, 2015.

Callaghan, Dympna. "Confounded by Winter: Speeding Time in Shakespeare's Sonnets." In *A Companion to Shakespeare's Sonnets*, edited by Michael Schoenfeldt, 105–18. New York: John Wiley & Sons, 2006.

Callaghan, Dympna. *Shakespeare's Sonnets*. Malden: Wiley-Blackwell, 2007.

Carruthers, Mary. *The Book of Memory: A Study of Memory in Medieval Culture*. 2nd edition. Cambridge: Cambridge University Press, 2008.

Cavafy, C. P. "Body, Remember." In *The Collected Poems: With Parallel Greek Text*, 107-9. Oxford: Oxford University Press, 2009.

Cavafy, C. P. "One Night." In *The Collected Poems: With Parallel Greek Text*, 71-3. Oxford: Oxford University Press, 2009.

Charney, Maurice. *Wrinkled Deep in Time: Aging in Shakespeare*. New York: Columbia University Press, 2009.

Chartier, Roger. *The Order of Books: Readers, Authors, and Libraries in Europe between the 14th and 18th Centuries.* Translated by Lydia G. Cochrane. Palo Alto: Stanford University Press, 1994.

Chess, Simone. "Male Femininity and Male-to-Female Crossdressing in Shakespeare's Plays and Poems." In *Queer Shakespeare: Desire and Sexuality*, edited by Goran Stanivukovic, 227–44. London: Bloomsbury, 2017.

Cicero. *On Friendship (Laelius de Amicitia) & The Dream of Scipio,* Translated by J.G.F. Powell. Warminster, U.K.: Aris and Phillips Ltd., 1990.

Cohn, Dorrit. *Transparent Minds: Narrative Modes for Presenting Consciousness in Fiction.* Princeton: Princeton University Press, 1978.

Connerton, Paul. "Seven Types of Forgetting." *Memory Studies* 1, no. 1 (2008): 59–71.

Conway, Martin. *Flashbulb Memories.* Brighton: LEA, 1995.

Conway, Martin. "Memory and Desire: Reading Freud." *The Psychologist* 19, no. 9 (2006): 548–50.

Cormack, Bradin. "Shakespeare's Narcissus, Sonnet's Echo." In *The Forms of Renaissance Thought: New Essays on Literature and Culture*, edited by Leonard Barkan, Bradin Cormack, and Sean Keilen, 127–39. New York: Palgrave Macmillan, 2009.

Correll, Barbara. "'Terms of 'Indearment': Lyric and General Economy in Shakespeare and Donne." *ELH* 75, no. 2 (Summer 2008): 241–62.

Crane, Mary Thomas. *Shakespeare's Brain: Reading with Cognitive Theory.* Princeton: Princeton University Press, 2000.

Crawforth, Hannah and Elizabeth Scott-Baumann. "Preface." In *On Shakespeare's Sonnets: A Poet's Celebration*, edited by Hannah Crawforth and Elizabeth Scott-Baumann, xiv–xv. New York and London: Bloomsbury, 2016.

Crawforth, Hannah, Elizabeth Scott-Baumann, and Clare Whitehead, eds. *The Sonnets: The State of Play.* New York: Bloomsbury Arden Shakespeare, 2017.

Crooke, Helkiah. *Microcosmographia: A Description of the Body of Man.* London: Jaggard, 1618.

Culler, Jonathan. "Apostrophe." In *The Pursuit of Signs: Semiotics, Literature, Deconstruction*, 135–54. Ithaca: Cornell University Press, 1981.

Culler, Jonathan. *Theory of the Lyric.* Cambridge, MA and London: Harvard University Press, 2015.

Dadabhoy, Ambereen. "The Unbearable Whiteness of Being (in) Shakespeare." *postmedieval: a journal of medieval cultural studies* 11, nos. 2–3 (2020): 228–35.

Damasio, Antonio. *The Feeling of What Happens: Body, Emotion, and the Making of Consciousness.* Orlando: Harcourt, 1999.

Damasio, Antonio. *Looking for Spinoza: Joy, Sorrow, and the Feeling Brain.* New York: Houghton Mifflin Harcourt, 2003.

Damasio, Antonio. *Self Comes to Mind: Constructing the Conscious Brain.* London: Heinemann, 2010.

Dean, Tim. "Bareback Time." In *Queer Times, Queer Becomings*, edited by E. L. McCallum and Mikko Tuhkanen, 75–100. Albany: State University of New York Press, 2011.

de Certeu, Michel. *The Practice of Everyday Life.* Translated by Steven Rendall. Berkeley: University of California Press, 1984.

de Grazia, Margreta. "Revolution in Shake-speare's Sonnets." In *A Companion to Shake-speare's Sonnets*, edited by Michael Schoenfeldt, 57–69. New York: John Wiley & Sons, 2006.

Deleuze, Gilles. "Coldness and Cruelty." In *Masochism: Coldness and Cruelty & Venus in Furs*, translated by Jean McNeil, 9–142. New York: Zone Books, 1991.

Deleuze, Gilles. *Difference and Repetition*. Translated by Paul Patton. London and New York: Bloomsbury, 2004.

Deleuze, Gilles. *Proust and Signs: The Complete Text*. Translated by Richard Howard. London: Continuum, 2008.

Deleuze, Gilles. "Desire and Pleasure." In *Between Deleuze and Foucault*, translated by Daniel W. Smith, edited by Nicolae Morar, Thomas Nail, and Daniel W. Smith, 223–31. Edinburgh: Edinburgh University Press, 2016.

Derrida, Jacques. *Of Grammatology*. Translated by Gayatri Spivak. Baltimore: Johns Hopkins University Press, 1976.

Derrida, Jacques. *Memoires for Paul de Man*. Translated by Cecile Lindsay, Jonathan Culler, and Eduardo Cadava. New York: Columbia University Press, 1986.

Derrida, Jacques. *Specters of Marx*. Translated by Peggy Kamuf. London and New York: Routledge, 1994.

Derrida, Jacques. *Archive Fever: A Freudian Impression*. Translated by Eric Prenowitz. Chicago and London: University of Chicago Press, 1995.

Derrida, Jacques. *The Work of Mourning*. Edited by Pascale Anne-Brault and Michael Naas. Chicago: University of Illinois Press, 2001.

Dinshaw, Carolyn. *How Soon Is Now? Medieval Texts, Amateur Readers, and the Queerness of Time*. Durham: Duke University Press, 2012.

Dixon, Dustin W. and John S. Garrison. "The Spectacle of Helen in Euripides' Helen and Marlowe's Doctor Faustus." *Classical Receptions Journal* 13, no. 2 (April 2021): 159–77.

Dolan, Frances E. *Marriage and Violence: The Early Modern Legacy*. Philadelphia: University of Pennsylvania Press, 2009.

Dollimore, Jonathan. *Death, Desire, and Loss in Western Culture*. London and New York: Routledge, 1998.

Donne, John. *The Complete English Poems*. Edited by A. J. Smith. London and New York: Penguin, 1996.

Donne, John. "Death's Duel. Preached before Charles I (25 February 1631)." In *The Major Works: Including Songs and Sonnets and Sermons*. Edited by John Carey, 401-8. Oxford: Oxford University Press, 2009.

Donne, John. "Elegy XX: To His Mistress Going to Bed." In *Selected Poetry*, edited by John Carey, 23. Oxford: Oxford University Press, 2009.

Dubrow, Heather. "'Incertainties now crown themselves assur'd': The Politics of Plotting in Shakespeare's Sonnets." *Shakespeare Quarterly* 47, no. 3 (1996): 291–305.

Dugan, Holly. *The Ephemeral History of Perfume: Scent and Sense in Early Modern England*. Baltimore: The Johns Hopkins Press, 2011.

Edelman, Lee. *No Future: Queer Theory and the Death Drive*. Durham and London: Duke University Press, 2004.

Edmondson, Paul and Stanley Wells. *Shakespeare's Sonnets*. Oxford: Oxford University Press, 2004.

Edmondson, Paul and Stanley Wells. "Introduction." In William Shakespeare, *All the Sonnets of Shakespeare*, edited by Paul Edmondson and Stanley Wells, 1–37. Cambridge: Cambridge University Press, 2020.

Einstein, Albert. *The Ultimate Quotable Albert Einstein*. Edited by Alice Calaprice. Princeton: Princeton University Press, 2010.

Eire, Carlos. *A Brief History of Eternity*. Princeton and Oxford: Princeton University Press, 2010.

Eng, David L. and David Kazanjian. "Introduction: Mourning Remains." In *Loss*, edited by David L. Eng and David Kazanjian, 1–28. Berkeley: University of California Press, 2003.

Engel, William E. *Death and Drama in Renaissance England: Shades of Memory*. Oxford: Oxford University Press, 2002.

Engel, William E., Rory Loughnane, and Grant William, eds. *The Memory Arts in Renaissance England: A Critical Anthology*. Cambridge: Cambridge University Press, 2016.

Erll, Astrid. *Memory in Culture*. Translated by Sara B. Young. Hampshire: Palgrave Macmillan, 2011.

Espinosa, Ruben. *Shakespeare on the Shades of Racism*. New York and London: Routledge, 2021.

Faulkner, William. *The Sound and the Fury: The Corrected Text*. New York: Vintage, 1991.

Fernyhough, Charles. *Pieces of Light: The New Science of Memory Illuminates the Stories We Tell about Our Past*. New York: Harper, 2013.

Ferrand, Jacques. *Erotomania, or A Treatise Discoursing of the Essence, Causes, Symptoms, Prognostics, and Care of Love, or Erotique Melancholy*. Translated by Edmund Chilmead. Oxford: L. Lichfield, 1640.

Ficino, Marsilio. *Commentary of Marsilio Ficino on the Symposium of Plato on the Subject of Love*. Translated by Sears Reynolds Jayne. New York: Columbia University Press, 1944.

Findley, Timothy. *Elizabeth Rex*. Winnipeg and Niagara Falls: Blizzard Publishing, 2002.

Fineman, Joel. *Shakespeare's Perjured Eye: The Invention of Poetic Subjectivity in the Sonnets*. Berkeley, Los Angeles, and London: University of California Press, 1986.

Finucci, Valeria and Regina Schwartz. "Introduction: Worlds within and without." In *Desire in the Renaissance: Psychoanalysis and Literature*, edited by Valeria Finucci and Regina Schwartz, 3–18. Princeton: Princeton University Press, 1994.

Fisher, Will. "Queer Money." *English Literary History* 66 (1999): 1–23.

Foucault, Michel. "Sexual Choice, Sexual Act." In *Foucault Live: Collected Interviews, 1961–1984*, edited by Sylvère Lotringer, 322-34. New York: Semiotext(e), 1996.

Freeman, Elizabeth. *Time Binds: Queer Temporalities, Queer Histories*. Durham: Duke University Press, 2010.

Freeman, Mark. *Rewriting the Self: History, Memory, Narrative*. New York: Routledge, 1993.

Freeman, Mark. *Hindsight: The Promise and Peril of Looking Backwards*. Oxford: Oxford University Press, 2010.

Freud, Anna. *The Ego and the Mechanisms of Defence*. London and New York: Routledge, 1993.

Freud, Sigmund. "Remembering, Repeating and Working-Through." In *The Standard Edition of the Complete Psychological Works of Sigmund Freud*, vol. 12, edited by James Strachey, 145-56. London: Hogarth Press, 1950.

Freud, Sigmund. *The Ego and the Id*. Translated by Joan Riviere. Edited by James Strachey. New York: W. W. Norton and Company, 1960.

Freud, Sigmund. "Jokes and Their Relation to the Unconscious." In *The Standard Edition of the Complete Psychological Works of Sigmund Freud*, vol. 8, edited and translated by James Strachey, 1–238. London: Hogarth Press, 1960.

Freud, Sigmund. "The Economic Problem of Masochism." In *The Standard Edition of the Complete Psychological Works of Sigmund Freud*, vol. 19, edited and translated by James Strachey, 155-70. London: The Hogarth Press, 1961.

Freud, Sigmund. "Inhibitions, Symptoms, and Anxiety." In *The Standard Edition of the Complete Psychological Works of Sigmund Freud*, vol. 20, translated by James Strachey, 77–175. London: The Hogarth Press, 1961.

Freud, Sigmund. "Mourning and Melancholia." In *The Standard Edition of the Complete Psychological Works of Sigmund Freud*, vol. 14, edited and translated by James Strachey, 152-70. London: Hogarth Press, 1964.

Freud, Sigmund. "Beyond the Pleasure Principle." In *On Metapsychology*. Edited by Albert Dickson, 269-338. Middlesex: Penguin Books, 1987.

Freud, Sigmund. *Civilization and its Discontents*. Translated by James Strachey. Edited by Peter Gay. New York: W. W. Norton and Co., 1989.

Freud, Sigmund. "Transience." In *On Murder, Mourning, and Melancholia*, translated by Shaun Whiteside, 195–200. New York: Penguin, 2005.

Fuery, Patrick. *Theories of Desire*. Melbourne: Melbourne University Press, 1995.

Fulwood, William. *The Castle of Memorie*. London, 1562.

Garrison, John S. "Shakespeare and Friendship: An Intersection of Interest." *Literature Compass* 9, no. 5 (May 2012): 371–9.

Garrison, John S. *Friendship and Queer Theory in the Renaissance*. New York: Routledge, 2014.

Garrison, John S. "Recollection and Preemptive Recollection in Shakespeare's Sonnets." In *Memory and Mortality in Renaissance England*, edited by William E. Engel, Rory Loughnane, and Grant Williams, 61–77. Cambridge: Cambridge University Press, 2022.

Garrison, John S. and Kyle Pivetti. *Sexuality and Memory in Early Modern England: Literature and the Erotics of Recollection*. New York: Routledge, 2015.

Genet, Jean. *Funeral Rites*. Translated by Bernard Frechtman. New York: Grove Press, 1994.

Gesualdo (Gesualdi), Filippo. *Plutosofia ... Nella quale si spiega l'Arte della Memoria con altre cose notabili pertinenti, tanto alla Memoria naturale quanto all'artificiale*. Padua, 1592.

Gil, Daniel Juan. *Before Intimacy: Asocial Sexuality in Early Modern England*. Minneapolis: University of Minnesota Press, 2006.

Glennie, Paul and Nigel Smith. *Shaping the Day: A History of Timekeeping in England and Wales 1300–1800*. Oxford: Oxford University Press, 2011.

Goldberg, Jonathan and Madhavi Menon. "Queering History." *PMLA* 120, no. 5 (October 2005): 1608–17.

Goldwell, Charles. "My Friend." In *The True Choice of a Friend*. London: for Benjamin Fisher, 1625.

Gordon, Colby. "A Woman's Prick: Trans Technogenesis in Sonnet 20." In *Shakespeare/Sex: Contemporary Readings in Gender and Sexuality*, edited by Jennifer Drouin, 268–89. New York: Bloomsbury Arden Shakespeare, 2020.

Gratarolo, Guglielmo. *De memoria reparanda, augenda confirmandaque ac de reminiscentia*. Basel, 1533.

Greene, Jody. "Introduction: The Work of Friendship." *GLQ* 10, no. 3 (2004): 319–37.

Grimald, Nicolas. "Of Friendship." In *Tottel's Miscellany*, edited by Richard Tottel. London, s.n., 1867.

Grosz, Stephen. *The Examined Life: How We Lose and Find Ourselves*. London: Random House, 2013.

Guy-Bray, Stephen. "Remembering to Forget: Shakespeare's Sonnet 35 and Sigo's 'XXXV.'" In *Sexuality and Memory in Early Modern England: Literature and the Erotics of Recollection*, edited by John S. Garrison and Kyle Pivetti, 43–50. London and New York: Routledge, 2015.

Halberstam, Jack J. *In a Queer Time and Place: Transgender Bodies, Subcultural Lives*. New York: New York University Press, 2005.

Halbwachs, Maurice. *On Collective Memory*. Translated by Lewis A. Coser. Chicago: University of Chicago Press, 1992.

Hall, Kim F. "'These Bastard Signs of Fair': Literary Whiteness in Shakespeare's Sonnets." In *Post-Colonial Shakespeares*, edited by Ania Loomba and Martin Orkin, 64–83. London: Taylor and Francis, 1998.

Halpern, Richard. *Sodomy and Sublimity in the Sonnets, Wilde, Freud, and Lacan*. Philadelphia: University of Pennsylvania Press, 2016.

Hardy, Barbara. "Shakespeare's Narrative: Acts of Memory." *Essays in Criticism* 39, no. 2 (1989): 93–115.

Harington, John. *A Preface, or rather a Briefe Apologie of Poetrie*, prefixed to the translation of *Orlando Furioso*. London, 1591.

Harris, Jonathan Gil. "The Smell of Macbeth." *Shakespeare Quarterly* 58, no. 4 (Winter 2007): 465–86.

Harrison, Matthew. "Desire Is Pattern." In *Shakespeare's Sonnets: The State of Play*, edited by Hannah Crawforth, Elizabeth Scott-Baumann, and Clare Whitehead, 185–208. New York: Bloomsbury Arden Shakespeare, 2017.

Hawes, Stephen. *The histoire of graunde Amoure and la bell Pucel, called the Pastime of plesure*. London: John Wayland, 1554.

Helfer, Rebeca. *Spenser's Ruins and the Art of Recollection*. Toronto: University of Toronto Press, 2012.

Herbert, Amanda. *Female Alliances: Gender, Identity, and Friendship in Early Modern Britain*. New Haven: Yale University Press, 2014.

Herbert, Mary. "To the Angell Spirit of the Most Excellent Phillip Sidney." In *The Collected Works of Mary Sidney Herbert, Countess of Pembroke*, vol. 1: *Poems, Translations, and Correspondence*, edited by Margaret P. Hannay, Noel J. Kinnamon, and Michael G. Brennan, 110–12. Oxford: Oxford University Press, 1998.

Hirsch, Marianne. "Family Pictures: Maus, Mourning, and Post-Memory." *Discourse* 15, no. 2 (Winter 1992–3): 3–29.

Hiscock, Andrew. *Reading Memory in Early Modern Literature*. Cambridge: Cambridge University Press, 2011.

Hiscock, Andrew and Linda Perkins Wilder, eds. *The Routledge Handbook of Shakespeare and Memory*. New York: Routledge, 2018.

Holderness, Graham. *Nine Lives of William Shakespeare*. New York: Continuum, 2011.

Holland, Abraham. *Hollandi posthuma*. London, 1626.

Holland, Peter, ed. *Shakespeare, Memory and Performance*. Cambridge: Cambridge University Press, 2006.

Hoskins, John. *Directions for Speech and Style*. Edited by Hoyt Hudson. Princeton: Princeton University Press, 1935.

Howard, Henry, Earl of Surrey. "Complaint of the Absence of her Lover, Being on the Sea." In *The Broadview Anthology of Sixteenth-Century Poetry and Prose*, edited by Marie Loughlin, Sandra Bell, and Patricia Brace, 192. Peterborough, ON: Broadview Press, 2011.

Huttner, Lee Benjamin. "Body Positive: The Vibrant Present of Derek Jarman's Edward II (1991)." *Shakespeare Bulletin* 32, no. 3 (2014): 393–412.

Hyman, Wendy Beth. "Patterns, the Shakespearean Sonnet, and Epistemologies of Scale." *Spenser Studies: A Renaissance Poetry Annual* 36 (2022): 323–36.

Innes, Paul. *Shakespeare and the English Renaissance Sonnet: Verses of Feigning Love*. New York: Macmillan, 1997.

Ivic, Christopher and Grant Williams, eds. *Forgetting in Early Modern English Literature and Culture*. London: Routledge, 2004.

Iyengar, Sujata. *Shades of Difference: Mythologies of Skin Color in Early Modern England*. Philadelphia: University of Pennsylvania Press, 2005.

Iyengar, Sujata. *Shakespeare's Medical Language: A Dictionary*. New York: Bloomsbury Arden Shakespeare, 2011.

Jakobson, Roman. *Language in Literature*. Edited by Krystyna Pomorska and Stephen Rudy. Cambridge, MA and London: Harvard University Press, 1987.

Jarman, Derek. *Queer Edward II*. London: British Film Institute, 1991.

Jarman, Derek. *Modern Nature*. Minneapolis: University of Minnesota Press, 2009.

Johanson, Kristine. "Ecclesiastes and Sonnet 59." In *The Sonnets: The State of Play*, edited by Hannah Crawforth, Elizabeth Scott-Baumann, and Clare Whitehead, 55–76. New York: Bloomsbury Arden Shakespeare, 2017.

Johnson, Barbara. "Apostrophe, Animation, and Abortion." *Diacritics* 16, no. 1 (Spring 1986): 28–47.

Johnson, Barbara. "Speech Therapy." In *Shakesqueer: A Queer Companion to Shakespeare's Works*, edited by Madhavi Menon, 328–32. Durham: Duke University Press, 2001.

Jones, Chris. "On a Rough Night, Queen Elizabeth I Hangs out with Actors." *Chicago Tribune*, December 9, 2011.

Jonson, Ben. "*De stilo et optimo scribendi genere*." In *The Cambridge Edition of the Works of Ben Jonson*, vol. 7, edited by David Bevington, Martin Butler, and Ian Donaldson, 556–8. Cambridge: Cambridge University Press, 2012.

Jordan, June. "Introduction." In *Soulscript: A Collection of Classic African American Poetry*, xix–xxiii. New York: Crown, 2004.

Jordan, June. *Directed by Desire: The Collected Poems of June Jordan*. Port Townsend: Copper Canyon Press, 2007.

Judt, Tony. *The Memory Chalet*. New York: Penguin, 2011.

Karremann, Isabel. *The Drama of Memory in Shakespeare's History Plays*. Cambridge: Cambridge University Press, 2015.

Kastan, David Scott. *Shakespeare and the Shapes of Time*. Hanover: University Press of New England, 1982.

Kavanagh, P. J. "Dream." In *On Shakespeare's Sonnets: A Poet's Celebration*, edited by Hannah Crawforth and Elizabeth Scott-Baumann, 15. London and New York: Bloomsbury, 2016.

Keats, John. *Selected Letters*. Edited by Robert Gittings. Oxford: Oxford University Press, 2009.

Khamsi, Roxanne. "Unpicking the Link between Smell and Memories." *Nature* 606, S2–S4 (June 22, 2022).

Kingsley-Smith, Jane. "Shakespeare's Sonnets and the Claustrophobic Reader: Making Space in Modern Shakespeare Fiction." *Shakespeare* 9, no. 2 (2013): 187–203.

Kingsley-Smith, Jane. *The Afterlife of Shakespeare's Sonnets*. Cambridge: Cambridge University Press, 2019.

Koestenbaum, Wayne. *Humiliation*. New York: Picador, 2011.

Kore-eda, Hirokazu, dir. *After Life* (known in Japan as *Wonderful Life*). Engine Film and TV Man Union, 1998.

Kunin, Aaron. "Shakespeare's Preservation Fantasy." *PMLA* 124, no. 1 (January 2009): 92–106.

Langley, Eric. *Shakespeare's Contagious Sympathies: Ill Communications*. Oxford: Oxford University Press; 2018.

Lees-Jeffries, Hester. *Shakespeare and Memory*. Oxford: Oxford University Press, 2013.

Lehrer, Jonah. *Proust Was a Neuroscientist*. New York: Houghton Mifflin Harcourt, 2007.

Lemnius, Levinus. *The Touchstone of Complexions*. London, 1576.

Levin, Richard. "Sonnet 129 as a 'Dramatic' Poem." *Shakespeare Quarterly* 16 (1965): 175–81.

Lombion, Sandrine, Blandine Bechetoille, Sylvie Nezelof, and Jean-Louis Millot. "Odor Perception in Alexithymic Patients." *Psychiatry Research* 177, nos. 1–2 (2010): 135–8.

Lowenthal, David. "Nostalgia Tells It Like It Wasn't." In *The Imagined Past: History and Nostalgia*, edited by Christopher Shaw and Malcolm Chase, 18–32. Manchester: Manchester University Press, 1989.

Lyly, John. *Euphues*. In *The Descent of Euphues: Three Elizabethan Romance Stories*, edited by J. Winny, 1–66. Cambridge: Cambridge University Press, 2015.

Lyne, Raphael. *Memory and Intertextuality in Renaissance Literature*. Cambridge: Cambridge University Press, 2006.

Lyne, Raphael. *Shakespeare, Rhetoric, Cognition*. Cambridge: Cambridge University Press, 2011.

MacDonald, Joyce Greene. *Women and Race in Early Modern Texts*. Cambridge: Cambridge University Press, 2002.

MacKendrick, Karmen. *Counterpleasures*. New York: State University of New York Press, 1999.

Magnusson, Lynne. "Non-Dramatic Poetry." In *Shakespeare: An Oxford Guide*, edited by Stanley Wells and Lena Cowen Orlin, 286–300. Oxford: Oxford University Press, 2003.

Marshall, Cynthia. *The Shattering of the Self: Violence, Subjectivity, and Early Modern Texts*. Baltimore: Johns Hopkins University Press, 2002.

Martin, Philip. *Shakespeare's Sonnets: Self, Love and Art*. Cambridge: Cambridge University Press, 1972.

Martin, Sandra. "Prize Play Hits Close to Home." *The Globe and Mail*, November 17, 2000. Accessed October 1, 2020. https://www.theglobeandmail.com/arts/prize-play-hits-close-to-home/article18427663/.

Masten, Jeffrey. "Is the Fundament a Grave?" In *The Body in Parts: Fantasies of Corporeality in Early Modern Europe*, edited by David Hillman and Carla Mazzio, 128–45. New York: Routledge, 1997.

Masten, Jeffrey. *Textual Intercourse: Collaboration, Authorship, and Sexualities in Renaissance Drama*. Cambridge: Cambridge University Press, 1997.

Masten, Jeffrey. *Queer Philologies: Sex, Language, and Affect in Shakespeare's Time*. Philadelphia: University of Pennsylvania Press, 2017.

Matthews, Paul M., Jeffrey McQuain, and Diana Ackerman. *The Bard on the Brain: Understanding the Mind through the Art of Shakespeare and the Science of Brain Imaging*. New York: Dana Press, 2003.

McEleney, Corey. *Futile Pleasures: Early Modern Literature and the Limits of Utility*. New York: Fordham University Press, 2017.

McFaul, Tom. *Male Friendship in Shakespeare and His Contemporaries*. Cambridge: Cambridge University Press, 2007.

McIntosh, Hugh. "The Social Masochism of Shakespeare's Sonnets." *Studies in English Literature, 1500–1900* 50, no. 1 (Winter 2010): 109–25.

McKay, John, dir. *A Waste of Shame: The Mystery of Shakespeare and His Sonnets*. London: BBC Four, 2005.

Menon, Madhavi. "Spurning Teleology in Venus and Adonis." *GLQ: A Journal of Lesbian and Gay Studies* 11, no. 4 (2005): 491–519.

Meres, Frances. *Paladis Tamia, Wit's Treasury*. London, 1598.

Milton, John. "On Shakespeare: 1630." In *John Milton: The Major Works*, edited by Jonathan Goldberg and Stephen Orgel, 20. Oxford: Oxford University Press, 2008.

Milton, John. "Sonnet 16 (When I consider how my light is spent)." In *John Milton: The Major Works*, edited by Jonathan Goldberg and Stephen Orgel, 81. Oxford: Oxford University Press, 2008.

Mitchell, Stephen. *Can Love Last? The Fate of Romance over Time*. New York: W. W. Norton & Co., 2002.

Mohamed, Feisal G. "On Race and Historicism: A Polemic in Three Turns." *English Literary History* 89, no. 2 (Summer 2022): 377–405.

Montaigne, Michel de. *The Essayes or Morall, Politike and Militarie Discourses of Lord Michaell de Montaigne*. Translated by John Florio. London: Val. Sims for Edward Blount, 1603.

Morrison, Toni. *The Bluest Eye*. New York: Vintage, 2007.

Morrison, Toni. *The Source of Self-Regard: Selected Essays, Speeches, and Meditations*. New York: Alfred A. Knopf, 2019.

Moten, Fred. "The Dark Lady and the Sexual Cut: Sonnet Record Frame/Shakespeare Jones Eisenstein." *Women and Performance: A Journal of Feminist Theory* 9, no. 2 (1997): 143–61.

Moul, Victoria. "English Elegies of the Sixteenth and Seventeenth Century." In *The Cambridge Companion to Latin Love Elegy*, edited by Thea S. Thorsen, 306–19. Cambridge: Cambridge University Press, 2013.

Moulton, Ian Frederick. "Catching the Plague: Happiness, Health, and Disease in Shakespeare." In *Disability, Health, and Happiness in the Shakespearean Body*, edited by Sujata Iyengar, 212–22. New York: Routledge, 2014.

Mullally, Sinéad L. and Eleanor A. Maguire. "Memory, Imagination, and Predicting the Future: A Common Brain Mechanism?" *Neuroscientist* 20, no. 3 (June 2014): 220–34.

Muñoz, José Esteban. *Cruising Utopia: The Then and There of Queer Futurity*. New York: NYU Press, 2009.

Muñoz, José Esteban. "The Sense of Watching Tony Sleep." In *After Sex? On Writing since Queer Theory*, edited by Janet E. Halley and Andrew Parker, 142–50. Durham: Duke University Press, 2011.

Musser, Amber. "Masochism: A Queer Subjectivity?" *Rhizomes* 11/12 (Fall 2005/Spring 2006), www.rhizomes.net/issue11/musser.

Nicholson, Catherine. "Algorithm and Analogy: Distant Reading in 1598." *PMLA* 132, no. 3 (May 2017): 643–50.

O'Connor, Sinead. "I Do Not Want What I Haven't Got." Chrysalis Records, 1990.

Ondaatje, Michael. *The Cinnamon Peeler: Selected Poems*. New York: Vintage, 1997.

Ong, Walter J. *Orality and Literacy: The Technologizing of the Word*. New York and London: Routledge, 2002.

Orgel, Stephen. "The Desire and Pursuit of the Whole." *Shakespeare Quarterly* 58, no. 3 (Fall 2007): 290–310.

Pasquier, Etienne. *Monophylo*. Translated by Sir Geoffrey Fenton. 1572.

Pastuzyn, Elissa D. "Are Our Memories Formed by an Ancient Virus?" *The Biologist* 65, no. 3 (2018): 14–17.

Pastuzyn, Elissa D. et. al. "The Neuronal Gene Arc Encodes a Repurposed Retrotransposon Gag Protein that Mediates Intercellular RNA Transfer." *Cell* 172, nos. 1–2 (January 11, 2018): 275–88.

Peacham, Henry. *The Garden of Eloquence*. London: R. F. for H. Jackson, 1593.

Pequigney, Joseph. *Such Is My Love: A Study of Shakespeare's Sonnets*. Chicago: University of Chicago Press, 1986.

Percy, William. *Sonnets to the Fairest Coelia*. London: Printed by Adam Islip, for W. P., 1594.

Philips, Katherine. "Ode against Pleasure." In *Poems*. London, 1664.

Phillips, Adam. *Side Effects*. New York: Harper Perennial, 2006.

Pivetti, Kyle. *Of Memory and Literary Form: Making the Early Modern English Nation*. Newark: University of Delaware Press, 2015.

Plat, Hugh. *The Jewell House of Art and Nature*. London, 1594.

Plato. *Phaedrus*. In *The Collected Dialogues of Plato*, edited by Edith Hamilton and Huntington Cairns. 475–525. Princeton: Princeton University Press, 1961.

Plato. *The Theaetetus of Plato*. Translated by Myles Burnyeat and M. J. Levett. Indianapolis: Hackett Publishing Company, 1990.

Plato. *Symposium*. Translated by Robin Waterfield. Oxford: Oxford University Press, 2009.

Pollack-Pelzner, Daniel. "What Shakespeare Actually Did during the Plague." *The New Yorker*, April 1, 2020.

Porta, Giovan Battista della. *L'Arte del ricordare* [The Art of Remembering]. Naples: Marco Antonio Passaro, 1566.

Proulx, Annie. *Close Range: Wyoming Stories*. New York: Scriber, 1999.

Proust, Marcel. *The Captive and The Fugitive*, vol. 5 of *In Search of Lost Time*. New York: The Modern Library, 1993.

Puttenham, George. *The Art of English Poesy*. Edited by Frank Whigham and Wayne A. Rebhorn. Ithaca and London: Cambridge University Press, 2007.

Ramsey, Paul. *The Fickle Glass: A Study of Shakespeare's Sonnets*. New York: AMS Press, 1979.

Ravenna, Peter of (Petrus). *The art of memory, that otherwyse is called the Phenix*. Translated by Robert Copland. London:William Middleton, 1548.

Reis, Bruce. *Creative Repetition and Intersubjectivity: Contemporary Freudian Explorations of Trauma, Memory, and Clinical Process*. New York: Routledge, 2020.

Riviere, Joan. "On the Genesis of Psychical Conflict in Earliest Infancy." In *Developments in Psychoanalysis*, edited by Melanie Klein, Paula Heimann, Susan Isaacs, and Joan Riviere, 37–66. New York: Routledge, 2018.

Rosmarin, Adena. "Hermeneutics versus Erotics: Shakespeare's Sonnets and Interpretive History." *Publications of the Modern Language Association of America* 100, no. 1 (January 1985): 20–37.

Ross, Michael and Anne E. Wilson. "Constructing and Appraising Past Selves." In *Memory, Brain, and Belief*, edited by Elaine Scarry and Daniel L. Schacter. 231–58. Cambridge, MA: Harvard University Press, 2000.

Rossetti, Dante Gabriel. "The House of Life: A Sonnet-Sequence." In *The Pre-Raphaelites: An Anthology of Poetry by Dante Gabriel Rossetti and Others*, edited by Jerome H. Buckley, 96–196. Chicago: Chicago Review Press, 2001.

Rudenstine, Neil L. *Ideas of Order: A Close Reading of Shakespeare's Sonnets*. New York: Farrar, Straus, and Giroux, 2014.

Ruiz, Sandra. "Waiting in the Seat of Sensation: The Brown Existentialism of Ryan Rivera." *Women & Performance: A Journal of Feminist Theory* 25, no. 3 (2015): 336–52.

Russell, Calum. "After Life: Hirokazu Koreeda's Meditative Analysis." *Far Out Magazine* (August 10, 2021): 1.

Sagaser, Elizabeth Harris. "Shakespeare's Sweet Leaves: Mourning, Pleasure, and the Triumph of Thought in the Renaissance Love Lyric." *ELH* 61, no. 1 (1994): 1–26.

Sanchez, Melissa E. "'Use Me but as Your Spaniel': Feminism, Queer Theory, and Early Modern Sexualities." *PMLA* 127, no. 3 (May 2012): 493–511.

Sanchez, Melissa E. *Queer Faith: Reading Promiscuity and Race in the Secular Love Tradition*. New York: New York University Press, 2019.

Sanchez, Melissa E. "Was Sexuality Racialized for Shakespeare?" In *The Cambridge Companion to Shakespeare and Race*, edited by Ayanna Thompson, 123–38. Cambridge: Cambridge University Press, 2021.

Sanchez, Melissa E. "Protestantism, Marriage, and Asexuality in Shakespeare." In *Shakespeare/Sex: Contemporary Readings in Gender and Sexuality*, edited by Jennifer Drouin, 98–122. London and New York: Bloomsbury Arden Shakespeare, 2022.

Saunders, Richard. "Physiognomie, and chiromancie ... whereunto is added the art of memory." In *The Memory Arts in Renaissance England: A Critical Anthology*, edited by William E. Engel, Rory Loughnane, and Grant Williams, 89–90. Cambridge: Cambridge University Press, 2016.

Scarry, Elaine. *Naming Thy Name: Cross-Talk in Shakespeare's Sonnets*. New York: Farrar, Straus, and Giroux, 2016.

Schacter, Daniel L. *Searching for Memory: The Brain, The Mind, and the Past*. New York: Basic Books, 1996.

Schacter, Daniel L. *The Seven Sins of Memory: How the Mind Forgets and Remembers*. Boston and New York: Houghton Mifflin Harcourt, 2001.

Schacter, Daniel L., Donna Rose Addis, Demis Hassabis, et al. "The Future of Memory: Remembering, Imagining, and the Brain." *Neuron* 76 (November 21, 2012): 677–94.

Schalkwyk, David. *Shakespeare, Love, and Service*. Cambridge: Cambridge University Press, 2012.

Schoenfeldt, Michael. "Introduction." In *A Companion to Shakespeare's Sonnets*, edited by Michael Schoenfeldt, 1–12. New York: John Wiley & Sons, 2006.

Schoenfeldt, Michael. *The Cambridge Introduction to Shakespeare's Poetry*. Cambridge: Cambridge University Press, 2010.

Schopenhauer, Arthur. *Studies in Pessimism*. Translated by T. Bailey Saunders. Whitefish, MT: Kessinger Publishing, 2010.

Sedgwick, Eve Kosofsky. *Between Men: English Literature and Male Homosocial Desire*. New York: Columbia University Press, 1985.

Shakespeare, William. *Poems: Written by Wil. Shake-speare. Gent*. London: Thomas Cotes for John Benson, 1640.

Shakespeare, William. *The Sonnets and a Lover's Complaint*. Edited by John Kerrigan. New York: Penguin, 2000.

Shakespeare, William. *The Oxford Shakespeare: The Complete Sonnets and Poems*. Edited by Colin Burrow. Oxford: Oxford University Press, 2008.

Shakespeare, William. *The New Oxford Shakespeare*. Edited by Gary Taylor, John Jowett, Terri Bourus, and Gabriel Egan. Oxford: Oxford University Press, 2016.

Shannon, Laurie. *Sovereign Amity: Figures of Friendship in Shakespearean Contexts*. Chicago: University of Chicago Press, 2002.

Shannon, Laurie. "'Nature's Changing Course': Asking Questions with Sonnet 18." Plenary Panel: "Queer Natures: Bodies, Sexualities, Environments," 45th Annual Meeting of the Shakespeare Association of America, Atlanta, GA, April 7, 2017.

Shrank, Cathy. "Reading Shakespeare's *Sonnets*: John Benson and the 1640 *Poems*." *Shakespeare* 5, no. 3 (September 2009): 271–91.

Sidney, Philip. "Astrophil and Stella." In *Sir Philip Sidney: The Major Works*, edited by Katherine Duncan-Jones, 153–211. Oxford: Oxford University Press, 2008.

Sidney, Philip. "The Defence of Poetry." In *Sir Philip Sidney: The Major Works*, edited by Katherine Duncan-Jones, 212–51. Oxford: Oxford University Press, 2008.

Sigo, Cedar. *Language Arts*. Seattle: Wave Books: 2014.

Singh, Jyotsna G. "'Th' expense of spirit in a waste of shame': Mapping the 'Emotional Regime' of Shakespeare's Sonnets." In *A Companion to Shakespeare's Sonnets*, edited by Michael Schoenfeldt, 277–89. New York: John Wiley & Sons, 2006.

Sinha, Anoushka. "King Lear under COVID-19 Lockdown." *Journal of the American Medical Association* 323, no. 18 (April 10, 2020): 1758–9.

Skuse, Alanna. "The Worm and the Flesh: Cankered Bodies in Shakespeare's Sonnets." In *Disability, Health, and Happiness in the Shakespearean Body*, edited by Sujata Iyengar, 240–59. New York: Routledge, 2014.

Smith, Bruce R. "I, You, He, She, and We: On the Sexual Politics of Shakespeare's Sonnets." In *Shakespeare's Sonnets: Critical Essays*, edited by James Schiffer, 411–29. New York: Routledge, 2000.

Smith, Bruce R. "Shakespeare's Sonnets and the History of Sexuality: A Reception History." In *A Companion to Shakespeare's Works: The Poems, Problem Comedies, Late Plays*, edited by Richard Dutton and Jean E. Howard, 4–26. Oxford: Blackwell, 2005.

Smith, Emma. "What Shakespeare Teaches Us about Living with Pandemics." *The New York Times*, March 28, 2020.

Smith, Ian. *Black Shakespeare: Reading and Misreading Race*. Cambridge: Cambridge University Press, 2022.

Smiths, The. "Cemetry Gates." By Morrissey and Johnny Marr. Recorded 1986. Track 5 on *The Queen Is Dead*. Rough Trade Records.

Sontag, Susan. *Illness as Metaphor and AIDS and Its Metaphors*. New York: Picador, 2001.

Spalding, John Lancaster. *Aphorisms and Reflections: Conduct, Culture and Religion*. Chicago: A. C. McClurg & Company, 1901.

Staniloiu, Angelica and Hans J. Markowitsch. "Towards Solving the Riddle of Forgetting in Functional Amnesia: Recent Advances and Current Opinions." *Frontiers in Psychology* 3 (November 2012): 403.

Stanivukovic, Goran. "Sex in the Sonnets: The Boy and Dishonourable Passions of the Past." In *Shakespeare/Sex: Contemporary Readings in Gender and Sexuality*, edited by Jennifer Drouin, 171–94. New York: Bloomsbury Arden Shakespeare, 2020.

Stewart, Alan. *Close Readers: Humanism and Sodomy in Early Modern England*. Princeton: Princeton University Press, 1997.

Stretter, Robert. "Cicero on Stage: Damon and Pithias and the Fate of Classical Friendship in English Renaissance Drama." *Texas Studies in Literature and Language* 47, no. 4 (Winter 2005): 345–65.

Sullivan, Garrett A., Jr. "Lethargic Corporeality on and off the Early Modern Stage." In *Forgetting in Early Modern English Literature and Culture: Lethe's Legacies*, edited by Christopher Ivic and Grant Williams, 41–58. London and New York: Routledge, 2004.

Sullivan, Garrett A., Jr. *Memory and Forgetting in English Renaissance Drama: Shakespeare, Marlowe, Webster*. Cambridge: Cambridge University Press, 2005.

Sullivan, Garrett A., Jr. "Voicing the Young Man: Memory, Forgetting, and Subjectivity in the Procreation Sonnets." In *A Companion to Shakespeare's Sonnets*, edited by Michael Schoenfeldt, 331–42. Malden and Oxford: Wiley-Blackwell, 2007.

Sutphen, Joyce. "'A dateless, lively heat': Storing Loss in the Sonnets." In *Shakespeare's Sonnets: Critical Essays*, edited by James Schiffer, 199–218. London and New York: Routledge, 2000.

Swann, Marjorie. "Vegetable Love: Botany and Sexuality in Seventeenth-Century England." In *The Indistinct Human in Renaissance Literature*, edited by Jean E. Feerick and Vin Nardizzi, 139–58. New York: Palgrave Macmillan, 2012.

Toffolo, Marieke Bianca Jolien, Monique Smeets, and Marcel van den Hout. "Proust Revisited: Odours as Triggers of Aversive Memories." *Cognition and Emotion* 26, no. 1 (2012): 83–92.

Toohey, Peter. *Boredom: A Lively History*. New Haven: Yale University Press, 2011.

Tosh, Will. *Male Friendship and Testimonies of Love in Shakespeare's England*. London: Palgrave Macmillan, 2016.

Traub, Valerie. "The Sonnets: Sequence, Sexuality, and Shakespeare's Two Loves." In *A Companion to Shakespeare's Works*, vol. 4: *The Poems, Problem Comedies, Late Plays*, edited by Richard Dutton and Jean E. Howard, 275–301. Oxford: Blackwell, 2003.

Traub, Valerie. "Friendship's Loss: Alan Bray's Making of History." *GLQ* 10, no. 3 (2004): 339–65.

Traub, Valerie. *Thinking Sex with the Early Moderns*. Philadelphia: University of Pennsylvania Press, 2016.

Tribble, Evelyn. *Cognition in the Globe: Attention and Memory in Shakespeare's Theatre*. Basingstoke: Palgrave Macmillan, 2011.

Tribble, Evelyn and John Sutton. "Cognitive Ecology as a Framework for Shakespearean Studies." *Shakespeare Studies* 39 (2011): 94–103.

Tribble, Evelyn and John Sutton. "Minds in and out of Time: Memory, Embodied Skill, Anachronism, and Performance." *Textual Practice* 26 (2012): 587–607.

Valbuena, Olga L. "The Dyer's Hand: The Reproduction of Coercion and Blot in Shakespeare's Sonnets." In *Shakespeare's Sonnets: Critical Essays*, edited by James Schiffer, 325–46. London: Taylor and Francis, 2013.

van de Vijver, Gertrudis, Ariane Bazan, and Sandrine Detandt. "The Mark, the Thing, and the Object: On What Commands Repetition in Freud and Lacan." *Frontiers in Psychology* 8 (December 2017): 1–10.

van der Kolk, Bessel. *The Body Keeps the Score: Brain, Mind, and Body in the Healing of Trauma*. New York: Viking, 2014.

Vasiliauskas, Emily. "The Outmodedness of Shakespeare's Sonnets." *ELH* 82, no. 3 (Fall 2015): 759–87.

Vendler, Helen. *The Art of Shakespeare's Sonnets*. Cambridge, MA: Harvard University Press, 1997.

Vendler, Helen. "Formal Pleasure in the Sonnets." In *A Companion to Shakespeare's Sonnets*, edited by Michael Schoenfeldt, 27–44. New York: John Wiley & Sons, 2006.

Vendler, Helen. *The Ocean, the Bird, and the Scholar: Essays on Poets and Poetry*. Cambridge, MA and London: Harvard University Press, 2015.

Walker, William. "Anadiplosis in Shakespearean Drama." *Rhetorica: A Journal of the History of Rhetoric* 35, no. 4 (Autumn 2017): 399–424.

Warley, Christopher. *Sonnet Sequences and Social Distinction in Renaissance England*. Cambridge: Cambridge University Press, 2005.

Warner, Michael. *The Trouble with Normal: Sex, Politics, and the Ethics of Queer Life*. Cambridge, MA: Harvard University Press, 1999.

Watson, Amanda. "'Full character'd': Competing Forms of Memory in Shakespeare's Sonnets." In *A Companion to Shakespeare's Sonnets*, edited by Michael Schoenfeldt, 343–60. Oxford: Blackwell Publishing, 2010.

Wells, Stanley. *Looking for Sex in Shakespeare*. Cambridge: Cambridge University Press, 2004.

Whitman, Walt. *The Complete Poems.* Edited by Francis Murphy. New York: Penguin, 2005.

Wilder, Lina Perkins. *Shakespeare's Memory Theatre: Recollection, Properties, and Charac-ter.* Cambridge: Cambridge University Press, 2010.

Williams, Grant. *Ars Reminiscendi: Mind and Memory in Renaissance Culture.* Toronto: Center for Reformation and Renaissance Studies, 2009.

Williams, Grant. "Monumental Memory and Little Reminders: The Fantasy of Being Remembered by Posterity." In *The Routledge Handbook of Shakespeare and Memory*, edited by Andrew Hiscock and Lina Perkins Wilder, 297–312. London and New York: Routledge, 2017.

Williams, Raymond. *The Country and the City.* London: Chatto and Windus, 1973.

Wilson, Katharine M. *Shakespeare's Sugared Sonnets.* London: Allen and Unwin, 1974.

Wilson, Thomas. *The Arte of Rhetoric.* Edited by G. H. Mair. Oxford: Clarendon Press, 1909.

Wilson, Timothy D. *Strangers to Ourselves: Discovering the Adaptive Unconscious.* Cam-bridge, MA: Harvard University Press, 2002.

Wojnarowicz, David. *Close to the Knives: A Memoir of Disintegration.* New York: Vintage Books, 1991.

Wolfson, Susan J. "Reading Intensity: Sonnet 12." In *Shakespeare up Close: Reading Early Modern Texts*, edited by Russ McDonald, Nicholas D. Nace, and Travis D. Williams, 146–53. London: Bloomsbury, 2012.

Wordsworth, William. "Nuns fret not in their narrow rooms." In *William Wordsworth—The Major Works: Including The Prelude*, edited by Stephen Gill, 286. Oxford: Oxford University Press, 2008.

Wright, George T. "The Silent Speech of Shakespeare's Sonnets." In *Shakespeare's Sonnets: Critical Essays*, edited by James Schiffer, 135–62. New York and London: Garland, 2000.

Zboya, Eric. "Sonnet 30." In *The Sonnets: Translating and Rewriting Shakespeare*, edited by Paul Legault, 48. Brooklyn: Nightboat Books, 2012.

Index

For the benefit of digital users, indexed terms that span two pages (e.g., 52–53) may, on occasion, appear on only one of those pages.